The Constitutional Review

Second Edition

Arne Mavčič

Vandeplas Publishing, LLC

United States of America

The Constitutional Review, Second Edition

Dr. Arne Mavčič

Published by:

Vandeplas Publishing, LLC – June 2013

801 International Parkway, 5th Floor
Lake Mary, FL. 32746
USA

www.vandeplaspublishing.com

ISBN 978-1-60042-193-8

Table of Contents

THE AUTHOR

Dr. Arne Mavčič

Arne Mavčič[1], D. Law (born 4 August 1948), completed his Bachelor of Law at the University of Ljubljana Law School, Slovenia in 1970, from which, after having completed his post-graduate studies in civil law at the Universities of Zagreb and Ljubljana Law Schools, he was awarded a Doctorate of Law in 1979.

From 1970 to 1973 he was legal advisor to the Slovenian Parliament, from 1974 to 1977 he was Head of the International Department of the Slovenian Health Insurance Association. Since 1978 he has been the Director of the Legal Information Center of the Constitutional Court of the Republic of Slovenia, a Senior Expert Councillor to the University of Ljubljana Law School, specializing in legal information systems and constitutional law, and a Senior Expert Counsellor to the Institute on Labour Law of the University of Ljubljana Law School.

Dr. Mavčič is the liaison officer for Slovenia on constitutional law and legal information systems to the (Venice) Commission for Democracy through Law under the Council of Europe, the liaison officer for Slovenia on constitutional law and legal information systems to the ACCPUF Paris, and Secretary of the Slovenian Constitutional Law Society, Secretary of the Slovenian Jurists Commission, a member of the Slovenian Labour Law and Social Security Association, a member of the International Constitutional Law Association, a member and the national President for Slovenia of the World Jurist Association, a member of the Law Association for Asia and the Pacific, a member of the Slovenian Informatics Society, a Fulbright Scholar, an editor of the Collected Slovenian Constitutional Case-Law series, national editor of the East European Case Reporter of Constitutional Law and national author for Slovenia of Kluwer's Encyclopaedia of Constitutional Law.

He is the editor and author of several other publications in the field of constitutional law as well as an author of over 100 papers and reports on national and international conferences, seminars and workshops. Of late, Dr. Mavčič has predominantly been engaged in practical and promotional activities in the fields of comparative constitutional judiciary and legal information systems.

[1] Dr. Arne Mavčič
Director of the Legal Information Center
The Constitutional Court
of the Republic of Slovenia
1000 Ljubljana
Beethovnova 10
Slovenia
Phone: +386 (1) 477 64 47
Fax: +386 (1) 425 43 47
e-mail: arne.mavcic@us-rs.si
Internet: www.us-rs.com

Preface

This comparative survey of constitutional systems is current as of April 2001. This book represents a reprint and up-dated version of author's part of a book entitled The Constitutional Review and its Development in the Modern World (A Comparative Constitutional Analysis) written together with Mr. G. Harutyunyan, which was published in Yerevan in 1999.

The author would like to take this opportunity to thank his English language editor Mr. Dean De Vos and his French language editor Mrs. Marie-Claude Oberti-Zupančič, whose expert linguistic help proved invaluable throughout the project.

The author is also extremely grateful to Mr. Edo Milavec for helping him with the computer aided editing and graphic design of tables and maps that the author was unable to work out by himself.

I. An Introduction to the Nature of the Origin and Function of Systems of Constitutional Review

One source of constitutionality is the tendency to limit the absolute powers of monarchs. This entails the process of establishing material constitutionality, which is older than the formal legal meaning of constitutionality. Under the influence of the philosophy of natural law, the definition of material constitutionality was developed, which states that the basis for any political system must be the recognition of basic human rights, and above all personal freedom and private property. Under this theory these rights are older than the State and have to be protected even against the State itself. Therefore power must be limited by legal regulation. In addition, the ability to appropriately implement such power is ordered in such a way that basic human rights are guaranteed. The principle of material constitutionality has to be realized on the basis of a written constitution which must include the mentioned basic elements, i.e. the limitation of power - it should be limited by an objectively determined legal system - and the recognition of basic human rights as well as sources of powers within the public sovereignty. If the written constitution does not have such elements, such a system can be treated as merely formal legal constitutionality.

Constitutionality is a political principle, which partly finds expression in the normative function of law, partly in real social existence. It entails a mechanism of political relations and powers as well as legal counterweights and guarantees by which the self-interest of power has to be limited. Constitutionality should not be treated statically, because it can change. Therefore we can speak about constitutionality and the constitution as a unique principle which finds complete expression in the written constitution. Material constitutionality is the structural essence of each democratic political system.

The introduction of constitutionality was based on the appropriate level of maturity of socio-political circumstances, which finds expression in the consideration of the following principles: the basic rights of humans and citizens, the principle of national sovereignty and the principle of the separation of powers. The principle of constitutionality involves a democratic source of power (the general voting right), the recognition of basic human rights, as well as the organization of the highest State bodies.

The written constitution is, in principle, the most important legal and political remedy for the implementation of constitutionality. Therefore it is necessary for the functioning of each democratic political system that a constitution is implemented. Only in a definitely democratic political system can the implementation of constitutionality and legality be provided. There is no constitutionality without democracy and vice versa.

II. Constitutional Justice and Practice:

A. The Character of Social Relations and the Constitutional Review

For the implementation of constitutionality, proper social circumstances and political and legal guarantees (remedies) must be provided[2].

The particular social conditions that are important for the implementation of constitutionality, and which are essential for democratic political systems are as follows:

- Social stability. This involves material stability for the protection of a particular constitutional system against eventual sudden changes which could be caused by social powers that do not favor the present political system. From the point of view of formal legal stability, the constitution should be the factor which stabilizes the political system and its institutions. However, the socio-political system is not dependent only on the strength of the constitution, but also on the socio-political basis of the constitution. The socio-political basis is the cause and consequence of the strength of the constitution. Generally we can speak about the social (material and formal) stability when the social and political sphere does not change too often and there are not any too big and sudden changes. Both elements of social stability, i.e. material and formal stability, are closed to each other and both influence the implementation of constitutionality. However, social instability requires a more active role of organized subjective powers with the implementation of constitutionality for social stability.
- Social homogeneity or heterogeneity. This involves the social group composition of society. If the society is more homogeneous concerning social position and social consciousness, there are advantages for implementing constitutionality and legality. The social structure of the society is the basis for determining the framework of the political system as well as the contents of the constitutionality. Social homogeneity and social peace are interwoven. All current societies are more or less heterogeneous (differentiated, structured). Therefore their social structure influences the implementation of constitutionality.
- Social consciousness and public opinion. Consideration of constitutionality and legality is dependent on social consciousness and public opinion and involves the understanding that the constitution and statutes must be considered. Such a democratic consciousness is dependent on the duration of the tradition and existence of democratic institutions. Within a concrete society, the belief must be stabilized that consideration of constitutionality and legality is a benefit and the goal of everyone. A developed social consciousness is one of the most important elements needed for the integration of a certain political system. A real democratic system also assures the creation of public opinion and guarantees its affirmation.

---

2 See Rupnik, J., Ustavnost, demokracija in politični sistem, Založba Obzorja Maribor 1975, p. 15-150.

> Such public opinion may be a support for the implementation of constitutionality and legality. Public opinion is also an important political factor for the limitation of power, and entails the condemnation of the violation of constitutionality and legality. Public opinion as a form of social consciousness became a very important political power within the social system and in such a way also a factor for the consideration of constitutionality and legality.

Constitutionality may be exercised within a certain political system only by the willful endeavor of those social powers who have adopted the constitution. Social stability as well as social heterogeneity influences the implementation of constitutionality. The creation of material conditions is an imperative of a stable social and political system, which in turn affects the contents and stability of political institutions.

The protection of the basic political relations determined by the constitution is guaranteed by the different guarantees or remedies (political and legal) for the protection of constitutionality and legality of a democratic political system. Constitutionality and legality can be exercised only within appropriate social circumstances. There are socio-political and legal remedies that guarantee the implementation of constitutionality and legality.

Socio-political guarantees include institutions and instruments that implement constitutionality and legality which are at least partially dependent on human will. The most important remedies are the following: democracy, the separation of powers, and reducing State power and State bureaucracy. The appropriate organization of power (the separation of powers) is one of the most important remedies. Socio-political guarantees insure the objective circumstances necessary for the functioning of the political system that assure that constitutionality and legality function more efficiently. Within a State governed by the rule of law, socio-political remedies only consist of guarantees of the efficient functioning of the political system (the prevention of a concentration of power).

In a contemporary State governed by the rule of law, the first legal remedies are the judiciary and constitutional justice. The judiciary as a legal form of the protection of constitutionality and legality was developed through many steps: civil, criminal, and administrative judiciary. The judicial protection of constitutionality, *i.e.* the constitutional review (exercised by constitutional justice), however, was introduced following the realization that regulations of State bodies can also violate the constitution, and was established with the introduction of written constitutions, and is the highest form of the legal protection of constitutionality.

The concentration of power can be limited only by the separation of powers into legislative, executive and judicial branches. The principle of the separation of powers is an essential component of constitutionality. It is a basic principle of democracy. The result of the introduction of the judicial review of constitutionality was a qualitative change as regards the principle of the separation of powers. Where it was introduced it has been become increasingly important in the political field, and it has become an increasingly essential component of the mechanism of State authority as its decisions actively intervene in political and social life.

The political guarantee for the implementation of constitutionality is the right of individuals to participate in public affairs. This requires de-bureaucratisation. The institutionalized guarantee against the bureaucracy of political functions is a multiparty system and general and equal voting rights, which assure the relatively quick change of political structures.

Constitutional review is also a remedy against anomalies concerning the concentration of powers within executive bodies. In particular, an excess of State legislative activities oppresses individuals within the political system. Constitutional review is a remedy for balancing processes which could lead to State intervention into certain fields of human activity.

The legal guarantees and/or legal remedies for the protection of constitutionality and legality are as follows:

The principle of the rule of law (the principle of legality) means that all State bodies must act on the basis of the constitution and statutes. Any self-interest which is imposed on the principle of expedience is, as a rule, excluded. The principle of the rule of law or the principle of legality is closely bound with the legislative function of a contemporary State. Because a statute is the most direct reflection of sovereignty, the activity of the administration and the judiciary must be subordinated to a statute; within this scope, the principle of legality and the rule of law are reflected. The principle of legality is bound with the idea of basic rights as well as with the separation of powers. In addition, the mentioned principle also has a certain other meaning: the request for the conformity of lower regulations with higher regulations. The principle of legality also reflects the desire to limit power and its political liability (the principle of the political liability of authority). Authority is limited, in particular, by legal norms. This principle of legality regulates the relationship of the executive-administrative and judicial power by statute. The principle of constitutionality means that all other general legal acts must be in accordance with the constitution, because the constitution has the position of the supreme act. Constitutionality has a formal (the process for adopting an act must be in conformity with the constitution) and a material character (the contents of all other general legal acts must be in conformity with the constitution). The principle of legality reflects the formal and material conformity of executive or individual acts of the administrative and judicial bodies with statutes.

B. Particularities of the Constitutional Review during the Transitional Period in Slovenia

In addition to its stronger position within the scope of the national system along with the power to decide constitutional complaints regarding violations of human rights, the most important novelty of the Slovenian Constitutional Court in comparison with other respective systems of the New Democracies is its conspicuous cassatory function with reference to statute. Under the 1991 *Constitution* the Constitutional Court may abrogate a statute. In some other systems of the New Democracies such a concentration of power in only one institution (the Constitutional Court) could even be limited by the power of the Parliament to adjudicate the constitutionality of statutes.

The Slovenian Constitutional Court acquired the status of an independent institution carrying out the constitutional review in relation to the Legislature characterized by the explicit power to abrogate statutes adopted by the Legislature. The former function of the Constitutional Court; due to the Principle of the Unity of Powers and the Supremacy of the Parliament, focused on the assessment of the unconstitutionality of a statute, changed into an active relationship not only involving the cassation of statute, but also guidance of the Legislature in its legislative activity. However, a concession by the Constitutional Court to the Legislature is still possible in that the Court may not abrogate a disputable statutorial provision, but rather enables the Legislature to reconcile the disputable statutorial regulation with the *Constitution* within a period of time, pursuant to the guidelines of the Constitutional Court in a specific decision (see Article 48 of the *Constitutional Court Act*).

In this period the Constitutional Court has played a more important role based on its new extended powers. In the sense of contemporary trends, the Slovenian Constitutional Court has assumed the role of a negative Legislature.[3] In this period of transition the Legislature is not always able to follow developments nor to impose standards for all shades of the legal system and its institutions. This results in the so-called interpretative decisions[4] taken by the Court or the appellative decisions or certain declaratory decisions that include certain instructions by the Constitutional Court to the Legislature on how to settle a certain question, or a specific issue (Article

---

[3] The basic difference between the so-called intervention of the Constitutional Court into the field which belongs to the Legislature, and other forms of intervention by which the Constitutional Court would exceed its authorization to be sometimes transformed into a **reserve Legislature**, would be in fact that the Constitutional Court abrogating a statute only "takes away", but the Legislature may also amplify. On the other hand, the abrogation of statute by a Constitutional Court decision does not create law to a low degree in comparison with writing new statutorial provisions. It may depend on the context where the abrogated legal provision is situated, on the type of provision, but sometimes only on pure coincidence concerning which legislative technique was used by the Legislature, if the Constitutional Court really executes its supposed undisputable function of negative Legislature, or participates in the creation of a new provision. How much space will belong to the Legislature concerning the extraction of determined unconstitutionalities and how much space has to be occupied by the Constitutional Court, may in cases of the highest degree partially depend also on the intensity of the activities of the Legislature (Testen, F., Techniques of the Decision-Making Process of the Constitutional Court in the Abstract Constitutional Review, Legal Journal (*Pravna praksa*), No. 1/99, p. 5).

[4] It is exactly by "interpretation" as a decision-making technique that the Constitutional Court can enter the space which is otherwise reserved for the Legislature. This interpretation entails a technique which is used in Constitutional Court sentences describing the particular contents of a legal norm in an affirmative manner (Testen, F., The Techniques of Constitutional Court Decision-Making Process in the Abstract Constitutional Review, Legal Journal (*Pravna praksa*), No. 1/99, p. 5).

48 of the *Constitutional Court Act*). However, in compliance with the Principle of Judicial Self-Restraint, a clear limit has been imposed on the Slovenian Constitutional Court due to the fact that the Court has actively been creating the legal rule both negatively (*e.g.* by abrogation) and positively (*e.g.* by appellative, interpretative and the declarative decisions), a function theoretically reserved for the Legislature. On the other hand there arises the question whether the Constitutional Court, in deciding on the existence or non-existence of a specific provision, actually creates the law, because it carries out a review of legislative activity. In any case, the Legislature cannot avoid the existence of constitutional case-law in its activity.

Furthermore, Slovenian Constitutional Case-Law, which has a certain tradition, can serve as an example of the knowledge and techniques of a national legislative practice. A comparison of certain topical views could as well add to the promotion of a national democratic process and culture. Accordingly, it could have direct applicative value in the search for systemic solutions in some other countries.

III. Historical Steps in the Development of Systems of Constitutional Review and Particularities of Their Basic Models

A. History

The establishment of supreme judicial bodies for the protection of constitutionality and legality is not an invention of contemporary legal systems, but is rather related to the development of constitutionality, in particular on the European Continent. Constitutional/judicial review has passed though several characteristic development stages[5]:

1. Development up to World War I

Ancient Athenian law distinguished between a *nomos* (which might in a certain sense be compared to contemporary constitutional laws), and a *psephisma*, which in present times might be called a decree[6]. The fundamental principle was introduced that the decree (a *psephisma*), whatever its content, could not conflict with the *nomoi* in either form or substance. Two consequences attended the enactment of an unconstitutional *psephisma*. First, the member of the legislature who had proposed the illegal decree incurred criminal liability, which gave rise to a public right of action. Second, *psephismata* that were in conflict with the nomoi were considered void. The Athenian judges, although in principle obliged to decide cases on the basis of both the laws and the decrees, were bound by the latter only in so far as they were consistent with the former.

Certain elements of constitutional review go back as far as the year 1180, i.e. to the old German Reich. At first the corresponding judicial bodies dealt primarily with jurisdictional disputes between individual rulers and partly even with infringements of rights. Certain elements of constitutional review kept emerging under different forms throughout German legal history, until it was introduced in the present sense of the word with the *Weimar Constitution*. Preliminary forms of constitutional review existed in France by the middle of the 13th Century. Portugal introduced its constitutional review in *Philip's Code* in the 17th Century. More serious projects of constitutional/judicial review appeared in the *Constitutions* of Norway, Denmark and Greece in the 19th Century.

In 1867 the Austrian Federal Court acquired the jurisdiction to deal with jurisdictional disputes concerning the protection of individual political rights *vis-à-vis* administration; the State Court, on the other hand, made decisions on constitutional complaints (*Staatliche Verfassungsbeschwerde*).

---

5 ct. Rousseau Dominique, *La justice constitutionnelle en Europe*, Montchrestien, Paris, 1996, pp. 1-10; Favoreu Luis, *Los tribunales constitucionales*, Editorila Ariel, S. A., Barcelona, 1994, p. 15 et al. and p. 137 et al.; Fromont Michel, *La justice constitutionnelle dans le monde*, Dalloz, Paris, 1996, pp. 5-38

6 Capeletti, M., The Judicial Process in Perspective, Chapt. 3, published in 58 Cal. L. Rev. 1017(1970), published also in Beatty D., Comparative Constitutional Law Faculty of Law, University of Toronto, Spring 1994, p. I-6.

Although some initial elements of constitutional review can be seen already in the *Federal Constitution of Switzerland* (1848), the Swiss Federal Court acquired broader powers only with the modification of the *Constitution in 1874*.

In Norway constitutional review originates in the jurisprudence dating from 1890. Romania introduced constitutional review before World War I following the American model.

While the modern English legal system knows no constitutional review, English legal history does include some of its elements, *i.e.* the principle of the supremacy of the *Constitution* dates back to 1610 and is of essential significance for the development of constitutional review in England. Another example of an English contribution to this development is the impeachment originating in the late Middle Ages. Ideas about the supremacy of the *Constitution* and the right to judicial review spread from England over to the United States. There, already at the end of the 18th Century, the Court proclaimed individual English Acts null and void on the territory of the North American States. However, according to the *1789 Constitution* the Supreme Court as the highest Federal Court did not have any express constitutional powers. The decisive impact on the development of constitutional review was exerted by the famous *Marbury v. Madison Case(1803)*, in which the Supreme Court arrogated the power of judicial review concerned with the conformity of statutes with the *Constitution*. This gave a basis for the enforcement of the power of the American Supreme Court to carry out the judicial review of statutes. Although the next similar case appeared in this Court only in 1857, the way to the constitutional review of regulatory measures had already been paved.

The American Supreme Court created the grounds for the new institution in practice, *i.e.* the judicial protection of constitutionality. Such an American system of constitutional review was adopted primarily in some particular South American countries. Some of them explicitly determined the matter by the their constitution. In Europe, except in some Scandinavian countries, such a system of (indirect) judicial review of constitutionality could not be introduced because of the too high reputation of the legislative bodies.

The French, on the other hand, have clung tenaciously to the idea that no judicial body should be given the power to review the conformity statutes with a supposed higher law. The legislature, therefore, as the voice of popular sovereignty, was seen as the best guarantor of fundamental rights. From the standpoint of the development of constitutional review in continental Europe, France has always been against the notion that the acts of superior bodies and especially of parliamentary assemblies, as representatives of national sovereignty, might be subjected to review by the judiciary[7].

[7] Capeletti, M., The Judicial Process in Perspective, Chapt. 3, published in 58 Cal. L. Rev. 1017(1970), published also in Beatty D., Comparative Constitutional Law Faculty of Law, University of Toronto, Spring 1994, p. I-7/I-8.

2. The Development Between the two Wars

The development between the two Wars is referred to as "the Austrian period". The *Constitution of 1920* marks the foundation of the Austrian Constitutional Court with the exclusive power to review the constitutionality of statutes (at first, however, only of a preventive nature), following the work of the Austrian legal theorists Adolf Merkl and Hans Kelsen.

Following the example of the Austrian model, before World War II constitutional review was introduced in the following countries: Czechoslovakia (1920), Liechtenstein (*Staatsgerichtshof*, 1925), Greece (1927), Egypt (1941), Spain (1931) and Ireland (1937). The trend to broader enforcement of constitutional review was interrupted by the War and the already founded institutions failed to become active in practice (*e.g.* from 1933 through 1945 Austria was without constitutional review, after 1938 Czechoslovakia was without constitutional review).

3. The development after World War II

Constitutional review in the proper sense of the word, taken from the theoretical point of view, was able to develop only when instead of the principle of the sovereignty of the Parliament[8]there prevailed the idea of the supremacy of the *Constitution*[9] and where constitutional review is performed by a special body, independent of the legislative and executive power.[10] Such approaches were characteristic of the development after World War II. On the other hand, constitutional review also involves the principle of the vertical separation of powers. It emerged in federal states, whereby constitutional review was supposed to exert supervision over the federal Legislature in relation to member states. This was also due to historical reasons: the painful experiences of the past War and Fascism as a counterweight gave birth to the idea that constitutional review was characteristic of democracy. There were also institutional and political reasons: constitutional review should also represent efficient protection *vis-à-vis* legislative and executive power. The final step was to provide a means for guaranteeing government's obedience to the constitution, separate it from the legislative power itself and embody it in the active work of judges or, in some systems, of a special constitutional court[11]. This active work of the judiciary makes the necessarily vague terms of constitutional provisions more concrete and gives them practical application. Through this work the static terms of the constitution come alive, adapting themselves to the conditions of everyday life. It is in this way that the values embodied in the Higher Law become practical realities. As such this framework of modern constitutions and judicial review synthesizes the ineffective and abstract ideals of natural law with the concrete provisions of positive law. Through modern constitutionalism, in short,

---

8 Where the representative body itself decides on the constitutionality of its laws

9 Where the Constitution is the basis and the source of all state power

10 Not by the Parliament itself, but either by the regular courts or by a special body, such as the Constitutional Court or some other body

11 Capeletti, M., The Judicial Process in Perspective, Chapt. 3, published in 58 Cal. L. Rev. 1017(1970), published also in Beatty D., Comparative Constitutional Law, Faculty of Law, University of Toronto, Spring 1994, p. I-4/I-11.

natural law, put on an historical and realistic footing, has found a new place in legal thought.

Therefore, most countries introduced constitutional review directly after World War II (previously this had been a specialty of American law), including Brazil (again in 1946), Japan (1947), Burma/Myanmar (1947), Italy (1948), Thailand (1949), Germany (1949), India (1949), France (1958), Luxembourg, Syria (1950) and Uruguay (1952). In addition, constitutional review spread with different practical efficiency in Asia, Central and South America and Africa.

4. A New Period of Development in the Seventies

This period was marked with political changes in certain South European countries which introduced constitutional review upon the abolition of dictatorships: Greece (1968), Spain (1978), and Portugal (1976). In this period constitutional review was also introduced in the following countries: Cyprus (1960), Turkey (1961), Algeria (1963), former Yugoslavia (1963), as well as in Slovenia and other federal units of the former Yugoslavia (1963). In the meantime, certain existing systems of constitutional review introduced systemic revisions (Austria, Germany, Sweden, France, and Belgium). As a result of the political and social changes in the Eighties, constitutional review started to change also in many countries in Central and South America. In that part of the world a special position was accorded to Argentina, where the process of democratic transformation in a federal state first developed in its units, marked by the gradually increasing introduction of the elements of constitutional review of different intensity by the individual provinces.

5. The Introduction of Constitutional Review in the New Democracy Countries

Subsequent development involves the introduction of constitutional review in the central and Eastern European countries and in the Commonwealth of Independent States (thereafter, CIS).[12] The introduction of constitutional review entails the dissolution of the former principle of the unity of powers, in view of which the then socialist systems as a rule did not have any constitutional review. In the past, the only exceptions were the former Yugoslavia, which in 1963 introduced constitutional review following the Austrian or German model, and Czechoslovakia, where constitutional review was introduced in 1968, but did not become active in practice.

[12] Poland (1982), already in the former Soviet Union (1988), Romania (1991), Albania (1992), Bulgaria (1991), Lithuania (1992), Estonia (1992), Hungary (first attempt in 1984, definitely in 1989), Slovakia (1992), the Czech Republic (1992), Slovenia (newly established Constitutional Court by the 1991 Constitution), Croatia (1991), after 1991 Armenia, Azerbaijan, Belarus, Bosnia, Georgia, Kazakhstan, Kyrgyzstan, Latvia, Macedonia, Moldavia, Mongolia, Montenegro, Serbia, the Serbian Republic of Bosnia, Tadjikistan, Ukraine, Uzbekistan, as well as the federal entities of the Russian Federation (Adigea, Altai, Baskiria, Buryatia, Chuvachia, Dagestan, Inguchia, Irkutska Oblast, the Kabardino-Balkar Republic, Kakasa, the Karachaewo-Cherkez Republic, Karelia, Khalmukia, Koma, Marii-El, Northern Ossetia, Tatarstan, Tuba, Udmurtia, Yakutia).

B. Models of Constitutional/Judicial Review

The Constitutional Court is a special body that as the bearer of the protection of constitutionality holds a certain legal superiority in relation to other branches of power. Its review covers all legislative acts that are the highest legal instruments of a specific legal and political system. The status of a true institution with the power to provide constitutional review should only be held by the institution that in the specific system of the separation of powers holds such a limiting relation to the legislative power (the Parliament) that it may annul statutes adopted by the legislative body. It is a judicial institution established in view of special and exclusive decision-making powers on constitutional matters. This institution is located outside the ordinary court system and is fully independent of other branches of public authorities.

Any particular system can be classified on the basis of a common model of constitutional court structures considering the following essential components:

DOSSIER OF THE CONSTITUTIONAL COURT OF ....

STATE:
TITLE:
YEAR OF FOUNDATION:
SEAT:

I. CHRONICLE
1. Date and context of establishment
2. Position in the hierarchy of courts

II. STANDARD LEGAL REFERENCE
1. The Constitution of....................
2. The Constitutional Court Act.....................
3. The Rules of Procedure.......................
4. Other Internal Rules..........................

III. COMPOSITION AND ORGANIZATION
1. Composition
   1.1. The number of judges:
   1.2. Electoral/appointment body:
      1.2.1. Appointment Based System (Without the Participation of a Representative Body):
      1.2.2. Election Based System:
      1.2.3. Mixed Systems (Appointment and Election):
      1.2.4. Predetermined Composition From High Judicial Officials:
   1.3. The Court members:
      1.3.1. The term of office:
   1.4. The Court President:
      1.4.1. The term of office:
   1.5. The qualifications and the required professional experience of constitutional court judges:
   1.6. Incompatibilities:
   1.7. Immunities:
   1.8. Release from office prior to the expiration of the term:
2. Proceedings
   2.1. Hearing in plenum:
      2.1.1. A quorum:
   2.2. Hearing in camera:
      2.2.1. A quorum:
   2.3. The Dissenting/Concurring opinion:
   2.4. Public hearing:
   2.5. Internal session:
3. Organization
   3.1. Administrative autonomy:
   3.2. The budget:

- *3.3. Administrative services:*
- *3.4. Secretary:*
- *3.5. Financial service:.*
- *3.6. Special services:*
  - *3.6.1. Legal information center:*
  - *3.6.2. Legal library:*
  - *3.6.3. Legal advisers:*
  - *3.6.4. Clerical staff:*

IV. POWERS

1. Constitutional Court Review
   - *1.1. Preventive review:*
   - *1.2. A posteriori review:*
     - *1.2.1. Abstract review:*
     - *1.2.2. Concrete review:*
2. Other powers
   - *2.1. Constitutional complaints:*
   - *2.2. Jurisdictional disputes:*
   - *2.3. The unconstitutionality of acts and activities of political parties:*
   - *2.4. Charges against the President of the Republic:*
   - *2.5. Charges against the Prime Minister or against any Minister of State:*
   - *2.6. Electoral matters:*
   - *2.7. Referendums:*
   - *2.8. Other matters with which the Court is charged by the Constitution or statute:*
3. Standing before the Constitutional Court
   - *3.1. State bodies:*
   - *3.2. Individuals:*

V. NATURE AND EFFECTS OF DECISIONS

1. Finality:
2. Binding force:
   - *2.1. Erga omnes:*
   - *2.2. Inter partes:*
3. Ex officio:
4. The temporary order:
5. Abrogation in whole or in part:
   - *5.1. Effectiveness immediately or within a certain period of time:*
6. Annulment in whole or in part:
7. The consequences of decisions, damage claims
8. The declaration of unconstitutionality and illegality:
9. The legislative omissions:
10. The abrogation, retroactive or prospective, of a general act while deciding on a constitutional complaint:
11. The final decision on a contested human right or freedom based on a constitutional complaint:
12. Stating the competent body:
13. Impeachment:
    - *13.1. Finding the proposal for impeachment to be unfounded:*
    - *13.2. Decision on the basis for impeachment/decision on the termination of the Presidents/Prime Ministers/Ministers office:*
14. The annulment of an unconstitutional act/activity of a political party act/activity or the ordering of a deletion from the register of legal political parties:
15. The annulment of decisions of the National Assembly and rulings on the election of representatives:
16. Obligatory opinions on the conformity of international treaties with the Constitution:
17. Declarations on the constitutionality of a proposal to call a referendum:
18. Other forms of decisions:

VI PUBLICATION OF CONSTITUTIONAL COURT DECISIONS

1. The Official Gazette:
2. The Official Digest:
3. Legal Journals:
4. Electronic Publishing:
5. Other forms:

VII THE LEGAL INFORMATION SYSTEM

From the organizational point of view, it is possible to distinguish different models of constitutional/judicial review, as follows:

- The "American" - Judicial Review Model (based on the *Marbury Case (1803)*, dealt with by the Supreme Court of the United States, and on John Marshall's doctrine), whereunder constitutional matters are dealt with by all ordinary courts (a decentralized or diffuse or dispersed review) under ordinary court proceedings (*incidenter*). It is a specific and *a posteriori* review, whereby the Supreme (high) Court in the system provides for the uniformity of jurisdiction. In the diffuse system, the decisions as a rule take effect only *inter partes* (except for the principle *stare decisis*, whereunder the courts in the future abide by the ruling). In principle the decision concerning the unconstitutionality of a statute is declaratory and retrospective, *i.e. ex tunc* (with *pro praeterito* consequences). This system was adopted by the following countries:
    - IN EUROPE: Denmark, Estonia, Ireland, Norway, Sweden;
    - IN AFRICA: Botswana, Gambia, Ghana, Guinea, Kenya, Malawi, Namibia, Nigeria, the Seychelles, Sierra Leone, Swaziland, Tanzania;
    - IN THE MIDDLE EAST: Iran, Israel;
    - IN ASIA: Bangladesh, Fiji, Hong Kong (until 1 July 1997), India, Japan, Kiribati, Malaysia, the Federal States of Micronesia, Nauru, Nepal, New Zealand, Palau, Papua New Guinea, Singapore, Tibet[13], Tonga, Tuvalu, Vanuatu, Western Samoa;
    - IN NORTH AMERICA: the Canada, USA;
    - IN CENTRAL AND SOUTH AMERICA: Argentina, Bahamas, Barbados, Belize, Bolivia, Dominica, the Dominican Republic, Grenada, Guyana, Haiti, Jamaica, Mexico, St. Christopher/Nevis, Trinidad and Tobago.
- The New (British) Commonwealth Model (Mauritius) cannot be classified either under the American or the European model. It is characterized by a concentrated constitutional review under the jurisdiction of the Supreme Court consisting of ordinary judges without political nomination; as a rule, it involves preventive (a priori) review and the consulting function of the Supreme Court, although repressive (a posteriori) review is also possible; decisions take an erga omnes effect.
- The "Austrian" (Continental - Constitutional Review) Model (based on Kelsen's Model of 1920, involving the interconnection of the principle of the supremacy of the Constitution and the principle of the supremacy of the Parliament), whereunder constitutional matters are dealt with by specialized Constitutional Courts with specially qualified judges or by ordinary Supreme Courts or high courts or their special chambers (concentrated constitutional review) in special proceedings (*principaliter*). As a rule it is an abstract review, although a concrete

[13] Under the *Charter of the Tibetans in Exile* of 14 June 1991.

review is also possible. In addition to the *a posteriori* review, *a priori* review is also foreseen. The decisions have an *erga omnes* effect with reference to the absolute authority of the institution by which they are taken. Bodies exercising constitutional review may be:

a) Constitutional Courts

- IN EUROPE: Albania, Andorra, Austria, Belarus, the Federation of Bosnia and Herzegovina (with the Constitutional Courts of the federal entities Bosnia and Herzegovina and the Serbian Republic of Bosnia), Bulgaria, Croatia, the Czech Republic, the FRY (with the Constitutional Courts of constituent republics Serbia and Montenegro), Germany (with the regional Constitutional Courts: Baden-Wuerttemberg, Bavaria, Brandenburg, Bremen, Hamburg, Hessen, Niedersachsen, Nordrhein-Westfalen, Rheinland-Pfalz, Saarland, Sachsen, Sachsen-Anhalt), Hungary, Italy, Latvia, Lithuania, Luxembourg, Macedonia, Malta, Moldavia, Poland, Romania, the Russian Federation (with the federal unit Constitutional Courts: Adigea, Altai, Baskiria, Buryatia, Chechnia, Chuvachia, Dagestan, Inguchia, Irkutska Oblast, the Kabardino-Balkar Republic, Kakasa, the Karachaewo-Cherkez Republic, Karelia, Khalmukia, Koma, Marii-El, Northern Ossetia, Tatarstan, Tuba, Udmurtia, Yakutia/Sakha), Slovakia, Slovenia, Spain, Turkey, Ukraine;
- IN AFRICA: Angola, Benin, Burundi, the Central African Republic, Egypt, Equatorial Guinea, Gabon, Madagascar, Mali, Rwanda, South Africa, Togo;
- IN THE MIDDLE EAST: Cyprus, former Iraq, Palestine, Syria;
- IN ASIA: Armenia, Azerbaijan, Georgia, Kyrgyzstan, Mongolia, South Korea, Sri Lanka, Tajikistan, Thailand, Uzbekistan (with the regional Constitutional Committee of the Republic of Karakalpakstan);
- IN CENTRAL AND SOUTH AMERICA: Chile, Surinam, Tucuman Province (Argentina) with the *Constitution of Tucuman* of 28 April 1990;

b) High Courts or their special chambers

- IN EUROPE: Belgium (the Arbitration Court), Iceland, Liechtenstein, Monaco, Kosovo (the FRY);
- IN THE MIDDLE EAST: Yemen;
- IN AFRICA: Burkina Faso, Cameroon, Chad, Eritrea, Niger, Sudan, Uganda (1995), Zaire, Zambia;
- IN ASIA: the Philippines;
- IN CENTRAL AND SOUTH AMERICA: Costa Rica, Nicaragua, Panama, Paraguay, Uruguay;

c) The Constitutional Council

- in the Middle East: Lebanon;
- IN AFRICA: Mauritania, Senegal;
- IN ASIA: Cambodia, Kazakhstan.

Institutions based on the European model of constitutional review share the following common characteristics:

- constitutional review is introduced under different circumstances, depending on the particular national system;
- institutionally independent institutions of constitutional review located outside the judicial branch;
- in the proceedings following a constitutional complaint problems are created by the separation of constitutional review from the ordinary courts;
- constitutional status (administrative and financial autonomy) is a prerequisite for the independence of the Court;
- a monopoly of constitutional review (specialization in constitutional review), the concentration of power in one institution, most often with the power to abrogate statutes adopted by the Parliament;
- constitutional court judges are appointed by bodies of political power;
- the special nature of the jurisdiction: decisions are of a legal and political nature although they may also have a purely consultative function;
- the prevailing constitutional review of statutes;
- generally such constitutional review is repressive, although to a minor extent constitutional review is of a preventive nature.

- The Mixed (American Continental) Model with the elements of both a diffuse and concentrated system; despite the constitutional review power of the central Constitutional or Supreme Court (or its special chambers), all ordinary courts in the particular country are entitled to not apply laws deemed as not in conformity with the *Constitution*:

a) Constitutional Courts

- IN EUROPE: Portugal;
- IN CENTRAL AND SOUTH AMERICA: Colombia, Ecuador, Guatemala, Peru;

b) High Courts or their special departments

- IN EUROPE: Greece, Switzerland (in view of the fact that in the Swiss system - a system of limited constitutional review - the Swiss Federal Court cannot evaluate federal statutes, generally binding resolutions and ratified international agreements: the principle of supremacy exists on the federal level);
- IN ASIA: Indonesia, Taiwan;
- IN AFRICA: Cape Verde;
- IN CENTRAL AND SOUTH AMERICA: Brazil, El Salvador, Honduras, and Venezuela.

- The "French" (Continental) Model (based on the model of the French Constitutional Council - Conseil *Constitutionnel* - of 1958), where constitutional matters are subject to review by special bodies of constitutional review (most often the Constitutional Council) or by special chambers of ordinary Supreme Courts (concentrated constitutional review) in special proceedings (*principaliter*), provided that constitutional review is mainly of a preventive (consultative) character (although these systems also have a repressive form of constitutional review, in particular with reference to electoral matters):
  - IN EUROPE: France;
  - IN AFRICA: Algeria, Comoros, Djibouti, Ivory Coast, Morocco, and Mozambique.

- Other Bodies with the Power of Constitutional/Judicial Review (the National Council, Parliament or specialized parliamentary bodies, *etc.*):
  - IN EUROPE: Finland;
  - IN THE MIDDLE EAST: Bahrain, Kuwait, Oman;
  - IN AFRICA: Congo, Ethiopia, Guinea-Bissau, Sao Tome and Principe, Tunisia, Zimbabwe;
  - IN ASIA: Afghanistan, Brunei, Burma/Myanmar, China (as well as Hong Kong after 1 July 1997), Laos, North Korea, Pakistan, Turkmenistan, Vietnam;
  - IN AUSTRALIA;
  - IN CENTRAL AMERICA: Cuba.

- Systems Without Constitutional/Judicial Review:
  - IN EUROPE: Great Britain[14], the Netherlands[15];
  - IN AFRICA: Lesotho, Liberia, and Libya[16].

- International judicial institutions with certain functions of constitutional review:
  - the European Court of Human Rights in Strasbourg (for the European complaint);
  - the Court of Justice of the European Community in Luxembourg (for legal action leading to annulment; legal action against the omission of action by the Council of Ministers or the Commission of the Community; the solution of previous issues as a concrete review upon the demand of a member state court);

[14] Although the powers of the House of Lords include some elements of the preventive constitutional review.

[15] Concerning the system of the Netherlands, there are a few exceptions concerning the powers of the Supreme Court to decide cases connected to European Communities institutions.

[16] However, certain functions of constitutional review may be exercised in Libya by the Supreme Court of Libya which is also a member of the Arab Group of the Constitutional Courts and Constitutional Councils.

- the Court of EFTA Geneva (for the settlement of disputes between EFTA member states, a concrete review requested by the court of a member state of EFTA);
- *Comision y la Corte Interamericanas de los Derechos Humanos;*
- *Tribunal de Justicia del Acuerdo de Cartagena;*
- *La Corte Centroamericana de Justicia como Tribunal Constitucional de Centroamerica;*
- *the African Court of Human Rights.*

With reference to such international institutions, there often arises the question of their role and the role of national institutions of constitutional/judicial review concerning the relation of supranational law (*e.g.* European Community Law) *vis-à-vis* the national legal systems, based either on the dualist tradition[17] or on a monist tradition[18].

[17] In the following countries it is not superior in rank, but has a special character of supranational law: Denmark, Germany, Italy, Portugal.

[18] In the following countries feature the recognition of the supremacy of supranational law over national law: Belgium, France, Luxembourg, the Netherlands, Spain.

IV. Relation of Constitutional Courts to Other State Institutions

Concerning the Legislature:

The influence of the constitutional bodies upon the appointment or elections of the members of the Constitutional Court differs from system to system. In the election based systems as a rule parliaments exercise greater influence upon the elections of constitutional court judges as compared to the elections of judges of the ordinary courts. In those systems[19] constitutional court judges are exclusively appointed by the legislative body. The same principle is followed by Portugal where constitutional court judges, appointed by the Parliament, co-opt a certain number of other constitutional court judges. In case these systems involve the participation of the executive power, its role is limited to the recruitment of candidates.

The nature of the relation between the parliament and the Constitutional Court is that the parliament as a legislature adopts statutes whose conformity with the *Constitution* is evaluated by the Constitutional Court. Beside this, the parliament regulates by statute the important questions of the status and functioning of the Constitutional Court and the status of the judges of the Constitutional Court. The Constitutional Court has an important influence on the activities of the parliament, as it is bound to consider and implement the decisions of the Constitutional Court.

Concerning the Executive, the Head of State and the Government:

The Appointment Based Systems (Without the Participation of a Representative Body): In France three members of the Constitutional Council are appointed by the President of the Republic, three by the President of the National Assembly and three by the President of the Senate. In Japan, Sweden and in many African countries with constitutional/judicial review, judges (of the Supreme Court) are appointed exclusively by the government. In Burundi, Cyprus, Denmark, Ireland, Senegal South Africa, Turkey and the USA, constitutional court judges are exclusively appointed by the State sovereign or by the Head of State. In the Argentinean Province of Tucuman one part of constitutional court judges are appointed by an electoral body composed of the judges of the Supreme Court and the rest of the judges are appointed by the executive power.

The mixed systems (appointment and election): In Andorra the appointment of constitutional court judges is subject to the influence of the Head of State (the executive) and the Parliament. In Albania, Armenia, Austria, Bosnia and Herzegovina,

---

[19] Adigea/Russia, Azerbaijan, Baden-Wuerttemberg/Germany, Bavaria/Germany, Bashkiria/Russia, Belgium, Berlin/Germany, Bosnia and Herzegovina, Bremen/Germany, Buryatia/Russia, Croatia, Dagestan/Russia, Estonia, FRY, Germany, Hamburg/Germany, Hessen/Germany, Hungary, Irkutska Oblast/Russia, the Kabardino-Balkar Republic/Russia, Karelia/Russia, Koma/Russia, Liechtenstein, Lithuania, Montenegro/FRY, Namibia, Niedersachsen/Germany, Nordrhein-Westfalen/Germany, Northern Ossetia/Russia, Poland, Rheinland-Pfalz/Germany, Saarland/Germany, Serbia/FRY, the Serbian Republic of Bosnia, Slovenia, Switzerland, Tatarstan/Russia, Tuba/Russia, Uzbekistan and Yakutia/Russia.

Bulgaria, Cambodia, Canada, the Czech Republic, Georgia, Kazakhstan, Romania, and Slovakia one part of constitutional court judges are elected by the Parliament or are appointed by the Head of State or by the President of the Parliament, and the rest by the executive power. In Italy, Peru and Spain one part of constitutional court judges are elected by the Parliament, one part is appointed by the government and the remaining part by the senior judicial officials. With mixed systems, too, the role of the Parliament is prevalent and the role of the executive power is sometimes limited to a mere recruitment of the candidates.

On the other hand, the Constitutional Court is empowered to decide the Proceedings Before the Constitutional Court for Establishing the Responsibility of the President of the Republic, the Prime Minister or Ministers (Impeachment proceedings). It is necessary to emphasize criminal liability and civil liability beside the political responsibilities of a Minister. The individual criminal liability of a Minister is made evident through a special procedure. In the case of civil liability, a minister is liable for material damages.

Furthermore, there is the possibility of discovering the responsibility of the Prime Minister and ministers as regards violations of the *Constitution* and statutes in the performance of their duties which result in charges of Impeachment against the Prime Minister or against any Minister of State. The parliament (*e.g.* the National Assembly in Slovenia) may summon the Prime Minister or any Minister of State before the Constitutional Court to answer charges relating to breaches of the *Constitution* or of statute, committed during the performance of office. Any such charges are determined by the Constitutional Court.

Concerning the Executive or Administrative Branch:

Constitutional court decisions are final and binding. There is no legal remedy against a decision issued by the constitutional court. However, some systems allow the constitutional court to change its decisions (*e.g.* Belarus, Latvia, Ukraine).

Concerning the Judiciary:

In particular systems the composition of the constitutional court is predetermined and is composed of top judicial officials. Because the body competent for constitutional/judicial review consists of representatives of the highest national courts in Greece and in some other countries (Hong Kong until 1 July 1997, Mauritius. Rwanda, Sudan) neither the Parliament nor the government exerts direct influence on the appointment of constitutional court judges.

See Chapter V.

Concerning State bodies in general:

In most systems only the Constitutional Court is entitled to decide on disputes concerning jurisdiction between State bodies.

In addition, all State bodies have in principle the status of a legitimate (privileged) petitioner in proceedings before the Constitutional Court.

V. The Constitutional Court and the Judicial Branch

The following relations between the constitutional court and the judicial branch are possible:

- One of the powers of constitutional courts may be a concrete constitutional review; the European system did not adopt a judicial review system - it is obligatory for ordinary courts to present a case of potential unconstitutionality to the Constitutional Court; In the event that a court, in deciding a concrete case, concludes that a statute which it must apply is unconstitutional, it must stay the proceedings and initiate proceedings before the Constitutional Court. The proceedings in the court may be continued after the Constitutional Court has issued its decision.
- The constitutional court may also decide on jurisdictional disputes between ordinary courts and bodies of the State administration.
- The constitutional complaint is a special subsidiary legal remedy before the constitutional court. The Constitutional Court is limited in its decisions on constitutional matters, and violations of constitutional rights. However, if a violation is determined, the decision may have a cassatory effect as a rule *inter partes* (and *erga omnes* if the subject-matter of the decision is a legislative act). The Constitutional Court here retains the position of the highest judicial authority. These courts can be referred to as superior courts of cassation, because constitutional courts reviewing decisions of ordinary courts act in fact as the third and the fourth instance. Although the Constitutional Court is not a court of full jurisdiction, in specific cases it is the only competent court to judge whether a ordinary court has violated the constitutional rights of a plaintiff. It involves the review of micro-constitutionality and perhaps the review of the implementation of a law, which, however, is a deviation from the original function of the Constitutional Court. Cases of constitutional complaint raise sensitive questions of defining constitutional limits. In any case, the Constitutional Court is limited strictly to questions of constitutional law. The Slovenian system is specific in that the Constitutional Court may, under specified conditions, make a final decision on constitutional rights or fundamental freedoms themselves (Para. 1 of Article 60 of the *Slovenian Constitutional Court Act*, Official Gazette RS, No. 15/94).

The protection of fundamental rights and freedoms is an important function of the majority of constitutional courts, irrespective of whether they perform the function of constitutional judgment in the negative or positive sense. Whenever a Constitutional Court has the function of a "negative legislature", constitutional review is strongest precisely in the field of fundamental rights. Even in other fields (the concretisation of State-organisational and economic constitutional principles) in which the legislature has the primary role even in principle, constitutional courts insure that fundamental rights be protected. Precisely in the field of the protection of rights, the Constitutional Court also has the function of the substitute "Constitution-maker" (a "positive function"), which means that in specific cases constitutional courts even supplement constitutional provisions.

The Constitutional Court is not a part of the judicial branch.

VI. Guarantees of the Independence of Constitutional Justice

A. The Financing (the Budget) of the Constitutional Court as the Basis of its Independence

Most constitutional/judicial review bodies have an independent budget[20] separate from the whole State budget, and they are fully independent concerning its control. In addition, the financing of some newly introduced Constitutional Courts (*e.g.* in the Russian Federation, Lithuania, Belarus) is regulated in greater detail than other formerly established Courts , *e.g.*:

Bulgaria: The Constitutional Court shall have an independent budget (Article 3 of the *Constitutional Court Act* of 30 July 1991).

Spain: Under the "second additional" Article of the *Constitutional Court Act No. 2/1979 of 3 October 1979*, the Constitutional Court proposes the budget, which is managed as a part of the whole State budget. The Secretary General of the Constitutional Court prepares the budget with the help of the Court administration; in addition, he implements the budget and prepares the closing balance.

Portugal: Under Article 5 of the *Organization, Activity and Proceedings of the Constitutional Court Act No. 28/82 of 15 November 1982*, the Constitutional Court disposes of its budget; which is adopted within the scope of "the general expenses" of the State budget.

Germany: Under Article 1 of the *Constitutional Court Act (of 12 March 1951 with amendments)*, the Constitutional Court has a more independent and autonomous position in comparison with other constitutional bodies. Therefore the Constitutional Court as a constitutional body is not financially subordinated to any ministry, but it is an autonomously managed and budgeted independent body. The Court budget may be adopted only as a particular autonomous plan to be included in the whole State budget. The Court may manage the budgetary funds independently. The budget is discussed and adopted by a plenary Court session (Article 1.2 of the *Rules of procedure of the Constitutional Court of 2 September 1975, amended on 5 December 1978*). Consequently, a Plenum of the Court forms a special Budgetary Council (Article 3.1.c of the *Rules of Procedure of the Constitutional Court*).

Hungary: The Constitutional Court draws up its own budget and submits it, as part of the State Budget, for approval to the Parliament (Article 2 of *Act No. XXXII of 1989 on the Constitutional Court*).

---

[20] Or not explicitly declared as an independent budget, but a part of the whole State budget, *e.g.* Article 30 of the *Constitutional Court of the Republic of Uzbekistan Act of 30 August 1995*, Article 11.1 of the *Constitutional Court of the Republic of Kyrgyzstan Act of 18 December 1993*; Article 39.1 of the *Constitutional Court of the Republic of Yakutia/The Russian Federation Act of 6 February 1992*.

Austria: The Court budget is not regulated either by a statute or by rules of procedure or any other internal regulation of the Constitutional Court. However, the Court has its own budget in practice, as per agreement with the Ministry of Justice. The Court may manage its budget as a part of the whole State budget, adopted by the Parliament. The Court budget constitutes a special section of the State budget, similar to budgets of other State bodies.

Italy: Under Article 14.2.1. of the *Organization and Proceedings of the Constitutional Court Act. No. 87/1953 of 11 March 1953*, the Constitutional Court may autonomously manage its expenditures within the scope of funding adopted by statute.

France: The funds required for the activity of the Constitutional Council are determined within the scope of the whole general State budget. The President of the Constitutional Council is empowered to provide budgetary expenses. (Article 16 of the *Decree on the Constitutional Council No. 58/1067 of 7 November 1958 with amendments*).

Belgium: The funds necessary for the functioning of the Court of Arbitration is allocated under the allocations budget (Article 123.1 of the *Special Law of 6 January 1989 on the Court of Arbitration*).

The Russian Federation: Under Article 124 of the *Constitution*, the courts are financed only from the Federal budget, thus providing for the complete and independent administration of justice in accordance with Federal Law. In addition, the *Federal Constitutional Law on the Constitutional Court of the Russian Federation of 24 June 1994* contains exhaustive provisions guaranteeing the activities of the Constitutional Court (Article 7 of the *Law*): the Federal Constitutional Court is independent of any other body in organisational, financial, and material and technical terms. Court funding is provided for in the federal budget and ensures the independent and comprehensive performance of constitutional judicial proceedings. The federal budget annually allocates the separate funding needed to ensure the activities of the Constitutional Court of the Russian Federation, and which is managed by the Court autonomously. Spending estimates of the Court may not be reduced as compared to a preceding financial year.[21] The Court autonomously and independently arranges information and personnel support for its activity. The property required by the Court to perform its activities and managed by it is federal property. The Court may vest the right to manage the mentioned property in the structural units comprising its staff. No restrictions of legal, organisational, financial, information, material, technical or other conditions on the activities of the Court, as prescribed by the present *Constitution*, are permitted.

Lithuania: The freedom and independence of the Constitutional Court from other institutions is ensured by financial, material, technical as well as organisational guarantees secured by law (Article 5-1.1 of the *Constitutional Court Act No. I-67 of 3 February 1993, as amended by Act No. I-1475 of 11 July 1996*). The Constitutional Court is

[21] See also a similar provision in Article 93 of the *Constitutional Court of the Republic of Azerbaijan Act*.

financed from the State budget by ensuring the Constitutional Court the ability to independently and properly perform the functions of constitutional review. The estimate of expenditures must be approved by the Constitutional Court, which also independently disposes of the funds that are allocated to it (Article 5-1.2 of the *Constitutional Court Act*). The buildings and other possessions which are used by the Constitutional Court are State property transferred into the possession, use and disposal of the Constitutional Court on trust. These possessions may not be seized or transferred to other subjects without the consent of the Constitutional Court (Article 5-1.3 of the *Constitutional Court Act*). Restrictions of legal, organisational, financial, information, material, technical and other conditions of Court activities provided by the *Constitutional Court Act* are prohibited (Article 5-1.5 of the *Constitutional Court Act*).

Belarus: Guarantees of the activity of the Constitutional Court: Funding for the Constitutional Court is drawn from the budget of the Republic and guarantees the complete independence of legal proceedings before the Court. A separate item in the annual budget of the Republic provides for the funds required to guarantee the work of the Constitutional Court, and the Court is free to use those funds as it sees fit (Article 24.1 of *Constitutional Court Act No. 2914/XII of 30 March 1994*).

The premises required by the Constitutional Court to carry out its duties are the property of the Republic; the Court is responsible for their day-to-day management (Article 24.2 of the *Constitutional Court Act*).

Latvia: The Constitutional Court is financed from the State budget (Article 37 of the *Constitutional Court Act of 5 June 1996*).

Georgia: Under Article 4.2 of the *Constitutional Court Act of 31 January 1996*, expenses connected with the organization and activities of the Constitutional Court are determined by a separate section of the State budget. The President of the Constitutional Court submits a draft of expenses connected with the activities of the Constitutional Court by a proceedings determined by law.

Romania: Under Article 50 of the *Organization and Activity of the Constitutional Court Act No.47/1992*, the Court has its own budget as a part of the whole State budget. A draft budget must be approved by the judges of the Constitutional Court by a majority of votes and proposed for adoption to the Government and included in the whole State budget.

Croatia: Under the *Constitutional Court Act* (Narodne novine, No. 13/1991, with amendments), the Constitutional Court has its own budget which is adopted as a special part of the State budget by the representative chamber of the Parliament on the proposal of the Constitutional Court.

Slovakia: The Constitutional Court has a separate section in the Sate budget (Article 77 of the *Act on the Organization of the Constitutional Court of the Slovak Republic, on the Proceedings before the Constitutional Court and the Status of Judges, of 20 January 1993*).

Turkey: The Constitutional Court, within the framework of the general budget, administers its own budget (Article 56 of the *Law of the Organization and Trial Proceedings of the Constitutional Court No. 2949 of 12 November 1983*). In the first instance, the President is responsible for covering expenses out of the budget. In the second instance, responsibility for expenses is assigned to the Secretary-General. Accounting is managed by the department of Accounts established within the Constitutional Court. The payment of expenses is administered by the Directorate of the Financial Department of the Court. The Minister of Justice, or by consent, the Secretary General of the Court participates in discussions relating to the budget and conducted before the Parliamentary Assembly. The President and members of the Court may not, however, be summoned to present oral explanations.

Ukraine: Financing the Constitutional Court is regulated by the State budget in a separate item (Article 31.1 of the *Constitutional Court Act*). Proposals as to the size of the budget of the Court as well as the draft of the respective estimate are submitted by the President of the Court to the Cabinet of Ministers of the State and the Parliament during the formulation of the proposed State budget for each following year (Article 31.2 of the *Constitutional Court Act*).

SLOVENIA:

The Slovenian system has the following general features:

- The special character of the *Budget Act*: The Slovenian system in force (under the *Referendum and Public initiative Act*) excludes from the referendum decision-making process all laws passed by the accelerated legal procedure, as well as laws implementing the adopted State budget (Article 10 of the *Referendum and Public Initiative Act*). As a representative body, the National Assembly also adopts the State budget (Article 148 of the *Constitution*; Articles 215-228 of the *Rules of Procedure of the National Assembly*).
- The Basic Principles of the State Budget: concerning the Principle of the Annuality of the State Budget, the Budget is adopted for one year and is valid for the year which it concerns (Article 14.2 of the *Public Consumption Financing Act*).
- The Principle of the Legality of the State Budget: Each year the National Assembly approves the budget as well as the budget account.
- The Principle of the Universality of the Budget: All revenues raised and all monies expended for public purposes by the State must be accounted for in their respective budgets (Article 148.1 of the *Constitution*). Where the budget of the State has not been officially adopted as and when due, the expenditures of the State are temporarily financed in accordance with the terms of the last preceding budget of the State (Article 148.2 of the *Constitution*).
- The Principle of Specialisation: A payment may only be made for the purpose the Budget Law has authorised such expenditure for (Article 20 of the *Public Consumption Financing Act*).

- The Public Nature of the Budget and the Accounts: For the budget and the accounts of the State to be approved by law, they must go through all stages of the legislative procedure, including publication in the Official Gazette RS (Article 154 of the *Constitution*).
- The Procedure for the Adoption of the State Budget and the Closing Balance in Slovenia: The *Rules of Procedure of the National Assembly* specify a special procedure concerning the adoption of the State Budget and the Closing Balance (Articles 215-228 of the *Rules of Procedure of the National Assembly*).[22]
- The general State Budget is proposed to the National Assembly by the Government at latest by 1 October of the then current year in the form of a proposal accompanied by a budgetary memorandum (Article 215 of the *Rules of Procedure of the National Assembly*). Amendments can be added to the proposed budget (Articles 217-221 of the *Rules of Procedure of the National Assembly*). After voting on the particular parts of the budget, depending on the situation, any necessary reconciliation takes place. In addition, the National Assembly votes on the State Budget as a whole (Article 222 of the *Rules of Procedure of the National Assembly*). During the year the Government may propose a Budget Adjustment which is adopted by the accelerated legislative procedure (Article 225 of the *Rules of Procedure of the National Assembly*).
- The Closing Balance concerning the previous year is proposed by the Government at latest by the session of the National Assembly in June (Article 226 of the *Rules of Procedure of the National Assembly*). The National Assembly votes on the Closing Balance as a whole (Article 228 of the *Rules of Procedure of the National Assembly*).
- Techniques of Financial Supervision in Slovenia: This traditional method is exercised by means of approving the budget and the accounts of the State (Article 148 of the *Constitution*).

The Budget of the Slovenian Constitutional Court: The material basis of the real autonomy and independence of the Constitutional Court also depends on autonomy as regards management of the budgetary funds. Therefore statute declares that the funds for the work of the Constitutional Court are determined by the National Assembly following the proposal of the Constitutional Court, and constitute a part of the Republic of Slovenia Budget (Article 8.1 of *the Constitutional Court Act*). The Constitutional Court is not dependent on the Government in proposing the budget, which otherwise proposes the State budget. The Constitutional Court decides on the use of the mentioned funds (Article 8.2 of the *Constitutional Court Act*).

Control of the use of these funds is performed by the Court of Auditors (Article 8.3. of the *Constitutional Court Act*), which is the body with the ultimate responsibility for

[22] Articles 215-228 of the *Rules of Procedure of the National Assembly*. The budget does not determine the rights and responsibilities of citizens and other persons, so it is not in conflict with Article 87 of the *Constitution* if it is not determined in the Standing Orders of the National Assembly that the National Assembly must adopt it as statute (Constitutional Court of the Republic of Slovenia, Decision No. U-I-40/96, 3 April 1997, *Official Gazette RS* No. 24/97; *OdlUS VI*, 46).

auditing State finances, the State budget and monies expended for public purposes (Article 150.1 of the *Constitution*).

B. The Payment of Fees in Constitutional Proceedings as a Source of Constitutional Court Funding

Some constitutional court systems have introduced as an additional financial source fees payable when filing for proceedings before the Constitutional Court. However, the Court may exempt a citizen from paying such fees or reduce the fees depending on financial status (*e.g.* Article 39 of the *Federal Constitutional Law on the Constitutional Court of the Russian Federation of 24 June 1994*). Sometimes the fee may be explicitly excluded or the petitioners may be exempt from taxes, fees, and other such financial impositions (*e.g.* Turkey - Article 52 of the *Law of the Organization and Trial Procedures of the Constitutional Court No. 2940 of 12 November 1983*). The majority of systems have not introduced such fees on principle. On the other hand, prescribing a fee deters the abuse of petitioning or a payment of the costs of proceedings is explicitly foreseen in cases of frivolous applications (*e.g.* Austria, Georgia, Germany, Malta, Portugal, Spain, Switzerland).

Ukraine: The costs incurred by parties in constitutional examinations are compensated by budgetary funds as decided by the Constitutional Court of Ukraine (Article 59 of the *Constitutional Court Act*).

Slovenia: In proceedings before the Slovenian Constitutional Court each participant bears his own costs, unless the Court decides otherwise (Article 34.1 of the *Constitutional Court Act*). If a party fails to provide the necessary information for the Court due to unexcused absence, lack of preparedness or some other reason and, as a result, the hearing must be postponed, the Court may decide that the postponement of the hearing shall be at the expense of this party (Article 34.2 of the *Constitutional Court Act*). Petitioners pay court fees in accordance with a special statute (Article 34.3 of the *Constitutional Court Act*). Such a statute has not been passed to date.

C. The Powers of Constitutional Courts as Proof of their Independence

The extent of the powers of constitutional/judicial review bodies is as follows: in the traditional approach constitutional review bodies have no positive power in relation to the legislature. They may only be a negative legislature, whereas the role of a positive legislature is reserved for the Parliament. However, the negative powers of constitutional courts in relation to the legislature are also subject to certain limits, whereby the function of cassation of constitutional justice is limited by certain rights reserved for the legislative and the executive branch (*e.g.* the principle of judicial self-restraint, the *political question doctrine*).

Today, however, constitutional review decisions are no longer limited to the mere function of cassation, and the so-called positive decisions issued by constitutional courts are gradually gaining importance:

- One of these forms involves **appellate decisions** (Germany, USA), in which the Constitutional Court instructs the legislature (explicitly or implicitly, with or without a time limit) to adopt certain regulations in a particular domain. Recently certain countries have even imposed special provisions regarding the right of constitutional/judicial review bodies to instruct the legislature. Such a "positive" authorization of constitutional justice in a rather narrow form exists in the German, Austrian and Polish systems, and even more intensely in the Italian, Portuguese, Hungarian and Brazilian systems of constitutional/judicial review. The Portuguese Constitutional Court is provided with the express constitutional authorization to identify the existence of unconstitutionality due to an omission. This does not involve the fact that the proceedings of an abstract review of rules might reveal legislative omissions due to the insufficient or incorrect solution to a specific issue, but aims at direct and independent evaluation and identification of omissions caused by the legislature. The nature of the *Portuguese Constitution*, which imposes upon the legislature the obligation of legislative activity, has influenced the fact that the Portuguese Constitutional Court actually acquired such power. Considering the sensitive nature of this power, the Constitutional Court can only be active in the particular domain on the basis of the role of a narrow circle of legitimate petitioners. The Hungarian Constitutional Court, too, has jurisdiction to eliminate an unconstitutional situation that has developed due to some omission of a government body; proceedings can be initiated by the Constitutional Court alone or on the proposal of any government body or aggrieved person. The Brazilian constitutional/judicial review system features a special abstract complaint due to omission whereby government bodies, political parties represented in the Parliament and political organisations act as the main legitimate petitioners of the proceedings. At the same time, this system has a special individual complaint against an omission caused by the legislature (*mandado de injuncao*). The Italian constitutional review system is, above all, characterized by so-called creative decisions with which the Constitutional Court may even change or add wording to the regulation in question.
- Another factor of the decision-making process are the **guidelines** issued following a constitutional/judicial review; such guidelines for the future action of the legislature, the government and the administration may include appellate decisions, and partly also other decisions (decisions of abrogation, decisions of annulment, possibly also declaratory decisions relating to conformity with the *Constitution*). Sometimes such decisions already clearly indicate the essential point of the legal regulation, so that the legislature has only to elaborate the details and to provide for official adoption of the statute. This phenomenon is sometimes referred to as the negative legislative activity of constitutional courts or as the paralegislative or superlegislative activity of modern constitutional courts.

Nevertheless, from a global point of view, positive decisions of constitutional justice are of a substitutional character. The extent of this function is proportional to the intensity with which constitutional rights are affected.

- The court may issue decisions on unconstitutionality with reservation or with interpretations created by the Constitutional Court itself (the **interpretative decisions**). In these decisions the Constitutional Court insures with its own interpretation that in the future the implementation of the statute complies with the *Constitution*.

One specific feature of the Slovenian system is the use of the so-called appellate judgment issued by the Constitutional Court, and of content-related guidelines. The novelty of the *Constitutional Court Act* is that it allows for the possibility of the Constitutional Court assessing whether the Legislature has omitted a necessary legal regulation arising out of the *Constitution*. If the Constitutional Court determines that a statute, a regulation or a general act for exercising public powers is unconstitutional or illegal because a certain matter which it should regulate is not regulated or is regulated in a manner which makes it impossible to be abrogated either retroactively or prospectively, a declaratory judgment is adopted. The Legislature or the body that issued such an unconstitutional or illegal general act must abolish the ascertained unconstitutionality or illegality within a period set by the Constitutional Court (Article 48 of the *Constitutional Court Act*). In this way the *Constitutional Court Act* offers new possibilities (techniques, modes) of Constitutional Court decision-making, among which the Constitutional Court is free to choose when looking for an adequate form for its decision. Thus, for example, interpretative decisions are necessary and reasonable whenever in practice a disputed provision is understood and applied in several ways whereof certain ones are constitutionally acceptable and others are not. In such a case abrogation of the provision would not be reasonable because it would also affect those who have already applied the provision in conformity with the *Constitution*; accordingly, it is necessary to use the interpretative decision, through which the Constitutional Court preserves the disputed provision in the legal system in its undisputed extent or its meaning that conforms with the *Constitution*, at the same time indirectly eliminating from the legal system the use of the disputed provision if it is inconsistent with the *Constitution* (through the duty of all government bodies to act in compliance with any decision issued by the Constitutional Court).[23]

[23] An indirect form of such power of the Constitutional Court was recognised by the *Constitution of 1974* in Articles 410 and 417. Nevertheless, in relation to the Legislature, the former system did not allow the abrogation of statutes or more severe forms of the relationship between the Constitutional Court and the legislature. Under Article 410 of the *Constitution of 1974* the Constitutional Court, however, had a certain "preventive function" of integrating current processes of coordination, complementing the further development of the legal system (along with consideration of the principle of the self-restraint of the Constitutional Court), hence the right and obligation to pursue the phenomena important for the implementation of constitutionality and legality, as well as to inform the Parliament of the situation and the problems in the respective domain and to provide it with the opinions and proposals for issuing, modifying or amending of statues, as well as with other measures granting constitutionality and legality. It referred to the phenomena encountered by the Constitutional Court in the cases in which it had already adopted a specific decision, but thereby discovered that in practice the interpretation of the *Constitution*, the existing statutorial regulations or the implementation of the *Constitution* or statute may involve certain ambiguities or gaps for which the statute or other legal measures should be modified or amended or replaced by an adequate measure. Under Article 417 of the *Constitution of 1974*, this applied also to the cases when the Constitutional Court discovered that the competent body had not issued a rule for the implementation of provisions of the *Constitution*, statute or other rule, although it had been obliged to do so.

Irrespective of the above, the Constitutional Court in its relation to the Legislature usually follows the principle of self-restraint: the interpretation of the provision does not exceed its limits, *i.e.* there is no direct amendment or modification of the provision by the Constitutional Court.

D. Immunities, Incompatibilities, Material Independence, and Protocol Rank

Most systems recognise the immunity of constitutional court judges and certain systems recognise explicit parliamentary immunity (*e.g.* Bulgaria, the Czech Republic, Italy, Slovenia, Spain). The independent position of constitutional court judges also implies the recognition of the corresponding material independence, as well as the adequate protocol rank. The respective matter is regulated mainly by the *Constitutional Court Acts* (passed by the Parliament), and sometimes by special parliamentary regulations or by internal regulations adopted by the Constitutional Court.

A special feature of the office of constitutional court judge is its incompatibility with certain activities. In almost all systems the office of constitutional court judge is compatible with scientific and artistic activities, but incompatible with political and commercial activities. With reference to political activities there may be various grades of restrictions, ranging from the absolute prohibition of membership in a political party (*e.g.* the Czech Republic) to the prohibition of membership for a certain period prior to election (*e.g.* Austria) or to the prohibition of membership in the bodies of a political party (*e.g.* Slovenia). The prevailing opinion regarding the activities of constitutional court judges in public is that they cannot be exclusively closed within the circle of their institution and that their activities in public contribute to the transparency of the Constitutional Court as well as to the pluralism of opinions.

Some significant systems in force are, as follows:

Georgia: Under Article 4.3 of the *Constitutional Court Act of 31 January 1996* the State is obliged to guarantee to a member of the Constitutional Court appropriate conditions for their work and life to ensure their independence. The State guarantees the security of members of the Constitutional Court and their family (Article 4.4 of the *Constitutional Court Act*). The social guarantees to the members of the Constitutional Court are regulated by special *Act No. 293-11G of 25 June 1996*.

Belarus: Guarantees of the independence of the Constitutional Court: The independence of Constitutional Court judges is guaranteed by their permanence of office, their immunity, their equal rights as judges, the procedure for the suspension and termination of the appointment of judges established by this Law, the right to a pension, the obligatory nature of the established procedure for constitutional legal proceedings, the prohibition of any form of interference in court activities, the guarantee of judges' material and social circumstances, and guarantees of security corresponding to their elevated status (Article 25.1 of the *Constitutional Court Act*).

The salaries of the President, Vice-President and judges of the Constitutional Court are determined on the same scale as that governing the salaries of the Chairman, First Vice-Chairman and Vice-Chairmen of the Supreme Council respectively (Article 25.2 of the *Constitutional Court Act*).

Constitutional Court judges not possessing living space, or who have flats with several tenants or need better accommodation for other reasons are to be granted comfortable, accommodation in the city of Minsk at the expense of the budget of the Republic, no later than six months after their election to the post of judge or the advent of the reasons mentioned hereinabove (Article 25.3 of the *Constitutional Court Act*).

If a Constitutional Court judge's term of office ceases before they reach retirement age or in the particular cases provided for in the *Constitutional Court Act*, they may, at their request, return to their former post or be offered equivalent work if the post is not available (Article 25.4 of the *Constitutional Court Act*).

The employment positions offered to former constitutional court judges is the responsibility of the Supreme Council of the Republic of Belarus. In this connection, the length of judges' service in the Constitutional Court is counted as part of the period of service completed in their previous work (Article 25.5 of the *Constitutional Court Act*).

Constitutional Court judges, including those who have resigned or retired, enjoy the guarantees provided for in legislation on the status of judges in ordinary courts. In the event of other legislative acts affording Constitutional Court judges greater guarantees of independence than provided for in this Law, the provisions of those acts shall apply (Article 25.6 of the *Constitutional Court Act*).

Ukraine: The Constitutional Court is the sole body exercising constitutional review in Ukraine (Article 1.1 of the *Constitutional Court Act* of 16 October 1996). Guarantees for the activity of judges of the Constitutional Court of Ukraine are as follows: the Independence of Judges (Article 27 of the *Constitutional Court Act*), the immunity of judges (Article 28 of the *Constitutional Court Act*), and the social and material provisioning of judges (Article 29 of the *Constitutional Court Act*).

Slovenia: The Position of the Constitutional Court in the National Hierarchy of the Courts: The Constitutional Court is the highest body of judicial power for the protection of constitutionality, legality, human rights and basic freedoms (Article 1.1 of the *Constitutional Court Act*).

Present Situation/Standard Legal Reference: The *Constitution of the Republic of Slovenia of 1991* again brought about changes in the position and powers of the Constitutional Court (Official Gazette RS, No. 33/91). A new *Constitutional Court Act* (Official Gazette RS, No. 15/94) specified in detail the provisions of the powers and proceedings. New *Internal Regulations of the Constitutional Court* are in the process of being adopted.

Incompatibilities and Immunities: The following activities are incompatible with judicial function (Article 166 of the *Constitution* and Article 16 of the *Constitutional Court Act*):

- Holding office in government bodies;
- Holding office in local government;
- Holding office in political parties;
- Holding other offices and activities deemed incompatible with the office of a judge of the Constitutional Court, in accordance with the *Constitutional Court Act*.

As regards immunities, members of the Constitutional Court enjoy the same immunities as members of the National Assembly (Article 167 of the *Constitution*).

A judge of the Constitutional Court may not be held legally responsible for an opinion or a vote expressed at a public hearing or session. They may not be detained, nor may criminal proceedings be instituted against them without the permission of the National Assembly, unless the judge commits a crime for which a sentence of over five years is prescribed (Article 18 of the *Constitutional Court Act*).

Working Conditions of Constitutional Court Judges

a) Salary and allowances

The President of the Constitutional Court is entitled to a salary and additional payment based on his office equal to the amount determined for the President of the National Assembly. Judges of the Constitutional Court are entitled to a salary and an additional payment based on their office equal to the amount determined for the Vice-President of the National Assembly. The Constitutional Court determines the salary of the Secretary of the Constitutional Court. It is determined proportional to the salary of a judge of the Constitutional Court (Article 71 of the *Constitutional Court Act*).

Judges of the Constitutional Court are entitled to compensation equal to their proportional salary for the period of their annual leave and for the first 30 days of absence from work due to illness or injury (Article 72 of the *Constitutional Court Act*).

b) Employment period and social insurance

The time during which judges of the Constitutional Court perform their office is counted as part of their employment period. During the performance of their office as judge of the Constitutional Court, judges enjoy social insurance in accordance with the social insurance regulations for persons in permanent employment (Article 73 of the *Constitutional Court Act*).

c) Other personal incomes and reimbursements

Judges of the Constitutional Court are entitled to:

- Reimbursement of travel expenses to and from work,
- Reimbursement of expenses for business trips (a travel allowance, daily allowance, hotel expenses),

- An allowance for meals during work,
- An annual leave allowance,
- A displacement allowance,
- Reimbursement for costs incurred for travelling from the place of their business residence to the place of permanent residence and back,
- Reimbursement of expenses for moving from their permanent residence to their business residence and back,
- Reimbursement of training costs,
- A long-service bonus,
- A retirement bonus (Article 74.1 of the Constitutional Court Act).

Conditions for and the amount of allowances and reimbursements are determined by the Constitutional Court (Article 74.2 of the *Constitutional Court Act*).

d) Annual leave and other days off

Judges of the Constitutional Court are entitled to annual leave of 40 days (Article 75.1 of the *Constitutional Court Act*). Judges of the Constitutional Court are entitled to extraordinary paid leave not exceeding 7 days each year for personal reasons (Article 75.2 of the *Constitutional Court Act*). In exceptional cases Judges of the Constitutional Court may be allowed to take extraordinary leave not exceeding 30 days each year (Article 75. 3 of the *Constitutional Court Act*). The conditions and examples mentioned in the preceding paragraphs are determined by the Constitutional Court (Article 75.4 of the *Constitutional Court Act*).

e) The rights of judges of the Constitutional Court after the expiration of their term of office

Judges of the Constitutional Court who, until their election as judge of the Constitutional Court, performed the office of court judge or some other permanent office in a State body, have the right, after the expiration of their office, to return to their previous office, if they fulfil all conditions for performing such office and if, within three months after the expiration of the said office, they notify the competent body of their wish to return to their previous function office (Article 76 of the *Constitutional Court Act*).

Judges of the Constitutional Court who, until their election as judge of the Constitutional Court, were employed in a State body, public company or public institution, have the right to return to their job within three months after the expiration of their office, or to another job corresponding to their education and their level of professional skill (Article 77 of the *Constitutional Court Act*).

Judges of the Constitutional Court whose office has expired and who, for objective reasons, are unable to perform their previous office, or who cannot find other suitable employment, and have not yet reached the age of retirement according to general regulations, have the right to compensation in the amount of the salary they received as a judge until such time as they find new employment or fulfil the conditions for retirement according to general regulations, but for no longer than one year after the termination of their office (Article 78.1 of the *Constitutional Court Act*).

The right to compensation under the preceding paragraph may be prolonged until the conditions for retirement are fulfilled according to general regulations, but for a period of no more than one further year (Article 78.2 of the *Constitutional Court Act*).

The period from the two preceding paragraphs is included in the employment period of judges of the Constitutional Court whose office has expired. During this period judges enjoy social insurance in accordance with the social insurance regulations for persons in permanent employment. If judges are entitled to annual leave during this period, they also are entitled to an annual leave allowance. They are entitled to a retirement bonus upon retiring (Article 78.3 of the *Constitutional Court Act*).

f) Wages, allowances, other incomes and reimbursements of other personnel of the Constitutional Court

The regulations which regulate the rights of officials in State bodies are applied mutatis mutandis when determining the rights of the Secretary of the Constitutional Court to receive wages, allowances, other incomes, reimbursements and other rights (Article 79 of the *Constitutional Court Act*).

The regulations which regulate the rights of officials in State bodies are applied mutatis mutandis when determining the rights of a director of a special service of the Constitutional Court or an adviser of the Constitutional Court to receive a salary, allowances, other incomes, reimbursements and other rights (Article 79.2 of the *Constitutional Court Act*).

The provisions of regulations concerning employees in State bodies are applied mutatis mutandis when determining the rights of other employees of the Constitutional Court to receive salaries, allowances, other incomes, reimbursements and other rights (Article 79.3 of the *Constitutional Court Act*).

E. The Appointment/Election of Judges to the Constitutional Court

The influence of constitutional bodies upon the appointment or election of members of the Constitutional Court differs from system to system. The varieties applicable to elections or appointment of constitutional court judges are as follows:

1. APPOINTMENT BASED SYSTEMS (Without the Participation of a Representative Body).
2. ELECTION BASED SYSTEMS: As a rule Parliaments exercise greater influence upon the election of constitutional court judges as compared to the election of judges of ordinary courts.
3. MIXED SYSTEMS (Appointment and Election): With mixed systems, too, the role of the Parliament is prevalent and the role of the executive power is sometimes limited to a mere recruitment of the candidates.

4. PREDETERMINED COMPOSITION FROM HIGH JUDICIAL OFFICIALS: Because the body competent for constitutional/judicial review consists of representatives of the highest national courts neither the Parliament nor the government exert direct influence on the appointment of constitutional court judges.

The independent position of the Constitutional Court is further symbolized by the mode of appointment of the President of the Constitutional Court. Its independence is even greater if the President is appointed by his/her colleagues - constitutional court judges themselves (Italy, Belgium, Cambodia, the FRY, Slovenia, Spain, Tuba/Russia, Yakutia/Russia); otherwise, the President is appointed by a qualified body outside the Constitutional Court (Austria, Bashkiria/Russia, France, Germany, the Kabardino-Balkar Republic/Russia, Karelia/Russia, Koma/Russia, Montenegro/the FRY, Northern Ossetia/Russia, Poland, Serbia/the FRY, the Serbian Republic of Bosnia, Tatarstan/Russia).

Nearly everywhere the qualifications and the required professional experience of constitutional court judges are subject to high standards: the candidates must not only have more than average legal expertise but also a high degree of sensibility for the political effects of their decisions. In practice constitutional court judges are selected exclusively from first-class lawyers with many years of experience, such as judges of ordinary courts, attorneys at law, senior government officials, professors of law, or politicians. Sometimes special qualifications are required (Belgium: command of the corresponding national language).

F. Public Control/the Public Nature of the Activities of the Constitutional Court

The public nature of the activities of the Constitutional Court is declared by the *Constitution*, but mainly by the *Constitutional Court Act*. This principle may be realized in some different forms:

PUBLIC HEARINGS;

Save where expressly provided by statute, all Court proceedings are conducted in public and all decisions are delivered in open Court (the public nature of court hearings; the public nature of delivering decisions). These public activities function as a control or supervision of the impartibility and legality of the decision making process. Beyond that, the *Constitution* sometimes provides for the so-called legal reservation: the exclusion of the public is reserved in order to protect the interests of a minor or public morality.

Slovenia: The activities of the Slovenian Constitutional Court are to be conducted in public in accordance with the *Constitutional Court Act* (Article 3 of the *Constitutional Court Act*). The principle of the public nature of the activities, declared by this provision, are of general importance concerning all kinds of proceedings; the purpose of the mentioned principle is to ensure a control on the activities of the Court to the parties of the proceedings and also other citizens (the unlimited circle of individuals). The respective function is ensured *e.g.* also by the statutorial provision on public hearings before the Constitutional Court (Article 35 and 36 of the *Constitutional Court Act*). The constitutional Court may exclude the public from a hearing or part thereof on the grounds of protecting public morals, public order, national security, the right to privacy and personal rights (Articles 37 and 38 of the *Constitutional Court Act*). The public nature of the activities of the Slovenian Constitutional Court results also from some internal regulations or systems adopted by the Constitutional Court[24] - the *Legal Information System of the Constitutional Court* introduced in 1987, the computerised database of Slovenian Constitutional Case-Law as a public database, in principle accessible to all users of legal information.

THE PUBLICATION OF COURT DECISIONS IN OFFICIAL GAZETTES, OFFICIAL DIGESTS, AS WELL AS IN LEGAL JOURNALS;

Slovenia: Providing information to the public concerning decisions of the Constitutional Court is, moreover, one of the functions, following the principle of the public nature of the activities of the Constitutional Court, set forth in laws and in other regulations[25]. The Constitutional Court applies this principle by publishing its decisions in official publications (Official Gazettes, *see* Article 42 of the *Constitutional Court Act* and Article 46 of the *Rules of Procedure of the Constitutional Court*) and by allowing access to information on its decisions in its database.

Slovenian constitutional case-law has been published and offered to interested parties:

- in *Odločbe in sklepi Ustavnega sodišča* (the Official Digest of the Constitutional Court; Slovenian full text version, including dissenting/concurring opinions, and English abstracts) since 1992;
- in the *Pravna Praksa* (Legal Practice Journal; Slovenian abstracts, with the full-text version of the dissenting/concurring opinions);
- since 1 January 1987 via the on-line *STAIRS database* (Slovenian full text version; since 1963; English full-text version since 1992); for this purpose a special English-Slovenian glossary was created containing terms on constitutional law;
- the first original CD-ROM containing the Slovenian Constitutional Case-Law (in Slovenian) was issued in May 1998;
- since 1993 in the *Bulletin on Constitutional Case Law* of the Venice Commission of the Council of Europe (including English and French summaries of the most

---

24 - Articles 4 and 39 of the *Rules of Procedure of the Constitutional Court* (Official Gazette SR, No. 10/74;
- Articles 39-41 of the *Regulation on Internal Office Administration* of 26 May and 7 July 1977 and of 16 January 1992;
- *Conclusions on the Assurance of the Public Nature of the Activities of the Constitutional Court Through the Public Media* of 13 January 1983 and 24 December 1987;

25 Article 3 of the Constitutional Court Act; Article 5, Para 2 of Article 37, Articles 6, 66 and 67 of the Rules of Procedure of the Constitutional Court; Official Gazette RS, No. 49/98, Articles 4 through 39 of the Regulation on Internal Office Administration; Conclusions on the Assurance of the Public Nature of the Activities of the Constitutional Court through the Public Media, adopted on 13 January 1983 and 24 December 1987.

important current decisions), as well as in the *CODICES database* issued on CD-ROM (Slovenian and English full-text versions and summaries in English and French), http://www.codices.coe.int; http://www.coe.fr/codices;

- since August 1995 on the Internet (Slovenian constitutional case law since 1990 (full text in Slovenian as well as in English - http://www.us-rs.si);
- since 1998 on the homepage of the A.C.C.P.U.F. (the French Speaking Group of Constitutional Courts) (http://www.accpuf.org);
- since 2000 on the website of the Ius-Info database of constitutional case-law (abstracts and full texts of decisions) and literature (abstracts) in Slovenian since 1963 (http://www.ius-software.si);
- since 1995 some important cases in English full-text versions in the *East European Case Reporter* on Constitutional Law, published by BookWorld Publications, The Netherlands. The *East European Case Reporter* is available also on the Internet (http://www.bwp-mediagroup.com/bookworld/eecrcl.htm).

THE CIRCULATION OF INFORMATION THROUGH SEVERAL COMPUTERIZED INFORMATION SYSTEMS;

Legal information on constitutional review matters as supported by different means of communication or media, taking into consideration the principle of the public nature of the activities of any Constitutional Court, circulate from the Constitutional Court as a decision issuer, to the public, the potential petitioners before the Constitutional Court, who receive information which may motivate their new petitions. This stream of information constitutes a certain procedural circle due to the nature of proceedings before any Constitutional Court, which are in principle proposed proceedings (*jurisdiccion voluntaria*): only a permanent inflow of petitions to the Constitutional Court actually justifies the existence, function and activities of the Constitutional Court.

Slovenia: The initial purpose of the legal databases of the Slovenian Constitutional Court was to provide more flexible processing of legal information, primarily constitutional case-law, as a support to the Constitutional Court in its decision-making processes. The activities of the Constitutional Court are conducted in public (Article 3 of the *Constitutional Court Act, Official Gazette RS*, No. 15/94; Article 5 and Articles 53 to 55 of the *Rules of Procedure of the Constitutional Court, Official Gazette RS*, No. 49/98). Therefore the corresponding databases were not created for internal users only (judges and legal advisers of the Court); from the very beginning they were intended for external users of legal information concerned with practice and theory related to constitutional review.

VII. The Independence and the Autonomy of the Organization of the Constitutional Court

Most systems of constitutional/judicial review allow for the organizational autonomy of the empowered body on the basis of the *Constitution* or on the basis of the *Constitutional Court Act*. This means they authorize the respective constitutional/judicial review bodies to follow their own rules regarding their internal organization. Special services of the Constitutional Courts are organized in a similar way: they consist of clerks and clerical staff, whereby the head of special services generally holds the status of a secretary general.[26]

Unless constitutional court acts especially provide otherwise, general labour laws apply to employees of the Constitutional Court (*e.g.* the Czech Republic - Article 10 of the *Constitutional Court Act*, Latvia - Article 40 of the *Constitutional Court Act*). In addition, in some systems constitutional courts may autonomously regulate the salaries of clerks and clerical staff, while the position of judges is regulated by the *Constitution*, or by a *Constitutional Court Act* (*e.g.* Slovenia - Articles 71-79 of the *Constitutional Court Act*; Latvia - Articles 38-39 of the *Constitutional Court Act*); Japan - Articles 50-51 of the *Court Organization Act No. 59 of 16 April 1947*; Turkey - Article 59 of the *Law of the Organization and Trial Proceedings of the Constitutional Court No. 2949 of 12 November 1983*), or by one special act (*e.g.* the Slovak Republic - Article 17 of the *Act on the Organization of the Constitutional Court of the Slovak Republic, and on Proceedings before Constitutional Court and the Status of Judges, of 20 January 1993*) or by many special acts (*e.g.* Georgia, Uzbekistan) or by general provisions regulating the position of State officers.

Some significant systems in force are as follows:

Belarus: The Constitutional Court independently acquires the information facilities and personnel required for its activities (Article 24.3 of the *Constitutional Court Act*).

The physical and technical resources required for the activities of the Constitutional Court, including means of transport and communication, are provided by the appropriate State bodies in accordance with a procedure established by the President of the Republic of Belarus with the agreement of the Constitutional Court.

The existing level of physical and technical resources required for the activities of the Constitutional Court may be reduced only with the consent of the Supreme Council of the Republic of Belarus (Article 244 of the *Constitutional Court Act*).

Latvia: The Constitutional Court freely and independently carries out information and organizational facilities procurement for its activities (article 5-1.4 of the *Constitutional Court Act*).

---

26 Some Courts have also established additional special services supporting the activities of the Court, *e.g.* the Constitutional Court of the Republic of Uzbekistan under the *Provisions on the Expert Advice Council of the Constitutional Court of the Republic of Uzbekistan of 5 July 1996*.

Ukraine: The Constitutional Court adopts acts which regulate the organization of its internal work in conformity with the *Constitutional Court Act* (Article 3.2 of the *Constitutional Court Act*) taking into consideration statutorial provisions on the Research consultants and assistants of judges of the Constitutional Court of Ukraine (Article 25 of the *Constitutional Court Act*), and the Organization and activities of the Constitutional Court of Ukraine (Articles 30-37 of the *Constitutional Court Act*), which involve: organization (Article 30), financing (Article 31), the Secretariat (Article 32), standing commissions (Article 33), temporary commissions (Article 34), the archive (Article 35),the library (Article 36) and the bulletin (Article 37). The organization of the activities of the Court is determined by the *Constitution*, by the *Constitutional Court Act*, as well as by internal acts of the Court.

Slovenia: The Constitutional Court of the Republic of Slovenia regulates its organization and work with its rules of procedure and other general acts (Article 2.2. of the *Constitutional Court Act*). The *Rules of Procedure* were adopted on 26 may 1998 (*Official Gazette RS*, No. 48/98).

The administrative services of the Slovenian Constitutional Court consist of: the secretary of the Constitutional Court (responsible for matters of organization and legal knowledge and the director/assistant secretary (responsible for financial organizational matters) (Article 7 of the *Constitutional Court Act*).

The special services of the Constitutional Court consist of: the Legal Information Centre with the legal library; legal advisers and clerical staff. The Constitutional Court appoints advisers to the Constitutional Court from among legal and other experts (Article 7.3 of the *Constitutional Court Act*). The Constitutional Court may employ probationers in accordance with statute (Article 7.4 of the *Constitutional Court Act*).

VIII. Bodies Exercising Constitutional Review and the Particularities of their Organization

The Composition of Constitutional Courts and Similar Bodies

The introduction of modern constitutional review is based on the Principle of the Separation of Powers and the Constitutional Court as the highest body for the protection of human rights. The Court's jurisdiction and proceedings are specified in detail by a Constitutional Court Act as well as in the Rules of Procedure adopted by the Constitutional Court itself.

In all new systems of constitutional review the Constitutional Court became the highest body of judicial power for the protection of constitutionality, legality, human rights and basic freedoms.

Most systems of constitutional/judicial review insure the **organisational autonomy** of the institution. This means they authorize respective constitutional/judicial review bodies to follow their own rules regarding their internal organization. Most constitutional/judicial review bodies also have an independent budget as a separate part of the whole State budget, and they are fully independent in its control. Services of constitutional courts are organised in a similar way: they consist of clerks and clerical staff, and the head of services generally holds the status of secretary general. Each constitutional court regulates its own internal organization in the exercise of its administrative autonomy and in principle it rules its own funds as a part of the State budget. The technical services of the Constitutional Court include the office of the General Secretary (concerning matters of organization and legal knowledge) and the office of the Head of Financial Services (financial organizational matters). The special services of the Constitutional Court also include the Legal Information Centre with its professional library; legal advisers and clerical staff.

The **decision-making process** may be organised in different ways:

- on the level of a PLENARY COURT (in France always);
- on the level of a PLENARY COURT AND CHAMBERS (*e.g.* Georgia, Germany, Portugal, Slovenia, Spain, Slovenia, Switzerland, where the reason for deciding in chambers involved mostly constitutional complaints; however, in these systems, too, important decisions are made in accordance with the plenary principle);
- on the level of task forces for individual legal domains (Italy).

The Constitutional Court decides *in camera* sessions or in public hearings.

The normal rule for deciding in the Constitutional Court is by a majority vote of all judges. Exceptions are nonetheless possible. As regards its composition when deciding, usually the Court deliberates *in plenum,* but it sits in chambers when deciding cases of constitutional complaints.

The **number of judges** performing the function of constitutional/judicial review differs from country to country, ranging from four (Andorra) or five (Senegal) to sixteen (Germany). As a rule, the appointment procedure for the members of the Court differs from that for the President of the Constitutional Court. The same applies to the duration of their term of office.

The **term of office of constitutional court judges** lasts between six (Portugal, Burundi), twelve years (Germany) or fifteen years (Kyrgyzstan); the average is nine years (which is also the case in Slovenia). The term of office of the members of the Serbian Constitutional Court/the FRY, of the US Supreme Court, as well as of the Constitutional Court of Tatarstan/Russia is permanent. A term of office that is too long may be dangerous for the evolution of the legal process, whereas a too short term of office could be detrimental for the continuity and the authority of the institution, as well as for the balance of the constitutional case-law. To assure the principle of the (political) independence of constitutional court judges, most systems do not allow their re-election. There is a variety of examples of how this is handled: the judges may have life tenure (the USA), they may perform their functions up to a certain age (a maximum of 70 years in Austria, Belgium, Bosnia and Herzegovina, Kyrgyzstan and Tatarstan/Russia, 60 years in Tajikistan), or their re-election after a limited term in office is explicitly excluded (France, Germany, Italy). Hungary, Portugal and Switzerland, do envisage the re-election of constitutional court judges, whereas in Spain immediate re-election is forbidden. The reappointment of Constitutional Courts and the frequency of the appointment of constitutional court judges do not coincide; in some countries the term of office of constitutional court judges expires successively, which results in the successive reappointment of a part of the Constitutional Court (Bulgaria, France, Romania, Spain). The minimum age acceptable for appointment of a constitutional court judge (40 years) is specified in Germany, Belgium and Slovenia, Georgia (35 years) and Tajikistan (30 years).

The influence of government bodies upon the **appointment or elections** of constitutional court judges differs from case to case (see Chapter VI)

Most systems recognise the **immunity of constitutional court judges** and certain systems recognise explicit parliamentary immunity (see Chapter VI).

A special feature of the office of constitutional court judge is its **incompatibility** with certain activities (see Chapter VI).

IX. The Powers of Constitutional Courts and Other Bodies of Constitutional Review

Powers

From a historical point of view, in many systems constitutional/judicial review emerged in jurisdictional disputes between various government bodies. Due to the fact there are numerous other controversial issues emerging today, constitutional review is no longer concerned only with the distinction of these powers .

The following countries feature the Constitutional Court functions listed:

I. PREVENTIVE REVIEW:

1. CONSTITUTIONAL PROVISIONS (Costa Rica, Chile, Moldavia, Switzerland - as regards the canton constitutions, the Central African Republic);

2. INTERNATIONAL AGREEMENTS (Albania, Algeria, Andorra, Armenia, Azerbaijan, Belarus, Bulgaria, Burkina Faso, Burundi, Buryatia/Russia, Cameroon, Cape Verde, the Central African Republic, Chile, Comoros, Congo, Dagestan/Russia, Estonia, France, Gabon, Georgia, Germany, Guatemala, Guinea, Hungary, the Ivory Coast, Karelia/Russia, Kazakhstan, Lithuania, Madagascar, Mali, Moldavia, Poland, Portugal, Russia, Slovenia, Spain, Tajikistan, Tunisia, Ukraine);

3. STATUTES (Afghanistan, Algeria, Austria - as regards the acts of federal entities, Belarus, Burkina Faso, Burundi, Cambodia, Cameroon, the Central African Republic, Chad, Chile, Comoros, Congo, Costa Rica, Cyprus, Djibouti, Ecuador, Finland, France, Gabon, Germany, Guatemala, Guinea, Hungary, Indonesia, Ireland, Italy, Ivory Coast, Kazakhstan, Madagascar, Mali, Mauritius, Morocco, Namibia, Niger, Northern Ossetia/Russia, Peru, Poland, Portugal, Romania, Russia, South Africa, Spain, Sri Lanka, Syria, Thailand, Togo, Tucuman/Argentina, Turkey, Tunisia, Venezuela, Zambia);

4. REGULATIONS (Belarus, Burundi, the Central African Republic, Comoros, Congo, Gabon, Madagascar, Namibia, Northern Ossetia/Russia, Portugal, Tucuman/Argentina);

5. ACTS OF THE HEAD OF STATE (Algeria, Guinea, Madagascar);

6. ACTS OF TERRITORIAL UNITS (South Africa);

7. OTHER REGULATIONS: BUDGET ACTS, PARLIAMENTARY INTERNAL REGULATIONS (Belarus, Burundi, Cameroon, the Central African Republic, Chad, Comoros, Cyprus, Djibouti, France, Madagascar, Niger, Romania, Thailand, Togo).

II. REPRESSIVE (A POSTERIORI) REVIEW:

1. Abstract review:

a) Concerning the Constitution, constitutional amendments, or basic constitutional provisions (Baden-Wuerttemberg/Germany, Brazil, Costa Rica, Cuba, Cyprus, Dagestan/Russia (the constitutions of administrative units), the FRY (the conformity of the *Constitution* of constituent republics with the *Constitution of the Federal State*); Kyrgyzstan, Rheinland-Pfalz/Germany, Russia (constitutions of federal entities), Saarland/Germany, Turkey, Ukraine, Uzbekistan (the conformity of the *Constitution of the Republic of Karakalpakstan* with the *Constitution of Uzbekistan*);

b) International agreements (including agreements between the Federal State and federal entities) (Adigea/Russia, Afghanistan, Austria, Azerbaidjan, Bashkiria/Russia, Cameroon, Chad, Comoros, Congo, Costa Rica, Greece, the Kabardino-Balkar Republic/Russia, Latvia, Liechtenstein, Lithuania, Madagascar, Mauritania, Moldavia, the Philippines, Russia, Senegal, Tatarstan/Russia, Tuba/Russia, Uzbekistan, Yakutia/Russia);

c) Statutes (Adigea/Russia, Afghanistan, Albania, Algeria, Angola, the Argentinean Province of Tucuman, Armenia, Austria, Azerbaidjan, Baden-Wuerttemberg/Germany, Bashkiria/Russia, Bavaria/Germany, Belgium, Benin, Berlin/Germany, Bolivia, Bosnia and Herzegovina, Brazil, Bulgaria, Buryatia/Russia, Cambodia, Cameroon, Cape Verde, Chad, Chile, Colombia, Congo, Comoros, Costa Rica, Cuba, Croatia, the Czech Republic (and the subsidiary power of the Supreme Court), Cyprus, Dagestan/Russia, Ecuador, Egypt, El Salvador, Equatorial Guinea, Eritrea, Estonia, the FRY, the FYROM, Georgia, Germany, Guatemala, Greece, Hamburg/Germany, Hessen/Germany, Honduras, Hungary, Irkutska Oblast/Russia, Italy, the Kabardino-Balkar Republic/Russia, Karelia/Russia, Koma/Russia, Kuwait, Kyrgyzstan, Latvia, Lebanon, Liechtenstein, Lithuania, Madagascar, Malawi, Malaysia, Mauritania, Mauritius, Moldavia, Mongolia, Montenegro/the FRY, Mozambique, Namibia, Nicaragua, Niedersachsen/Germany, Nordrhein-Westfalen/Germany, Northern Ossetia/Russia, Palestina, Panama, Paraguay, Peru, the Philippines, Poland, Rheinland-Pfalz/Germany, Russia, Rwanda, Saarland/Germany, Senegal, Serbia/the FRY, the Serbian Republic of Bosnia, the Seychelles, Slovakia, Slovenia, South Africa, South Korea, Spain, Sudan, Syria, Taiwan, Tajikistan, Tatarstan/Russia, Tuba/Russia, Turkey, Uganda, Ukraine, Uruguay, Uzbekistan, Karakalpakstan/Uzbekistan, Venezuela, Zaire, Zambia, Yakutia/Russia, Yemen);

d) Resolutions of the Parliament (Latvia);

e) Regulations (Adigea/Russia, Afghanistan, Albania, Angola, Armenia, Austria, Azerbaidjan, Buryatia/Russia, Cape Verde, Comoros, Congo, the Czech Republic, Dagestan/Russia, Ecuador, Egypt, El Salvador, Eritrea, the FRY, Georgia, Guatemala, Hungary, Irkutska Oblast/Russia, the Kabardino-Balkar

Republic/Russia, Karelia/Russia, Koma/Russia, Kuwait, Latvia, Liechtenstein, Lithuania, Madagascar, Mauritania, Moldavia, Mongolia, Montenegro/the FRY, Mozambique, Northern Ossetia/Russia, South Africa, Panama, the Philippines, Poland, Russia, Serbia/the FRY, the Serbian Republic of Bosnia, Slovakia, Slovenia, Sudan, Tajikistan, Tatarstan/Russia, Tucuman/Argentina, Ukraine, Uzbekistan, Karakalpakstan/Uzbekistan, Yakutia/Russia, Yemen);

f) Acts of the Head of State (Adigea/Russia, Algeria, the Argentinean Province of Tucuman, Armenia, Azerbaidjan, Bashkiria/Russia, Bulgaria, Buryatia/Russia, Ecuador, El Salvador, Georgia, Latvia, Lithuania, Madagascar, Moldavia, Mongolia, Northern Ossetia/Russia, Panama, the Philippines, Russia, Tajikistan, Tatarstan/Russia, Ukraine, Uzbekistan, Karakalpakstan/Uzbekistan, Yakutia/Russia, Yemen);

g) Rules and other acts of national administrative units (federal member states, (autonomous) provinces, local communities, *etc.*) (Azerbaidjan, Bashkiria/Russia, Buryatia/Russia, Cyprus, Dagestan/Russia, the FRY, Georgia, Irkutska Oblast/Russia, Karelia/Russia, Koma/Russia, Latvia, Northern Ossetia/Russia, Serbia/the FRY, Slovakia, Slovenia, Spain, Russia, Tajikistan, Ukraine, Uzbekistan, Yakutia/Russia);

h) Proclaimed regulatory measures of statutory authorities (Slovenia);

i) The conformity of national legal norms with international agreements (Albania, Bulgaria, the Czech Republic, the FRY, Hungary, Latvia, Poland, Slovakia, Slovenia);

j) Regional agreements/the agreements of constituent republics closed with the Federal State (Buryatia/Russia, Dagestan/Russia, Irkutska Oblast/Russia, the Kabardino-Balkar Republic/Russia, Karelia/Russia, Koma/Russia).

k) Other rules (Austria, Bolivia, Croatia, Ecuador, the FYROM, Hungary, the Kabardino-Balkar Republic/Russia, Madagascar, Mali, Northern Ossetia/Russia, the Philippines, Poland, Tajikistan, Serbia/the FRY, Slovakia, Slovenia, Turkey, Uganda);

2. CONCRETE REVIEW - SPECIALIZED CONSTITUTIONAL/JUDICIAL REVIEW BODIES REQUESTED BY ORDINARY COURTS (Adigea/Russia, Austria, Azerbaidjan, Bashkiria/Russia, Bavaria/Germany, Bremen/Germany, Bulgaria, Buryatia/Russia, Cambodia, Cape Verde, Congo, Costa Rica, Croatia, Cuba, the Czech Republic, Cyprus, Dagestan/Russia, Djibouti, Estonia, Gabon, Georgia, Germany, Guatemala, Hamburg/Germany, Honduras, Hungary, Iran, Italy, Karelia/Russia, Kazakhstan, Koma/Russia Kyrgyzstan, Lithuania, Madagascar, Malaysia, Malta, Niedersachsen/Germany, Niger, Panama, Paraguay, Poland, Romania, Russia, the Seychelles, Slovenia, South Africa, South Korea, Spain, Taiwan, Thailand, Togo, Uruguay, Zambia, Yakutia/Russia).

III. THE INTERPRETATION OF RULES (as an interpretative function):

1. CONCERNING THE CONSTITUTION (Adigea/Russia, Albania, Azerbaidjan, Bashkiria/Russia, Bulgaria, Burundi, Buryatia/Russia, Cambodia, Dagestan/Russia, Eritrea, Gabon, Germany, Hungary, Irkutska Oblast/Russia, Kazakhstan, Koma/Russia, Kyrgyzstan, Madagascar, Moldavia, Namibia, Niger, Papua New Guinea, Russia, Slovakia, Sri Lanka, Sudan, Taiwan, Uganda, Uzbekistan, Zaire, Yakutia/Russia);

2. CONCERNING STATUTES AND OTHER RULES (Azerbaidjan, Cambodia, Dagestan/Russia (in relation to federal legislation), Egypt, Equatorial Guinea, France, Indonesia, Madagascar, Palestina, Poland, Sudan, Taiwan, Uzbekistan).

IV. THE IMPLEMENTATION OF RULES - DECIDING ON MATTERS RELATING TO THE CONFORMITY OF A RULE'S IMPLEMENTATION WITH THE *CONSTITUTION* (Bashkiria/Russia, Ecuador, Irkutska Oblast/Russia, the Kabardino-Balkar Republic/Russia, the Philippines, Rheinland-Pfalz/Germany, Russia, Tuba/Russia).

V. THE OMISSION OF (STATUTORY) REGULATIONS - LEGAL *GAPES* (Brazil, Hungary, Italy, Portugal, the Seychelles, Uganda).

VI. (CITIZEN'S) LEGISLATIVE INITIATIVES:

1. CITIZEN'S INITIATIVES (Austria, Hungary, Romania, Spain);

2. Constitutional Court Legislative initiatives (Adigea/Russia, Bashkiria/Russia, Burundi, Buryatia/Russia, Dagestan/Russia, the Kabardino-Balkar Republic/Russia, Karelia/Russia, Koma/Russia, Northern Ossetia/Russia, Tatarstan/Russia, Tuba/Russia, Yakutia/Russia);

3. Participation in the legislative procedure (the Central African Republic).

VII. JURISDICTIONAL DISPUTES:

1. BETWEEN TOP GOVERNMENT BODIES (Adigea/Russia, Albania, Andorra, Austria, Azerbaidjan, Baden-Wuerttemberg/Germany, Bashkiria/Russia, Bavaria/Germany, Berlin/Germany, Bremen/Germany, Bulgaria, Buryatia/Russia, Cameroon, the Central African Republic, Chad, Croatia, Cyprus, Dagestan/Russia, Ecuador, El Salvador, the FRY, the FYROM, Gabon, Georgia, Germany, Guatemala, Hamburg/Germany, Hessen/Germany, Irkutska Oblast/Russia, Italy, the Kabardino-Balkar Republic/Russia, Karelia/Russia, Kazakhstan, Koma/Russia, Madagascar, Mali, Mongolia, Mozambique, Nicaragua, Niedersachsen/Germany, Niger, Nordrhein-Westfalen/Germany, Peru, Poland, Russia, Saarland/Germany, Senegal, the Serbian Republic of Bosnia, Slovakia, Slovenia, Spain, South Africa, South Korea, Taiwan, Tajikistan, Tatarstan/Russia, Thailand, Ukraine, Yakutia/Russia);

2. BETWEEN THE STATE AND REGIONAL OR LOCAL UNITS (Adigea/Russia, Albania, Austria, Bashkiria/Russia, Bosnia and Herzegovina, Brazil, Bulgaria, Buryatia/Russia, Cameroon, the Central African Republic, the Czech Republic (and the subsidiary power of the Supreme Court), Dagestan/Russia, the FRY, the FYROM, Germany, Hungary, India, Irkutska Oblast/Russia, Italy, Karelia/Russia, Koma/Russia, Madagascar, Malaysia, Mexico, Montenegro/the FRY, Nicaragua, Nigeria, Pakistan, Russia, the Serbian Republic of Bosnia, Slovenia, South Africa, South Korea, Spain, Switzerland, Tatarstan/Russia, Ukraine, Yakutia/Russia);

3. BETWEEN LOCAL OR REGIONAL UNITS (Austria, Bashkiria/Russia, Bolivia, Bosnia and Herzegovina, Brazil, Buryatia/Russia, Cameroon, the FRY, Germany, Irkutska Oblast/Russia, Italy, Karelia/Russia, Koma/Russia, Mexico, Montenegro/the FRY, Nicaragua, Nigeria, Peru, Russia, Slovenia, South Africa, South Korea, Spain, Switzerland, Tatarstan/Russia, Tucuman/Argentina, Ukraine);

4. BETWEEN THE COURTS AND OTHER GOVERNMENT BODIES (Austria, Egypt, Greece, Montenegro/the FRY Serbia/the FRY, Slovenia, Tucuman/Argentina);

5. OTHER SPECIFIC JURISDICTIONAL DISPUTES (Austria, Croatia, Cyprus, Hungary, Nicaragua, Tucuman/Argentina, Ukraine, Yakutia/Russia, Yemen);

6. Between the constitutional courts of the constituent republics of the federation (the FRY).

VIII. POLITICAL PARTIES - DECISIONS RELATED TO MATTERS OF UNCONSTITUTIONAL ACTS AND ACTIVITIES (Albania, Armenia, Azerbaidjan, Bashkiria/Russia, Bulgaria, Burkina Faso, Chile, Croatia, the Czech Republic, the FRY, the FYROM, Georgia, Germany, Moldavia, Montenegro/the FRY, Poland, Portugal, Romania, Russia, Serbia/the FRY, the Serbian Republic of Bosnia, Slovakia, Slovenia, South Korea, Yakutia/Russia).

IX. REFERENDUMS - DECISIONS REGARDING A REFERENDUM'S CONFORMITY WITH THE *CONSTITUTION* (Algeria, Armenia, Austria, Berlin/Germany, Burkina Faso, Cameroon, Chad, Chile, Comoros, Congo, Croatia, Djibouti, Equatorial Guinea, France, Gabon, Georgia, Greece, Hessen/Germany, Hungary, Ivory Coast, Kazakhstan, Madagascar, Mali, Mauritania, Moldavia, Mongolia, Montenegro/the FRY, Mozambique, Niger, Nordrhein-Westfalen/Germany, Portugal, Romania, Saarland/Germany, Slovakia, Slovenia, Zaire).

X. ELECTIONS - DECISIONS REGARDING THE CONFORMITY OF ELECTION PROCEEDINGS WITH THE *CONSTITUTION* AND STATUTE (Albania, Algeria, Armenia, Austria, Baden-Wuerttemberg/Germany, Bavaria/Germany, Berlin/Germany, Bulgaria, Burkina Faso, Burundi, Cambodia, Cameroon, the Central African Republic, Chad, Comoros, Congo, Croatia, the Czech Republic, Cyprus, Djibouti, Ecuador, Equatorial Guinea, France, the FRY, Gabon, Georgia, Germany, Greece, Guinea, Hamburg/Germany, Ivory Coast, Kazakhstan, Kyrgyzstan, Lebanon, Lithuania, Madagascar, Mali, Malta, Mauritania, Mauritius,

Moldavia, Mongolia, Montenegro/the FRY, Morocco, Mozambique, Namibia, Niedersachsen/Germany, Niger, Nigeria, Nordrhein-Westfalen/Germany, Portugal, Rheinland-Pfalz/Germany, Romania, Saarland/Germany, Serbia/the FRY, Slovakia, Sri Lanka, Syria, Togo, Tucuman/Argentina, Zaire, Yemen).

XI. THE CONFIRMATION OF THE ELECTION OF REPRESENTATIVES (Austria, Baden-Wuerttemberg/Germany, Bavaria/Germany, Berlin/Germany, Bulgaria, Chile, France, Georgia, Germany, Greece, Hamburg/Germany, Kazakhstan, Mongolia, Niedersachsen/Germany, Nordrhein-Westfalen/Germany, Saarland/Germany, Slovakia, Slovenia, Ukraine).

XII. THE PROTECTION OF HUMAN RIGHTS (constitutional complaints and similar constitutional remedies):

1. HUMAN RIGHTS PROTECTION (Adigea/Russia, Albania, Andorra, Austria, Azerbaidjan, Bavarian/Germany, Bashkiria/Russia, Benin, Berlin/Germany, Brazil, Bremen/Germany, Burundi, Buryatia/Russia, Cape Verde, Colombia, Congo, Croatia, the Czech Republic, Cyprus, Dagestan/Russia, Djibouti, Ecuador, El Salvador, Equatorial Guinea, the FRY, the FYROM, Georgia, Germany, Guatemala, Hessen/Germany, Honduras, Hungary, Israel, the Kabardino-Balkar Republic/Russia, Karelia/Russia, Koma/Russia, Kyrgyzstan, Liechtenstein, Montenegro/the FRY, Mali, Malta, Mauritius, Mongolia, Nicaragua, Panama, Papua New Guinea, Poland, Russia, Saarland/Germany, Senegal, Slovakia, Slovenia, South Africa, South Korea, Sudan, Spain, Sri Lanka, Switzerland, Syria, Taiwan, Tucuman/Argentina, Ukraine, Uzbekistan);
2. CONSTITUTIONAL COMPLAINTS REQUESTED BY COMMUNES (Baden-Wuerttemberg/Germany, the Czech Republic, Germany, Nordrhein-Westfalen/Germany);
3. CITIZENS' LEGISLATIVE INITIATIVES (Spain, Saarland/Germany);
4. NATIONALISATION (Rheinland-Pfalz/Germany, Saarland/Germany).

XIII. CAPACITY TO HOLD THE OFFICE:

1. CONCERNING THE HEAD OF STATE (Adigea/Russia, Algeria, Armenia, Azerbaidjan, Bashkiria/Russia, Bulgaria, Burundi, the Central African Republic, Croatia, Cyprus, France, Kazakhstan, Kyrgyzstan, Lithuania, Mauritania, Moldavia, Mozambique, Poland, Portugal, Romania, Yakutia/Russia);
2. CONCERNING OTHER STATE REPRESENTATIVES (Bulgaria, Cyprus, France, Russia, Yakutia/Russia);
3. Accepting the oath of the Head of State upon assuming office (Burundi).

XIV. IMPEACHMENT:

1. CONCERNING THE HEAD OF STATE/OR A MEMBER STATE OF THE FEDERATION (Adigea/Russia, Albania, Algeria, Armenia, Austria, Azerbaidjan, Bashkiria/Russia,

Bolivia, Bulgaria, Buryatia/Russia, Chile, Colombia, Croatia, the Czech Republic, Dagestan/Russia, Eritrea, the FYROM, Georgia, Germany, Hungary, Irkutska Oblast/Russia, Ireland, Italy, the Ivory Coast, Karelia/Russia, Kazakhstan, Koma/Russia, Lithuania, Madagascar, Mongolia, Montenegro/the FRY, Namibia, Russia, Rwanda, Slovakia, Slovenia, Tatarstan/Russia, Turkey, Ukraine, Yakutia/Russia);

2. OTHER STATE REPRESENTATIVES (Austria, Baden-Wuerttemberg/Germany, Bavaria/Germany, Bolivia, Bremen/Germany, Bulgaria, Comoros, Dagestan/Russia, Georgia, Italy, South Korea, Karelia/Russia, Koma/Russia, Lithuania, Mongolia, Niedersachsen/Germany, Nordrhein-Westfalen/Germany, Rheinland-Pfalz/Germany, Saarland/Germany, Slovenia, Taiwan, Tucuman/Argentina, Turkey, Ukraine).

XV. SPECIAL POWERS (violations of international law, decisions relating to the appointment of constitutional court judges and their immunity, opinions relating to the declaration of martial law, the implementation of decisions issued by international courts, proposals for the amendment of the *Constitution*, consultative functions, *etc.*) (Afghanistan, Algeria, Armenia, Austria, Berlin/Germany (membership in the *Richterwahlausschuss*); Bulgaria, Burundi, Cambodia, Chad, Cuba, the Czech Republic, Cyprus, Egypt, France, Germany, Hamburg/Germany (Representatives Rights), the Ivory Coast, Mauritania, Moldavia, Russia, Spain, Sri Lanka, Togo, Uzbekistan (concerning the dissolution of the Parliament, or the approval of a Head's of State decision)).

XVI. OTHER TASKS WHICH THE COURT IS CHARGED WITH BY THE *CONSTITUTION* OR STATUTE (Adigea/Russia, Azerbaidjan, Baden-Wuerttemberg/Germany, Bashkiria/Russia, Bavaria/Germany, Berlin/Germany, the Central African Republic, Chile, Croatia, Dagestan/Russia, Ecuador, the FYROM, Georgia, Germany, Guatemala, Hamburg/Germany, Hessen/Germany, Koma/Russia, Montenegro/the FRY, Nicaragua, Niedersachsen/Germany, Nordrhein-Westfalen/Germany, Portugal, Rheinland-Pfalz/Germany, Slovenia, South Africa, Spain, Tajikistan, Tuba/Russia, Turkey, Ukraine, Uzbekistan).

PARTICULAR COMPONENTS OF CONSTITUTIONAL COURT POWERS:

IN PREVENTIVE (*A PRIORI*) REVIEWS of constitutional provisions, international agreements signed by a particular country, statutes and other legislative acts, regulations and some other rules, the constitutional/judicial review body has in fact a consultative function, when on the demand of a petitioner (mostly privileged government bodies) it discusses a rule and issues the corresponding decision prior to the promulgation of a rule or its enforcement. Such power is held by the Constitutional Court of Italy with reference to provincial statutes; by the Constitutional or High Courts of Austria, Germany and Chile; (especially) by African systems following the French model; by Portugal, Ireland, Finland, Cyprus, Hungary, Romania, Syria, Turkey, Poland, Russia (only with reference to certain statutes), and until 1985 also by Spain. On the international level, this form of constitutional review has been subject to much criticism; in particular on the occasion of the abolishment of the preventive review in Spain, numerous weaknesses were pointed out: that the legislature neglects its own constitutional review, that in this way legislative procedure is delayed, that due to the short terms provided for, this review is questionable anyway. The preventive review provided by the French Constitutional Council applies mainly to statutes. Except for France and certain African countries, which are not familiar with the repressive review of statutes and executive regulations, but practice a wide preventive review of statutes, no country has adopted any pure system of preventive review.

THE REPRESSIVE (*A POSTERIORI*) REVIEW is applicable to the rules in force and has been adopted by most systems. Certain systems, however, tend to combine the essentially repressive review with the preventive review of the international agreements signed by the particular country; a few other systems practice a combination of the preventive and repressive review of other rules (Cyprus, Romania). Repressive review may be abstract or specific. In individual systems both forms may appear individually or jointly. Abstract (direct) review may refer to constitutional provisions, international agreements signed by a particular country, statutes, regulations, presidential decrees, legislative acts and other rules of administrative units as well as to some other categories of rules. It may be introduced independently of the proceedings in a specific case, on the basis of applications lodged by specially qualified petitioners. The abstract review is, in comparison with other forms, less frequent; its importance lies in the fact that it deals with theoretical questions relating to constitutional law. Constitutional court judges are concerned only with the question of the constitutionality of the rule as the main dispute; this may require the cassation of an unconstitutional rule or a declaratory dispute. The latter may also be of a preventive character. Cassation itself may have an *ex tunc* effect (annulment, setting aside) or an *ex nunc* effect (abrogation). Hence, cassation (of statutes) involves two versions: from the point of view of the authority of statute and the principle of notice, the cassation of a statute is supposed to take effect only following the adoption of a decision of the Constitutional Court onwards - an *ex nunc* effect (as in Austria). An abrogated statute represented the legal basis for issuing individual acts until its abrogation. From the point of view of the standing of the aggrieved citizens (parties) and the principles of equity and legality, the cassation of a statute is supposed to function retrospectively from the time of the adoption of the rule - *ex tunc* (as in Germany) - an unconstitutional statute cannot have any legal effect at all and it is necessary to "repair" everything that had been done on the grounds of an unconstitutional statute. A decision issued by the Constitutional Court has a retroactive effect going back to the adoption of the rule, as if the rule were erased from the legal system. The nullity of such an act is identified by the Constitutional Court only in a declaratory way. Nevertheless, this nullity cannot negate the fact that the respective statute was in force for a certain time and that legal affairs were regulated on that respective basis. In both cases individuals have the right to require the modification of individual acts issued on the respective basis.

THE SPECIFIC (CONCRETE, INDIRECT, ACCESSORY) REVIEW of rules arises out of proceedings in progress before an ordinary court which, however, has to be convinced of the unconstitutionality of a certain rule (Germany), or that the court's doubt about the unconstitutionality of the rule not be obviously unfounded (Italy). This approach envisages judicial review by an ordinary court whereby the Constitutional Court is relieved of its immediate duties (the character of a prejudicial question). The consequence of this review is that an unconstitutional rule (statute) is not applied to a specific dispute. The accessory constitutional review of a statute is rooted in the American system wherefrom it spread particularly into certain countries of the American continent and elsewhere. With a specific constitutional review the Constitutional Court issues decisions concerning the constitutionality and legality of legal measures as a prejudicial question and not a disputed individual act, as is the case with the constitutional complaint.

X. The Objects and Subjects of Constitutional Review

The Objects of constitutional review may be as follows:

- a constitution;
- a constitutional act;
- international agreements;
- statutes (organic or systemic statutes, ordinary statutes);
- legal *gapes*;
- parliamentary rules of procedure;
- other parliamentary regulations (ordinances, *etc.*);
- acts of the Head of State (having the force of law or not having the force of law);
- executive regulations of the Government (decrees, ordinances, budget acts, decisions, resolutions, *etc.*);
- governmental rules of procedure;
- executive regulations of the State administration (rules, orders, decisions, resolutions, *etc.*);
- individual acts of the State administration;
- rulings of territorial units (charters, ordinances, executive regulations *etc.*);
- collective agreements;
- judgments;
- interpretation of rules;
- the implementation of rules;
- legislative initiatives (*ex officio* duty o the Constitutional Court, citizen's initiatives *etc.*);
- jurisdictional disputes;
- the protection of human rights (the constitutional complaint, the popular complaint, other forms);
- election matters;
- referendum matters;
- capacity for offices;
- impeachment;
- other objects.

Subjects/Standing/Legal Interest Before the Constitutional Court:

- individuals (citizens, non-citizens)[27]. Some constitutional review systems also allow for a private individual's access to the Constitutional Court (concerning the abstract as well as concrete review, based on a constitutional complaint, or on a popular complaint (*actio popularis*) or on other forms of constitutional rights' protection (see chapter XI/A);.
- legal entities[28];
- associations, trade unions *etc.*
- State bodies (*i.e.* privileged, legitimate petitioners):
    - the legislature;
    - the executive (the Head of State, the Government, the State administration);
    - other State bodies or institutions;
    - territorial units;
    - the judiciary (ordinary courts; special courts; the Public Prosecutor);
    - the Central Bank;
    - the Court of Auditors;
    - the Ombudsman.

[27] Adigea/Russia, Albania, Andorra, Argentina, Austria, Azerbaidjan, Bavaria/Germany, Bashkiria/Russia, Benin, Berlin/Germany, Brazil, Bremen/Germany, Burundi, Buryatia/Russia, Cambodia, Cape Verde, the Central African Republic, Chad, Colombia, Congo, Costa Rica, Croatia, the Czech Republic, Cyprus, Dagestan/Russia, Djibouti, Ecuador, El Salvador, Equatorial Guinea, the FRY, the FYROM, Georgia, Germany, Guatemala, Hessen/Germany, Honduras, Hungary, Israel, Japan, the Kabardino-Balkar Republic/Russia, Karelia/Russia, Koma/Russia, Kyrgyzstan, Liechtenstein, Montenegro/the FRY, Mali, Malta, Mauritius, Moldavia, Mongolia, Nicaragua, Niger, Panama, Papua New Guinea, Paraguay, Peru, Poland, Rheinland-Pfalz/Germany, Russia, Saarland/Germany, Senegal, Seychelles, Sierra Leone, Slovakia, Slovenia, South Africa, South Korea, Sudan, Spain, Sri Lanka, Switzerland, Syria, Taiwan, Tucuman/Argentina, Ukraine, Uganda, Uzbekistan, Venezuela.

[28] Those entitled to lodge a constitutional complaint are generally individuals but in Austria, Germany, Spain, Switzerland, the FRY and Montenegro, legal entities explicitly may also, while in the Croatian system legal entities are explicitly excluded as a potential appellant.

XI. The Various Forms of Constitutional Review and their Implementation in Practice

According to statistical data there are 215 different current systems of constitutional and judicial review around the world. Among them there are 115 of a European character, 52 of an American character, 14 of a mixed character, 7 of a French character, 1 of New Commonwealth character, 21 of other forms of Constitutional/judicial review and 5 constitutional systems without constitutional/ judicial review.

The European model is the most wide spread current model of constitutional review in practice. Such a situation is first of all the result of the introduction of constitutional review, supported by the German experience as well as by the respective general models of constitutional systems created within some international organizations and/or associations (*e.g.* the Council of Europe), in Central and Eastern Europe, in the CIS as well as in several federal entities of the Russian Federation.[29] In addition, the European model was introduced also as an additional system in some systems in Central and South America, which were based in the past on the judicial review system of the American type.

On the other hand, the introduction of certain models was a result of traditional, historical, cultural, political and commercial links among some countries and/or among several groups of countries, always depending on the specific circumstances in a particular country.

[29] Adigea, Altai, Baskiria, Buryatia, Chuvachia, Dagestan, Inguchia, Irkutska Oblast, the Kabardino-Balkar Republic, Kakasa, the Karachaewo-Cherkez Republic, Karelia, Khalmukia, Koma, Marii-El, Northern Ossetia, Tatarstan, Tuba, Udmurtia, Yakutia/Sakha.

XII. CONSTITUTIONAL REVIEW IN THE FIELD OF HUMAN RIGHTS PROTECTION

A. The Individual as an Applicant Before the Constitutional Court

Proceedings before the Constitutional Court have the nature of proposed proceedings (*juridiccion voluntaria*). In principle, the Constitutional Court cannot itself initiate proceedings; as a rule, the proceedings before the Constitutional Court are based on (restricted to) the corresponding application lodged by a special, duly qualified (privileged) constitutional institution (the so-called legitimate petitioners).

The initiation of constitutional review proceedings on the initiative of the Constitutional Court (*ex officio*) is quite rare. It may most often be traced to some of the constitutional review systems of Eastern Europe; further, it is strictly preserved in Croatia and in Slovenia[30], elsewhere *ex officio* proceedings are not as frequent. The Austrian Constitutional Court, for example, may on its own initiative begin proceedings of the constitutional review of a statute or a regulation only if it refers to a prejudicial question in some proceeding before the respective Constitutional Court. All the above cases may be referred to as objective forms of constitutional review.

On the other hand, some constitutional review systems also allow for a private individual's access to the Constitutional Court (concerning abstract as well as concrete review, based on a constitutional complaint, or on a popular complaint (*actio popularis*) or on other forms of constitutional rights' protection. This involves the so-called subjective constitutional review, the violation of individual rights and the protection of individual rights against the State (in particular against the legislature). In the countries with a diffuse constitutional review and in some countries with a concentrated constitutional review, the individual citizen is offered the possibility of requesting the constitutional review of statutes, administrative measures or judgments in special proceedings. Only after the complaint has been lodged with the Constitutional Court do proceedings begin. Even then, as a rule, the complainant may withdraw their complaint in order to thereby terminate the respective proceedings.

The individual's standing as complainant before the Constitutional Court has been influenced by extensive interpretation of provisions relating to the constitutional complaint, as well as by ever more extensive interpretation of provisions relating to concrete review[31]. In some systems the individual's access to constitutional courts has become so widespread that it already threatens the functional capacity of the Constitutional Court[32]. Therefore, the legislature is trying to find some way for constitutional courts to eliminate less important or hopeless proceedings (*e.g.* the

30 Para. 2 of Article 15 of the *Croatian Constitutional Court Act* or in Article 39, Article 58 and Para. 4 of Article 61 of the *Slovenian Constitutional Court Act*.

31 Greece, Italy, Switzerland, the USA.

32 Germany.

restriction of abstract reviews by standing requirements). All these proceedings envisage the condition that the complainant must be affected by a certain measure taken by the public authority. With a growth in the number of complaints, efficiency decreases. Nevertheless, citizens should have many opportunities to apply for the protection of their constitutional rights.[33]

B. Bodies Empowered for Human Rights Protection and the Forms of such Proceedings

The petition of an affected individual whose constitutional rights are claimed to have been violated is generally the basis for appropriate proceedings of protection in which the protection of rights by the Constitutional Court is only one of a number of legal remedies for protection. Even the bodies intended to provide protection are different, depending on the specific system.

1. Basic rights may be protected in ordinary Court proceedings.

   a) Some legal systems provide protection of rights predominantly in proceedings before ordinary courts (general courts); for the most part these are countries which have also adopted the so-called diffuse or American model of judicial review34.

   The following are specific forms of the protection of rights by ordinary courts:

   b) The *Habeas corpus* proceedings, *i.e.* the protection against unjustified deprivation of liberty; an appropriate application is lodged with an ordinary court having such jurisdiction. Such proceedings are characterised by speed, simplicity and openness.[35]

   c) *Habeas data*, which is a sub-form of *habeus corpus* and was introduced in Brazil by the *Constitution of 1988*. It is a constitutional guarantee of a personal decision about information, in essence the protection of personal data.

   d) Further proceedings are recognised mainly by countries which have adopted the American model of judicial review, and include the following:[36]

   - *mandamus*, whereby it is possible to annul a mistake of a lower court by order of a higher court;

[33] France is a specific exception among these systems, as private individuals have no access to the Constitutional Council, except with reference to elections. In France, the protection of individual rights is, however, the responsibility of the National Council acting on the basis of a complaint against administrative acts.

[34] Australia, Barbados, Denmark, Finland, Great Britain, Greece, Guyana, Iceland, Ireland, Jamaica, Japan, the Netherlands, Norway, Sweden, Trinidad and Tobago, and the USA.

[35] *Habeas corpus* is mainly used in Argentina (as well as in the following Argentinean provinces: Chaco, Neuquen and Formosa); Bolivia, Brazil, Canada, Chile, Colombia, Costa Rica, Cuba, the Dominican Republic, Ecuador, El Salvador, Guatemala, Honduras, Mexico, Nicaragua, Panama, Paraguay, Peru, Uruguay, the USA, and in Venezuela; in Africa: Botswana, Ghana, Kenya, Lesotho, Malawi, Mauritius, Nigeria, Sierra Leone, Swazi, Tanzania, Uganda, Zambia and Zimbabwe; in Asia: Bangladesh, Hong Kong, India, Indonesia, Malaysia, Nepal, Pakistan, the Philippines, Singapore, Sri Lanka, and Taiwan.

[36] the USA; in Africa: Botswana, Ghana, Kenya, Lesotho, Malawi, Mauritius, Nigeria, Sierra Leone, Swazi, Tanzania, Uganda, Zambia, Zimbabwe; in Asia: Bangladesh, India, Nepal, the Philippines, Sri Lanka.

- *prohibition*, which prevents a higher court from usurping the jurisdiction of a lower court;
- *certiorari*, which involves the right of a higher court to resolve a case from the jurisdiction of a lower court;
- *quo-warranto*, which prevents a specific person from performing a function of a public nature which they have usurped.
- *Respondeat superior*, which is a compensation claim by an individual against the State37.

2. A specific form of the protection of rights which is reminiscent of the constitutional complaint, is the so-called *amparo*. This is a universal and a traditional form of human rights' protection in the Hispanophone legal system: the protection of an individual against violations of constitutional rights by government acts of all categories. In the main, the Supreme Courts of the State in question are responsible for this form of protection. The aim of such proceedings is to restore the violated right to the individual prior to its violation. It is also a characteristically accelerated proceedings. Mexico is the classic *amparo* country. It is followed by many Central and South American countries[38] as well as by the Seychelles.

3. Subsidiary amparo is still more similar to the constitutional complaint. This is a particular *sub-species* of *amparo*, in that the proceedings takes place before the Constitutional Court[39]. This form of protection is also called *accion de tutela*. Colombian *accion de tutela* is comparable to the constitutional complaint. It was introduced by the *Colombian Constitution of 1991*. It is characterised by the fact that the circle of protected constitutional rights is explicitly defined. It is possible to annul legal or administrative acts (in addition to the popular complaint (*actio popularis*) and proceedings of *habeus corpus* in Colombia).

4. Brazil introduced a number of specific legal remedies for the protection of human rights in the *Constitution of 1988*, including:
   - *mandado de seguranca*, which is a wider form of protection, for which the Supreme Court is competent, for the protection of rights not covered by *habeas corpus*;
   - *mandado de injuncao*, which is a special individual complaint for a case involving the negligence of the legislature.

5. Chile introduced a special modified version of amparo, the so-called *recurso de proteccion* in the *Constitution of 1980*.

---

37 The USA, and on the American model, also Taiwan.

38 Argentina, Bolivia, Colombia, Costa Rica, Cuba, the Dominican Republic, Ecuador, El Salvador, Guatemala, Haiti, Honduras, Nicaragua, Panama, Paraguay, Peru, Uruguay, Venezuela.

39 Colombia, Spain.

6. A popular complaint (*actio popularis*) may, equally, be lodged by an individual, generally without restrictions[40]. It is a special, individual legal remedy for the judicial protection of rights, although intended for the protection of fundamental rights in the public interest (while a constitutional complaint is lodged in the interest of the individual). A popular complaint is normally directed against a general act (usually a statute) which is considered to have violated a constitutional right.[41] The Constitutional Court is generally the competent body for reaching a decision which deals with the disputed act in the sense of an abstract review of rules. The popular complaint is less common in Europe[42]. In Israel the popular complaint is common in cases arising within Israel proper, the right to standing is decided mostly by the Court's willingness to grant it. It is most extensive in Central and South America[43]Argentina is an interesting example where there is no popular complaint (*actio popularis*) on a federal level, but individual provinces have introduced it: Buenos Aires, Chaco, Entre Rios, La Rioja, Nequen, Rio Negro and Santiago del Estero.. The popular complaint is a relatively common approach in Africa[44], while in Asia, the popular complaint is only recognised in Cambodia, in Japan, and only in electoral matters (as a *peoples' action* or *objective action*) as well as in Iran (a complaint before the Court of Administrative Justice).

7. A specific group of systems of constitutional law guarantees the individual only indirect protection, such that the individual does not have direct access to the Constitutional Court or other body of constitutional review. These are systems that consider the protection of the rights of the individual to be satisfied through:
   - an abstract review of rules[45]; or
   - a specific (concrete) review of rules[46]; or
   - a preventive abstract review of rules[47].

[40] The exceptions are Hungary and Slovenia, where it is restricted by a demonstration of standing by the complainant.

[41] Kelsen considers the popular complaint (*actio popularis*) as the strongest guarantee, however he does not recommend such solution because of the possible abuse of the right to initiate a dispute as well as because of the risk of the unbearable burdening of the Constitutional Court by such complaints.

[42] Bavaria - although in other German provinces and on a federal level there is no popular complaint, Croatia, partly the Czech Republic, the FRY, the FYROM, Hungary, Liechtenstein, Malta, Montenegro/the FRY, Slovenia.

[43] Argentina, Brazil, Colombia, Costa Rica, El Salvador, Panama, Paraguay, Peru, Venezuela.

[44] Burundi, the Central African Republic, Chad, Congo, Djibuti, Niger, Seychelles, Sierra Leone-according to the 1991 Constitution, South Africa and Uganda.

[45] Belarus, Belgium, Bulgaria, Cambodia, Italy, Latvia.

[46] Azerbaijan, Bosnia, Bulgaria, Estonia, Italy, Kazahstan, Lithuania, Yakutia.

[47] France.

C. The Constitutional Complaint and its Extent in the World

A constitutional complaint is a specific subsidiary legal remedy against the violation of constitutional rights, primarily by individual acts of government bodies which enables a subject who believes that their rights have been affected to have their case heard and a decision issued by a Court authorised to provide a constitutional review of disputed acts. Generally, the indictment refers to individual acts (all administrative and judicial acts), in contrast to the popular complaint (*actio popularis*), although it may also indirectly[48] or even directly[49] refer to a statute.

Is constitutional appeal a right? The Slovenian Constitutional Court has taken the view that it is an institute of judicial proceedings, or a special legal remedy[50].

The constitutional complaint is not an entirely new institute; its forerunner may be found in the Aragon law of the 13th to 16th Century[51]; and in Germany from the 15th Century onwards[52]; while Switzerland introduced a special constitutional complaint[53] in the *Constitution of 1874* and in the *Statutes* of 1874 and 1893.

The constitutional complaint is very common in systems of constitutional/judicial review. It is most widespread in Europe[54]. In Germany, the constitutional complaint appears on the federal and on provincial levels.[55]

In addition to Europe, some Asian systems recognise a constitutional complaint[56]. It should also be noted that other Arabian countries, if they recognise judicial review at all, have in the main adopted the French system of the preventive review of rules following the model of the French Constitutional Council of 1958, which does not recognise the right of the individual to direct access to specific constitutional/judicial review bodies. In Africa some countries recognise the constitutional complaint[57]. The only example of constitutional complaint in Central and South America is the Brazilian *mandado de injuncao, i.e.* an individual complaint in case of negligence by the legislature (under the jurisdiction of the Brazilian Supreme Court) unless we also count the

---

48 Slovenia, Spain.

49 Germany.

50 Ruling No. U-I-71/94 of 6 October 1994, OdlUS III, 109.

51 In the form of *recurso de agravios, firme de derecho, manifestacion de personas.*

52 Incorporated in the institution *Reichskammergericht* of 1495, envisaged in the famous constitutional text, *Paulskirchenverfassung*, of 1849, and in Bavaria it was provided for in the *Constitutions of 1808, 1818, 1919 and 1946.*

53 *Staatliche Verfassungsbeschwerde.*

54 Albania, Andorra, Austria, Croatia, the Czech Republic, Cyprus, the FRY, the FYROM, Germany, Hungary, Liechtenstein (1992), Malta, Montenegro/the FRY, Poland, Portugal, Russia, Slovakia, Slovenia, Spain, Switzerland-Supreme Court, Ukraine.

55 The federal constitutional complaint is the responsibility of the Federal Constitutional Court, the provincial constitutional complaint is the responsibility of certain Provincial Constitutional Courts: Bavaria, Berlin, Hessen and Saarland.

56 Baskiria (under the jurisdiction of the Constitutional Court), Georgia (under the jurisdiction of the Constitutional Court), Kyrghyzia (under the jurisdiction of the Constitutional Court), Mongolia (under the jurisdiction of the Constitutional Court since the *Constitution of 1992*), Papua-New Guinea (under the jurisdiction of the Supreme Court), South Korea (under the jurisdiction of the Constitutional Court since the *Constitution of 1987*), Taiwan (under the jurisdiction of the Supreme Court), Syria (under the jurisdiction of the Constitutional Court), Uzbekistan (under the jurisdiction of the Constitutional Court); the Constitutional Courts of Member states of the Russian Federation (Adigea, Buryatia, Dagestan, the Kabardino-Balkar Republic, Karelia, Koma).

57 Benin (Constitutional Court), Cape Verde (the Supreme Court of Justice), Mauritius (the Supreme Court), Senegal (the Constitutional Council) and Sudan (the Supreme Court).

Colombian *accion de tutela* (the jurisdiction of the Constitutional Court), usually considered to be a subsidiary *amparo*.

The particularity of individual systems is that they recognise a cumulation of both forms, the popular and the constitutional complaint[58]. The two forms may compete in their functions. The rationale for both forms is the protection of constitutional rights: the popular complaint (*actio popularis*) in public and the constitutional complaint in the private interest. In both cases the plaintiff is an individual. As a rule, the subject disputed is different: the popular complaint (*actio popularis*) refers to general acts and constitutional complaints refer to individual acts[59]. The standing of the plaintiff or that the remedy might have a personal effect upon the plaintiff is a precondition for a constitutional complaint. Although it should be possible to exclude the standing of the appellant as a precondition for the popular complaint (*actio popularis*), individual systems do require it[60], such that for both the constitutional and the popular complaint (*actio popularis*), the standing or the personal effect on an individual works as a corrective with the aim to prevent the abuse and overburdening of the Constitutional Court or other constitutional/judicial review body. In both cases the same aim may be pursued through the introduction of a filing fee. It is, however, characteristic that in practice the number of constitutional complaints is increasing everywhere. Therefore, many constitutional courts have adapted the organization of their work following this trend either in the form of specialised individual chambers for constitutional complaints[61] or by narrower units of the Constitutional Court (chambers, sub-chambers)[62] issuing decisions on constitutional complaints .

D. The Fundamentals of the Constitutional Complaint

The following are the elements of the system of the constitutional complaint:

- the preliminary selection of complaints (the integration of filters into proceedings). This is most highly developed in the German system with the intent to sift out potentially unsuccessful complaints, and as such the space for manoeuvre of the Constitutional Court in rejecting a frivolous complaint is extended. This, in fact, involves the narrowing of the constitutional complaint as a legal remedy in principle open to everybody. One general problem of constitutional courts is how to separate the wheat from the chaff and at the same time secure the efficient protection of human rights in a democratic system. In addition, in certain systems the proposals for introducing the constitutional complaint are recent; some tend to introduce prior selection systems; on the other hand, certain systems tend towards the abolition of this legal institution;

58 Bavaria, Brazil, Colombia, Croatia, partially the Czech Republic, the FRY, the FYROM, Hungary, Liechtenstein, Malta, Montenegro/the FRY, Slovenia.

59 Except for the possibility of indirectly impugning a statute in the FRY, Montenegro/the FRY, Slovenia and Spain, and the direct impugning of a statute in Germany.

60 the FYROM, Slovenia.

61 *e.g.* the German Federal Constitutional Court and the Spanish Constitutional Court.

62 *e.g.* in the Czech Republic, Georgia and Slovenia.

- protection through the constitutional complaint generally refers to constitutional rights and freedoms, and the circle of rights protected by the constitutional complaint is less specifically defined in individual systems (*e.g.* Slovenia, Croatia, the FRY and Montenegro, where "all" constitutionally guaranteed fundamental rights are supposed to be protected), while other systems mostly define the (narrow) the circle of protected constitutional rights.[63] Special forms of constitutional complaint may also protect special categories of rights[64];
- as a rule, acts disputed by the constitutional complaint refer to individual acts, with some exceptions[65];
- those entitled to lodge a constitutional complaint are generally individuals but in Austria, Germany, Spain, Switzerland, the FRY and Montenegro, legal entities explicitly may do so also, while in the Croatian system legal entities are explicitly excluded as a potential appellant; in some systems, the complaint may be lodged by the Ombudsman (Spain, Slovenia, the FRY) or by the public prosecutor (Spain, Portugal).
- the standing, or the personal effect the remedy might have upon the plaintiff is a mandatory element, although in most systems the concept of standing is fairly loosely defined;
- the prior exhaustion of legal remedies is an essential precondition, but with exceptions when the Constitutional Court may deal with a case irrespective of the fulfilment of this condition (Germany, Slovenia, Switzerland);
- the time limit for lodging an application ranges from 20 days to three months with an average of one month from the day of receipt or delivery of the final, legally binding (individual) judgment or decision or act of the State administration;
- the contents of applications are prescribed in detail in a majority of systems: in written form, sometimes with the language explicitly stated (Germany, Austria), along with the particular country, the disputed act, and a definition of the violation of the relevant constitutional right, *etc.*;
- a majority of systems (but not the systems of Middle and Eastern Europe) envisage the issuing of a temporary restraining order (injunction) or ruling (of the Constitutional Court) *i.e.* an order temporarily suspending the implementation of the disputed act until the adoption of a final decision;

---

63 *See also* Klucka, J., *Suitable Rights for Constitutional Complaints*, Report on the Workshop on the "Functioning of the Constitutional Court of the Republic of Latvia", Riga, Latvia, 3-4 July 1997, Offprint.

64 In Germany, Hungary, Slovenia and in the Czech Republic municipalities are entitled, in order to protect self-government, to file a **"communal" constitutional complaint** (Germany recognises the "communal" constitutional complaint on a federal level and on a provincial level in the provinces of Wuerttemberg and North Westphalia). The German system also recognises a special constitutional complaint by an individual in relation to constitutional conditions for the nationalisation of land (*Sozialisierung*) in the province of Rheinland-Pfalz. A special form of constitutional complaint exists in Spain: there, the institute of the citizens' legislative initiative is also protected by constitutional complaint.

65 In Switzerland and Austria a constitutional complaint can impugn only an administrative act, while in Germany, it can impugn acts of all levels (including a statute); in Spain, Slovenia, the FRY and Montenegro a statute may also be an indirect subject of a constitutional complaint; legislative negligence may be directly impugned by a constitutional complaint in Brazil, and also in the practice of the German Federal Constitutional Court and the Bavarian Constitutional Court.

- in some systems the payment of the costs of the proceedings is explicitly foreseen in cases of frivolous applications (Germany, Austria, Portugal, Spain, Switzerland);
- the effects of the decision: the Constitutional Court is limited to decide on constitutional matters, on the violation of constitutional rights. However, if a violation is found, a decision may have a cassatory effect which is, as a rule, *inter partes* (and *erga omnes* in a case in which the subject-matter of the decision is a legislative act). The Constitutional Court here retains the position of the highest judicial authority. These Courts can be referred to as the "high ranking courts of cassation", because Constitutional Courts reviewing the decisions of ordinary courts act in fact as the third and the fourth instance. Although the Constitutional Court is not a court of full jurisdiction, in specific cases it is the only competent court to judge whether a ordinary court has violated the constitutional rights of the plaintiff. It involves the review of micro-constitutionality, perhaps the review of the implementation of a law, which, however, is a deviation from the original function of the Constitutional Court. Constitutional complaint cases raise sensitive questions on defining constitutional limits. In any case, the Constitutional Court in its activities is limited strictly to questions of constitutional law. The Slovenian system is specific in that the Constitutional Court may, under specified conditions, make a final decision on constitutional rights or fundamental freedoms themselves (Para. 1 of Article 60 of the *Slovenian Constitutional Court Act*, Official Gazette RS, No. 15/94).

The protection of fundamental rights and freedoms is an important function of a majority of constitutional courts, irrespective of whether they perform the function of constitutional judgment in the negative or positive sense. Whenever a Constitutional Court has the function of a "negative legislature", constitutional review is strongest precisely in the field of fundamental rights. Even in other fields (the concretisation of State-organisational and economic constitutional principles) in which the legislature has the primary role even in principle, constitutional courts insure that fundamental rights are protected. Precisely in the field of the protection of rights, the Constitutional Court also has the function of a substitute "Constitution-maker" (the "positive function"), which means that in specific cases constitutional courts even supplement constitutional provisions.

E. Various International Forms of the Individual Complaint

1. The concept of "constitutional complaint" is usually connected with the national constitutional protection of fundamental rights. However, certain international documents also envisage specific legal remedies for the protection of fundamental rights and freedoms in the form of a complaint[66].

2. The *European Convention for the Protection of Human Rights and Fundamental Freedoms* of 4 November 1950 gives individuals the right to the so-called individual complaint[67]. An individual may lodge a complaint with the European Court of Human Rights following an alleged violation of rights guaranteed by the *Convention*. It is an explicit international legal remedy comparable to a national constitutional complaint. It fulfils the function of an individual complaint where national law does not guarantee any appropriate protection of rights. Individual complaints are a subsidiary legal remedy (preconditioned on the exhaustion of national legal remedies), it is not a popular complaint (*actio popularis*) and it does not have retroactive or cassatory effect. It differs from the constitutional complaint in the way that, contrary to the latter, it leads merely to a finding (*declaratory relief*).

The position of the *European Convention for the Protection of Human Rights and Fundamental Freedoms* in national law specifies whether an individual may refer to the *Convention* or even base a national constitutional complaint thereon. It further narrows the space for manoeuvre of the Constitutional Court itself in the interpretation of the provisions of the *Convention*. It actually connects the national Constitutional Court to European bodies in cases in which a judicial final national decision becomes the subject of an individual complaint to a European forum.[68]- it sometimes does not have a direct internal state effect: *e.g.* Great Britain, Iceland, Ireland, Norway, and Sweden. Some countries of Anglophone Africa are an exception regarding the latter group of systems (*e.g.* Kenya, Nigeria, Tanzania, and Uganda), as they expressly adopted the system of the protection of rights from the *European Convention for the Protection of Human Rights and Fundamental Freedoms* (*e.g.* Nigeria in the Constitution of 1960), influenced by the extension clause to the *European Convention* in terms of Article 63, which Great Britain

---

[66] *e.g.* Article 2 of the *Facultative Protocol of the General Assembly of the UN to the International Pact on Citizenship and Political Rights* of 19 December 1966 (Resolution No. 2000 A (XXI)) since the Council for human rights must accept and debate reports from individual persons who claim that they are the victims of the violation of any right defined in this Pact. The right to file an individual complaint is contained in the following: Article 23 of the *Declaration on Fundamental Rights and Freedoms of the European Parliament* of 12 April 1989; section 18(2) of the *Document of the Moscow Meeting of CSCE* of 3 October 1991; Article 25 of the *American Convention on Human Rights* of 22 November 1969; Article 28 of the *Contract on the European Community* of 1 February 1992; Charter of 1979 of the *Comision y la Corte Interamericanas de los Derechos Humanos*; Statute of 1980 of the *Inter-American Court on Human Rights*; the *American Convention on Human Rights* of July 18, 1978 (Article 44); Articles 55 through 59 of the *African (Banjul) Charter on Human and People's Rights* of June 27, 1981.

[67] Article 34 of the *Convention*.

[68] The *European Convention for the Protection of Human Rights and Fundamental Freedoms*:
- has constitutional status in Austria;
- is the basis for filing an internal national constitutional complaint in Switzerland, where it has a status comparable to the constitutional level;

In both cases it is permissible to base a national constitutional complaint on the provisions in the *Convention*.
- it is sometimes higher than ordinary law (Belgium, Cyprus, France, Luxembourg, Malta, The Netherlands, Portugal, Spain);
- it is sometimes ranked as Common Law: Denmark, which introduced the national use of the *Convention* by special *Statute* on 1 July
1992, Germany, Finland, Italy, Liechtenstein, San Marino, Turkey;

signed on 23 October 1953, whereby only the *Convention* itself and *Protocol 1* apply in these regions.

The institution of the constitutional complaint and the European complaint and the function of European bodies (above all the European Court of Human Rights) raises the question of national and supranational (final) instance. The national (final) instance would entail that the Constitutional Court as the highest body of judicial authority in a particular country for the protection of constitutionality and legality and human rights and fundamental freedoms[69] would be limited to the investigation of constitutional-legal questions only. The review of the correct findings of the actual circumstances and the use of simple rules of evidence are matters for the ordinary courts. The subsidiary nature of the constitutional complaint lies in the division of responsibility between the Constitutional and the ordinary courts. The gradation of instance could be established as ascending from the national Supreme Court through the national Constitutional Court to the European Court. In fact, instance is not the essence of this gradation although it is essential in the role of supplementing, in that the national constitutional complaint supplements national judicial protection while the supra-national European complaint supplements the national constitutional complaint.

F. The Core of the Judicial Protection of Human Rights

The core of the judicial protection of human rights lies in the constitutional complaint, since:

- Human rights are attributes of any democratic legal system;
- The constitutional complaint is (only) one of the legal remedies for protecting constitutional rights;
- The constitutional complaint is an important remedy for the protection of human rights and can be considered a human right itself[70]; the *Constitution* guarantees the constitutional complaint, in the same way as the rights it protects; at the same time, the constitutional complaint is limited by statute to the operational capacity of the Constitutional Court;
- Its effectiveness is disputed, since successful constitutional complaints are in a clear minority, although that should be no reason for its restriction or abolition. Such a number of unsuccessful constitutional complaints is also very often the result of the great number of the same kind of case filed before Constitutional Courts;

69 The status of the Constitutional Court is thus defined in *e.g.* Para. 1 of Article 1 of the *Constitutional Court Act* of 1994.

70 Ruling issued by the Slovenian Constitutional Court No. U-I-71/94 of 6 October 1994.

However, despite the internal contradictory properties of this institution, individuals should still have access to justice or to the judicial protection of their constitutional rights. The very existence of the constitutional complaint ensures a more effective review of violations of constitutional rights on the part of government bodies, especially during the process of transforming the social and legal order.

XIII. The Particularities of Current Constitutional Proceedings

A. The Dissenting/Concurring Opinion

There is an essential difference between decisions issued by constitutional courts in Europe and those of the Anglo-American type. The former are issued "impersonally" by the Court as a whole, whereas in the latter, individual judges make their personal contributions. In the first case the decision itself does not show whether it was adopted unanimously or by a majority of votes; moreover, it is absolutely not clear in any decision the way an individual judge actually voted. In the second case, however, it is not only evident when a majority or unanimous decision was adopted and how individual judges voted, and the judges who do not agree with the majority add their interpretation of the decision in either:

- a concurring opinion, when a judge agrees with the ruling but differs as to its reasoning,

  or

- a dissenting opinion, when a judge objects to the ruling itself.

At first the dissenting/concurring opinion was recognised only in the USA as well as in other Common Law based or American tradition based countries of the British Commonwealth, Central and South America, Scandinavia and Japan. After many theoretical and political objections the dissenting/concurring opinion became gradually accepted in the countries with Continental (European) legal systems. Although individual European systems of constitutional/judicial review departed from the decision-making mode characteristic of the Austrian model, they remained half-way to an American type of decision that introduced the dissenting/concurring opinion into Constitutional Court decisions.

As far as publication is concerned, a distinction may be made between two types of dissenting/concurring opinions:

- open, published together with the respective decision;
- anonymous, only added in writing to the internal part of the case.

Some constitutional judicial review systems do not accept dissenting/concurring opinions but keep the voting results secret, without publishing either the voting results or the names of judges[71]. The dissenting/concurring opinion is known above all in Croatia[72], Germany[73], Greece[74], Hungary[75], Portugal[76], Slovenia[77], Chile[78] and Spain[79]. In Portugal, however, the publication of votes including names is a matter of judicial tradition because the decisions issued by the Constitutional Court strictly include names also. On the other hand, much attention was aroused by the frequent occurrence of the dissenting/concurring opinion in Spain, where this practice appeared in both forms (dissenting opinion, concurring opinion). The dissenting/concurring opinion is, however, not recognised by the Court of Justice of the European Community in Luxembourg, but was recognised by the European Commission[80] and is recognised by the European Court of Human Rights in Strasbourg[81].

B. Temporary Orders

Pursuant to the regulation in force, a temporary order may refer to both a general and an individual act. It could be applied in the proceedings of an abstract review, a constitutional complaint as well as impeachment. The Constitutional Court considers this type of decision-making to be its own discretionary right. The disputed provision formally still remains in force, but it is prohibited to use it. Accordingly, the temporary order (because of the temporary situation as well as due to legal security) can not be legally implemented by itself, unless the Constitutional Court itself specifies the respective implementation mode.

The Constitutional Court can adopt a temporary order either with a special ruling (if the proceedings is initiated on the request of a privileged applicant) or with a ruling on a general subject. If the Constitutional Court adopts a special ruling on a temporary order, but the constitutional proceedings are subsequently discontinued, the Constitutional Court, by issuing a ruling that discontinues the proceedings, explicitly orders that the temporary order itself is no longer in force either. Otherwise the term of the temporary order is considered to expire according to the final Court decision.

---

71 *e.g.* Austria, Belgium, France, Ireland, Italy.

72 Para. 4 of Article 19 of the *Constitutional Court Act*.

73 Para. 2 of Article 30 of the *Federal Constitutional Court Act*. In addition, some Provincial Constitutional Courts adopted the dissenting opinion, *e.g.* Bavaria (Para. 5 of Article 25 of the *Constitutional Court Act*; Article 4 of the *Rules of Procedure of the Constitutional Court*), Berlin (Para. 2 of Article 29 of the *Constitutional Court Act*), Bremen (Para 3 of Article 13 of the *Rules of Procedure of the Constitutional Court*), Hamburg (Para. 4 and 5 of Article 22 of the *Constitutional Court Act*; Articles 27 and 28 of the *Rules of Procedure of the Constitutional Court*), Niedersachsen (Para. 2 of Article 11 of the *Rules of Procedure of the Constitutional Court*).

74 Para. 3 of Article 93 of the *Constitution*; Articles 35 to 38 of *Act* No. 184/1975.

75 Article 22 of the *Constitutional Court Act*.

76 Para. 4 of Article 42 of the *Constitutional Court Act* No. 28/1982.

77 Para. 3 of Article 40 of the *Constitutional Court Act*; Articles 48 to 50 of the *Rules of Procedure of the Constitutional Court*.

78 Para. 2 of Article 31 of the *Constitutional Court Act*.

79 Para. 2 of Article 90 of the *Constitutional Court Act* No. 2/1979.

80 Para. 1 of Article 31 of the *European Convention on Human Rights and Basic Freedoms*.

81 Para. 2 of Article 51 of the *European Convention on Human Rights and Basic Freedoms*.

Whether the applicant's proposal for a temporary order is accepted or refused depends on the decision of the Constitutional Court. The Court weighs whether not-easily-reparable damages are probable, which could justify the temporary order. On the other hand, it may also weigh the possible damages following the adoption of the temporary order. Accordingly, the Court decides not to adopt the temporary order if it is of the opinion that the damages resulting from the temporary order might exceed the risk of an unconstitutional interpretation of the disputed legal provision in a concrete case. The Constitutional Court may refuse the applicant's request for a temporary order with a special ruling, but may do it in a ruling on the non-acceptance of a popular complaint.

Suspending the implementation of an act can be total or only partial provided that the implementation thereof could involve not-easily-reparable consequences . If during the term of the temporary order the consequences of the respective ruling are interpreted in different ways, the Constitutional Court may, by a special decision, specify the manner its decision must be implemented.

With reference to the Slovenian system, a temporary order is not limited in time, as in the German constitutional review system (Para. 6 of Article 32 of the *Federal Constitutional Court Act/BverfGG*). The ultimate limit of its duration extends to the issuance of the relevant final Constitutional Court decision. However, the Constitutional Court is free to order the termination of its validity at any time during its term.

Concerning temporary orders in the Slovenian system, the constitutional court decisions may be as follows:

1. The Abstract Review

- An abstract review can result in the possible stay of the implementation of a general act pending a final decision.

2. The Constitutional Complaint

- A ruling on the suspension of the implementation of an individual act which is the subject of a constitutional complaint can be issued while deciding on a constitutional complaint.
- A ruling on the possible suspension of the implementation of a general act pending a final decision can be issued while deciding on a constitutional complaint. The above mentioned possibility of a temporary order parallels the temporary order foreseen in the abstract review proceedings.

The Constitutional Court may decide on a temporary order on a general act only in a plenary session, not also in an *a camera* session.

The Constitutional Court decides on temporary orders in proceedings examining a constitutional complaint and/or may suspend the implementation of a disputed individual act only if the constitutional complaint is accepted. If procedural prerequisites are lacking and/or if the constitutional complaint is not accepted, the Constitutional Court does not decide on the applicant's request for a temporary order.

3. Other (Specific) Proceedings

- The court may issue a decision suspending the President/Prime Minister/Ministers from office - while deciding on impeachment. The Constitutional Court may decide for such a temporary prohibition by a two-thirds majority of votes of all judges.

XIV. The Character of the Decisions of Constitutional Courts and their Publication

A. CONTENTS AND THE EFFECTS OF DECISIONS

1. Contents

1.1. Abstract Review

The following forms are possible, particularly concerning the Slovenian system of constitutional review:

- The abrogation (*ex nunc*) in whole or in part of unconstitutional statutes is effective immediately or within such a period of time, not exceeding one year, as specified by the Constitutional Court.

The regulation in force allows to the Constitutional Court to abrogate a general act with deferred effect, *i.e.* the respective decision comes into effect on the expiry of the period specified by the Constitutional Court. In this case, too, the Constitutional Court evaluates whether the specific circumstances of the respective case justify such a measure. On one hand the reasons for an abrogation with deferred effect are opposite to the reasons for a temporary order: the absence of the direct risk that the further implementation of the general act could cause considerable or even irreparable damage. On the other hand, however, the Constitutional Court may, as a rule, impose this measure whenever it chooses to avoid a legal gap resulting from abrogation when it presumes that the legislature would be able to change the unconstitutional or unlawful provision in the respective period and to bring it into conformity with the Court's decision.

Besides deciding upon constitutional complaints regarding violations of human rights, the most important new element is that the Slovenian Constitutional Court is empowered to abrogate (*ex nunc*) a statute directly. Due to the Principle of the Unity of Powers and the Supremacy of the Parliament, the former function of the Constitutional Court focused on assessing the unconstitutionality of a statute. This changed into an active relationship not only involving the abrogation of statutes, but also offering guidance to the legislature for the creation of Law. However, the Constitutional Court agreed to allow the legislature the opportunity to review disputable regulations within a due period of time, following the guidelines of the Constitutional Court in a specific decision.

In this way the Court assumed the role of a "negative legislature". In a period of transition the legislature is not always able to follow developments nor to impose standards for all shades of the legal system and its institutions. The so-called interpretive decisions issued by the Constitutional Court and the appellate decisions include certain instructions from the Constitutional Court to the Legislature on how to settle certain questions or specific issues. However, in compliance with the Principle of Judicial Self-Restraint, a clear limit has been imposed on the Slovenian Constitutional Court by the Court itself, which indicates that the Constitutional Court has already been creating legal rule (usually reserved for the Legislature). On the other hand, there is the question whether the Constitutional Court actually creates the law, because it also involves the review of legislative activity. In any case, the Legislature cannot avoid the existence of contemporary Slovenian Constitutional Case-Law in its activity.

- The abrogation (*ab initio/ex tunc* or prospectively/*ex nunc*) of other unconstitutional or unlawful executive regulations and other general acts.
- The declaration of the unconstitutionality and illegality of statutes, other general acts or general acts for the exercise of public powers which were made to conform to the *Constitution* and statute or which cease to be valid if the consequences of their unconstitutionality or illegality are not eliminated.
- The declaration of the unconstitutionality or illegality of a statute, other general act or a general act for the exercise of public powers because a certain matter which it should have regulated was not regulated or is regulated in a manner which makes it impossible to be abrogated retroactively (*ex tunc*) or prospectively (*ex nunc*). The Legislature or body which issued such unconstitutional or illegal general act must abolish the ascertained unconstitutionality or illegality within the period set by the Constitutional Court. The *Constitutional Court Act* has not foreseen any "sanction" if the Legislature fails to bring the disputed provision into conformity with the *Constitution* following the Court decision. The Legislature is bound only by the general provision on legally binding decisions of the Constitutional Court. The disputed regulation remains in force, and this has been confirmed by constitutional case-law.
- Any affected person is entitled, based on a Constitutional Court decision regarding the constitutional review of general acts, to request an amendment or retroactive abrogation (*ex tunc*) of an individual act or the elimination of detrimental consequences or even claim damages within three months from the day of the publication of a Constitutional Court decision.

1.2. The Constitutional Complaint

The following results are possible:

- The abrogation, retroactive (*ex tunc*) or prospective (*ex nunc*), of an individual act and return of the case to the empowered body.
- The abrogation, retroactive (*ex tunc*) or prospective (*ex nunc*), of a general act (while deciding on a constitutional complaint).
- The final decision on a contested human right or freedom based on a constitutional complaint (entailing the replacement of the disputed individual act by the Court decision), in the case of a retroactive abrogation (*ex tunc*) of an individual act, if such proceedings is necessary in order to eliminate consequences

that have already occurred on the basis of the abrogated individual act, or if such is the nature of the constitutional right or freedom, and if a decision can be reached on the basis of the information in the document. At first the above power of the Constitutional Court gave rise to a discussion of whether in this case the Constitutional Court represented an instance above the ordinary courts (especially above the Supreme Court). Present constitutional case-law, however, proves that the Constitutional Court is limited to the evaluation of pure constitutional issues, *e.g.* to the strict evaluation of breaches of certain constitutional rights.

1.3. Other (Specific) Proceedings

Other proceedings, mainly adopted by systems of constitutional review, can result in the following:

- Stating the empowered body in jurisdictional disputes.
- Finding a proposal for impeachment to be unfounded.
- Deciding on the grounds for an impeachment/deciding on the suspension of the President's/Prime Minister's/Ministers office.
- The annulment of an unconstitutional political party act or activity, or an order requiring a deletion from the register of political parties.
- The annulment of a decision of the National Assembly, or a decision on a representative's election.
- An obligatory opinion on the conformity of international treaties with the *Constitution*.
- A declaration of the unconstitutionality of a request concerning a call for a referendum.

2. The Appointment of a Body Empowered to Implement Court Decisions

If necessary, the Court specifies which body must implement its decisions (regarding the constitutional review of general acts), and in what manner. The Constitutional Court may order the temporary suspension of the implementation of individual acts, based on a general act abrogated by the Court decision.

The replacement of a disputed individual act by a Court decision is implemented by the body empowered for the implementation of the individual act retroactively abrogated (*ex tunc*) by the Constitutional Court and replaced by the decision of the same. If there is no such empowered body according to the current regulations, the Constitutional Court appoints one.

3. Effects

Under the main accepted principle of constitutional review systems, the decisions of the Constitutional Court are binding and produce effects *erga omnes*.

Exceptions to this rule are constitutional complaints and jurisdictional disputes where decisions have effect only *inter partes*, but even here effects are felt *erga omnes*, when the Constitutional Court acts *ex officio*

THE REHEARING OF PROCEEDINGS BEFORE THE CONSTITUTIONAL COURT

The decisions of the Constitutional Court are binding (*e.g.* Para. 3 of Article 1 of the *Slovenian Constitutional Court Act*, Official Gazette RS, No. 15/94) and executable (Para. 2 of Article 40 of the *Slovenian Constitutional Court Act*). The rules concerning the proceedings before the Constitutional Court do not include any exceptional legal remedy against a Constitutional Court decision, which also includes any rehearing or, in general, repetition of proceedings concerning an already adjudicated constitutional dispute.

The problem of rehearing proceedings was discussed in constitutional theory and practice in the eighties[82]. The discussions looked for inspiration in foreign systems, however not in the American system, which includes accessory constitutional review in ordinary cases with an in *inter partes* judgment effect of the judgment, but first of all in the Austrian and Italian systems[83]; even though also in these systems the rehearing of proceedings is excluded. Therefore, there were some proposals[84] concerning the subsidiary implementation of rules of other proceedings for the rehearing of proceedings before the Constitutional Court following the example of the regulation governing re-hearings in administrative disputes: *i.e.* on the grounds of a worse violation occurring during the proceedings, or on the grounds of a particular criminal offence, when a party uncovers new facts or they have an opportunity to be able to submit new evidence with which a case may have been adjudicated more advantageously for the party if such facts or evidence had been submitted in the previous proceedings. First of all, a rehearing in a constitutional dispute (taking into consideration its particularities, because the object of adjudication in such a dispute is a normative act) would be reasonable if after the issuance of the Constitutional Court decision, new facts or evidence were uncovered which, if they had been known and applied previously, would have caused a different Constitutional Court decision. The rehearing of proceedings would be reasonable in all kinds of Constitutional Court decisions, except when the Constitutional Court by its previous decision has abrogated or annulled a particular normative act[85]. If the re-hearing could be implemented in the case of such a normative act, and the previous Constitutional Court decision on an abrogation or annulment were abolished, the Constitutional Court would without competency, in fact, enter into the normative function of the legislature or other author of normative acts which determine the legal order in a particular field.

Concerning the conditions or reasons for rehearing, the same reasons may be applied as for the rehearing of an administrative dispute. In view of what has been explained

82 Globevnik, *Problem obnove v ustavnem sporu*, Pravnik, No.. 4-6/82,p. 82.

83 Globevnik, *Problem obnove*, p. 82.

84 Globevnik, *Problem obnove*, p. 83.

85 Globevnik, *Problem obnove*, p. 84.

above, in a constitutional dispute it would not be reasonable in a rehearing to abolish a previous Constitutional Court decision and to replace such a decision with a new one on the grounds that in the confrontation of a normative act with a certain constitutional or statutorial provision, such a provision had not been correctly interpreted and was mistakenly legally implemented. However, this does not mean that the Constitutional Court may not even without a formally held rehearing proceeding following a request of a party in the same case, and in a special proceeding, revise the Court's previous decision. In the constitutional case-law of the former Yugoslavia, in some cases a case before the Constitutional Court was reheard, the previous Constitutional Court decision was overturned and replaced by a new one[86]. The rehearing of a Constitutional Court case is not a rehearing in the classical judicial sense (despite the subsidiary implementation of rules concerning judicial proceedings). As a matter of fact, it is a special kind of rehearing of Constitutional Court proceedings that may result in the overturning of the previous Constitutional Court decision and its replacement with a different new decision.

Properly speaking, the Constitutional Court is internally procedurally bound by the text of its decision and/or with the "irrevocability" of the decision[87]. Such irrevocability means that the Constitutional Court may not abrogate or change a decision which has already been issued. "Any promulgated or issued decision is no longer in the disposition of the Constitutional Court "[88].

Consequently, the decisions of the Constitutional Court are indisputable for the parties. However, as an exception it is necessary to consider the *European Convention for the Protection of Human Rights and Fundamental Freedoms* of 4 November 1950, which gives individuals the right to the so-called individual complaint against a national final Constitutional Court decision.[89] Because there is no (national) legal remedy against Constitutional Court decisions, they become formally final when issued.

---

86 Globevnik, *Problem obnove*, p. 85.

87 *Unwiderruflichkeit*, Jochen Abr. Frowein - Thilo Marauhn, Grundfragen der Verfassungsgerichtsbarkeit in Mittel- und OstEuropa, Cremer, *Die Wirkungen verfassungsgerichtlicher Entscheidungen*, Springer, Band 130, 1998, p. 249.

88 Jochen Abr. Frowein, Thilo Marauhn, *Grundfragen der Verfassungsgerichtsbarkeit in Mittel- und Osteuropa*, Springer, Band 130, 1998, p. 249.

89 The individual complaint under Article 25 of the Convention is an extraordinary legal remedy similar to the constitutional complaint (Stackelberg, 87). The Court deals with the case only if all national legal remedies have already been exhausted in accordance with generally accepted principles of international law. **Furthermore, the constitutional complaint before the Constitutional Court (if it is introduced in a particular national legal system), which is the sole subsidiary legal remedy, follows the exhaustion of legal remedies; this is confirmed also by permanent European constitutional case-law)** (Stackelberg, 93; Matscher, Der Rechtsmittelbegriff, 266; Nedjati, 16 in 18, Klecatsky, 544; Schmalz, 132). The individual has to exhaust, in a particular case, all legal remedies allowed by the national legal order, including the constitutional complaint (Bleckmann, 45).

Sources:

1. dr. Bleckmann Albert, Staatsrecht II - Die Grundrechte, 3. Auflage, Koeln, 1989, p. 29-46
2. Klecatsky-Oehlinger, Gerichtsbarkeit des oeffentlichen Rechts, Manz Verlag, Wien, 1984, p. 517, 540.
3. Matscher dr. Franz, Der Rechtsmittelbegriff der EMRK, Festschrift fuer Winifried Kralik, Wien, 1968, p. 257
4. Nedjati Zaim M., Human Rights under the European Convention, North-Hollang Publishing Company, Amsterdam-New York-Oxford, 1978, p. 13-20
5. Schmalz Dieter, Grundrechte, 2. Auflage 1991, Nomos Verlagsgesellschaft, Baden-Baden, p. 25-26, 131-133
6. Von Stackelberg Curt Freiherr sen.& jun., Das Verfahren der deutschen Verfassungsbeschwerde und der europaeischen Menschenrechtsbeschwerde, Koeln, 1988, p. 85.

In a majority of Constitutional Court systems, Constitutional Court decisions are declared final, sometimes they are explicitly defined as irrevocable[90]. In this way, constitutional courts are prevented from changing their decisions after their enforcement, with the exception of corrections of obvious incorrectness[91]. So, constitutional courts are completely internally-procedurally bound by their own decisions.

However, the generally accepted principle of the irrevocability of constitutional court decisions are loosened or even partially waived by particular systems. A certain "relaxation" of the aforementioned principle means that such systems authorise the constitutional courts to interpret their own decisions[92]. Such systems relativise the finality of Constitutional Court decisions.[93]

On the other hand, the Byelorussian, Lithuanian and Ukrainian systems authorise the Constitutional Court to change its decision *ex officio* subsequently, without any external request or petition[94]. The Byelorussian and Lithuanian system require the necessary condition that some circumstances become known which had not been known by the Constitutional Court when issuing its decision, or that the constitutional provision which was the basis for the Constitutional Court decision was changed[95]. The Lithuanian system requires that in such cases the Constitutional Court have an appropriate new decision[96]. Under the Ukrainian system the required condition is that new circumstances are discovered connected with the case which were not previously discussed which existed at the time the case was discussed and decided[97]. In addition, the Byelorussian Constitutional Court is empowered to intervene in such cases *ex officio*[98]. The Lithuanian Constitutional Court, however, may react only on the basis of an "external" request[99]. Otherwise, the mentioned systems do not determine a legal remedy against Constitutional Court decisions. Therefore, Constitutional Court decisions are indisputable. An exception is the suspensive veto against a Constitutional Court decision which may be submitted by the President of State and the President of the Parliament, as determined by the Constitution of Kazakhstan[100].

---

90 *e.g.* Para. 3 of Article 26 of the Albanian *Constitution* (No. 7561); Para. 4 of Article VI of the *Constitution of the Federation of Bosnia and Herzegovina;* Para. 5 of Article 14 of the *Bulgarian Constitutional Court Act;* Para. 2 of Article 107 of the *Lithuanian Constitution* and Article 59 of the *Lithuanian Constitutional Court Act;* Para. 3 of Article 112 of the *Macedonian Constitution*; Para. 2 of Article 140 of the *Moldavian Constitution*; Para. 1 and 4 of Article 82 of the *Constitution of Kyrgyzstan.*

91 *e.g.* Article 58 of the *Lithuanian Constitutional Court Act.*

92 Para. 5 of Article 26 of the *Albanian Constitution*, No. 7561; Article 61 of the *Lithuanian Constitutional Court Act*; Article 83 of the *Russian Constitutional Court Act* and Article 41 of the *Belorussian Constitutional Court Act.*

93 In addition, it is interesting to note that by the provision of Para 3 of Article 61 of the *Lithuanian Constitutional Court Act*, the Constitutional Court has to interpret its own decisions in such way that the contents do not change. The request for such an interpretation is not permissible if the request does not concern the same disputed object, but may lead to the issuing of a new decision (Decision of the Lithuanian Constitutional Court of 21 September 1994, published in the Official Digest, No. 3/1995, 111).

94 Article 42 of the *Belorussian Constitutional Court Act*; Article 62 of the *Lithuanian Constitutional Court Act*; Article 68 of the *Constitutional Court Act.*

95 Article 42 of the *Belorussian Constitutional Court Act*, Para, 1 of Article 62 of the *Lithuanian Constitutional Court Act.*

96 Para 2 and 3 of Article 62 of the *Lithuanian Constitutional Court Act.*

97 Article 68 of the *Ukrainian Constitutional Court Act.*

98 Para. 2 of Article 127 of the *Belorussian Constitution.*

99 Articles 105 and 106 of the *Lithuanian Constitution* and Articles 64 and 74 of the *Lithuanian Constitutional Court Act.*

100 Para. 3 to 5 of Article 131 of the *Constitution of Kazakhstan.* In a certain "milder" form a similar "intervention" in a Constitutional Court decision was determined by the former Polish system; similar forms exist in Latvia and Romania, but they are limited to the abstract control of norms.

B. THE PUBLICATION OF CONSTITUTIONAL COURT DECISIONS

1. Publication

Decisions and certain resolutions (if the Constitutional Court so chooses) are published in the Official State Gazette, local official gazettes and/or official gazettes of territorial units and in the official journal in which the respective general act had been published (in Slovenian).

2. The Effect of Publication

One day after the publication of decisions or on the expiry of the period specified by the Constitutional Court, abrogation decisions (*ex nunc*) come into effect. A general act abrogated (*ex nunc*) by the Constitutional Court does not apply to relationships that had arisen before the day such abrogation came into effect, if by that day such relationship had not been entered into.

Within three months from the day of the publication of the Constitutional Court decision, any affected person is entitled, based on a Constitutional Court decision, to request an amendment or retroactive abrogation (*ex tunc*) of an individual act or the elimination of detrimental consequences or even claim damages.

XV. Particularities of the Constitutional Review in Some Countries

Specific systems of Constitutional/Judicial Review Classified by Certain Main Regions (Middle/Eastern Europe and the CIS, the Arab World, Africa, Asia, Central & South America)

In some regions systems of constitutional/judicial review show certain specialities; such regions primarily include the former socialist countries of Middle and Eastern Europe and the CIS, the Arab World, Africa, Asia and the countries of Central and South America.

A. Constitutional Review in the New Democracies

1.1. Development in the so called New Democracy countries has involved the introduction of constitutional review in the so-called New Democracy countries[101]. The introduction of constitutional review has meant a break-up of the former Principle of the Unity of Powers, in view of which socialist systems, as a rule, did not have any constitutional review. The only real exception was the former Yugoslav Federation, which in spite of the Principle of the Unity of Powers, introduced a constitutional review system in 1963 on the federal level as well as on the level of member republics, following the European (Austrian/German) Model. However, it is necessary to mention the Romanian experiment that introduced the constitutional review before World War I. In addition, in Czechoslovakia the respective institution was first introduced in 1920. The trend to broader enforcement of the constitutional review in Czechoslovakia was interrupted by World War II and the already founded institutions failed to become active in practice. Subsequently the constitutional review in Czechoslovakia was newly introduced in 1968, but did not become active in practice.

1.2. The development of constitutional review in the countries of former socialist regimes is characterized by the following:

- Except in the former Yugoslav Federation and some attempts in Romania and Czechoslovakia, constitutional review has no tradition.
- Even after World War II constitutional review (contrary to its affirmation in West European countries) was not instituted due to the fundamental incompatibility with the existing national political systems. These systems adopted the principle according to which the legislative branch is held responsible

[101] Poland (1982), the former Soviet Union (1988), Romania (1991), Albania (1992), Bulgaria (1991), Lithuania (1992), Estonia (1992), Hungary (first attempt in 1984, definitely in 1989), Slovakia (1992), the Czech Republic (1992), Slovenia (newly established Constitutional Court by the 1991 Constitution), after 1991: Armenia, Azarbaijan, Belarus, the Federation of Bosnia and Herzegovina, The (International) Constitutional Court of Bosnia and Herzegovina, the FRY, the FYROM, Georgia, Kazakhstan, Kyrgyzstan, Latvia, Moldavia, Mongolia, Montenegro/the FRY, Serbia/the FRY, the Serbian Republic of Bosnia, Tadjikistan, Ukraine, Uzbekistan (with the Constitutional Committee of the Autonomous Republic of Karakalpakstan), as well as the federal entities of the Russian Federation (Adigea, Altai, Baskiria, Buryatia, Chuvachia, Dagestan, Inguchia, Irkutska Oblast, the Kabardino-Balkar Republic, Kakasa, the Karachaewo-Cherkez Republic, Karelia, Khalmukia, Koma, Marii-El, Northern Ossetia, Tatarstan, Tuba, Udmurtia, Yakutia/Sakha).

for the constitutionality of regulations and according to which constitutional review cannot be practiced by an extra-parliamentary body. Therefore, the power of constitutional review was in principle reserved for the legislative bodies[102].

- The introduction of constitutional review systems following the European Model is of more recent date, arising in general at the end of the Eighties and continuing in the Nineties, along with the development of the democratic process in the above mentioned countries. Accordingly, the introduction of constitutional review brought about a significant change in the above countries where previously such a system had been completely unknown.

1.3. The generally adopted constitutional review model in these respective countries has been the so-called European (Austrian/German, Continental, Concentrated) Model[103]. Bodies exercising constitutional review include the following:

a) Constitutional Courts: Albania, Armenia, Azerbaijan, Belarus, the Federation of Bosnia and Herzegovina, The (International) Constitutional Court of the Republic of Bosnia and Herzegovina, Bulgaria, Chechnya, Croatia, the Czech Republic, the FRY, Georgia, Hungary, Latvia, Lithuania, Moldavia, Mongolia, Montenegro/the FRY, the FYROM, Kazakhstan, Kyrgyzstan, Poland, Romania, the Russian Federation (with the Constitutional Courts of the federal entities of Adigea, Altai, Baskiria, Buryatia, Chuvachia, Dagestan, Inguchia, Irkutska Oblast, the Kabardino-Balkar Republic, Kakasa, the Karachaewo-Cherkez Republic, Karelia, Khalmukia, Koma, Marii-El, Northern Ossetia, Tatarstan, Tuba, Udmurtia, Yakutia/Sakha), Serbia/the FRY, the Serbian Republic of Bosnia and Herzegovina, Slovakia, Slovenia, Tajikistan, Ukraine, Uzbekistan (with the Constitutional Committee of the Autonomous Republic of Karakalpakstan);

b) (Concentrated or specific) constitutional review performed by the highest ordinary court in the country: Estonia;

c) Other forms of the constitutional review based to a large degree on the principle of self-review inside the parliamentary system: Turkmenistan.

1.4. Institutions based on the European constitutional review model share the following characteristics:

- in comparison with the more consistent systems of constitutional review of Western Europe, the constitutional review systems introduced in the New

---

[102] Such as the Presidency of the Supreme Soviet of the Soviet Union and the State Council of Poland, where the right to petition was held by the general state attorney. Subsequently such constitutional review bodies were also introduced in Romania (the Constitutional Committee by the Constitution of 1965) and in Hungary (by the Constitution of 1984). The Hungarian Council for Constitutional Law was in charge of cooperation with other government bodies concerned with the protection of the constitutionality and legality of all statutes, decrees and ordinances. The 11 to 17 member council was elected by the National Assembly from among the deputies and politician. The first Constitution of the former Democratic Republic of Germany granted constitutional review jurisdiction to the so-called Constitutional Committee. Before 1963 in Slovenia the system of the protection of constitutionality and legality included the review of rules under the principle of self-review inside the parliamentary system.

[103] Based on Kelsen's Model of 1920, involving the interconnection between the principle of the supremacy of the Constitution and the principle of the supremacy of the Parliament, whereunder constitutional matters are dealt with by specialized Constitutional Courts with specially qualified judges or by regular Supreme Courts or High Courts or their special senates (a concentrated constitutional review) in special proceedings (*principaliter*). Usually abstract reviews are carried out, although specific reviews are also possible. In addition to the *a posteriori* review, *a priori* reviews are also foreseen. The decisions have an *erga omnes* effect with reference to the absolute authority of the institution by whom they are issued.

Democracies have been exercised with a higher or lower intensity, depending on the particular national system;

- a monopoly of constitutional review (specialisation in constitutional review) concentrated in one institution. In some systems this is combined with the power of cassation of statutes adopted by the Parliament;
- not all the systems insure individuals access to the Constitutional Court;
- in the proceedings following a constitutional complaint problems occur due to the separation of constitutional review from the ordinary courts;
- constitutional court judges are elected or appointed mainly by bodies of political power (the legislature, the executive);
- the decisions of the constitutional courts are of a legal as well as of a political nature, although they may also have a purely consultative function;
- as a rule the constitutional review is repressive, although to a minor extent constitutional review is of a preventive nature;
- the object of such a preventive review of acts are primarily international agreements[104];
- administrative and financial autonomy is a prerequisite for the independence of the Court.

[104] Armenia, Azerbaijan, Belarus (as well as statutes and other regulations), Bulgaria, Buryatia/Russia, Dagestan/Russia, Estonia (as well as statutes), Georgia, Hungary (as well as statutes), Lithuania, Karelia/Russia, Kazakhstan (as well as statutes), Moldavia (as well as constitutional provisions), Romania (as well as statutes and other regulations), Russia (as well as statutes), Tadjikistan, Ukraine. The Slovak system on the other hand explicitly excludes the possibility of any preventive review, while the Northern Ossietian system includes the preventive review of statutes and regulations.

1.5. Essential Elements of the Constitutional Review:

- the timing of reviews: preventive/*a priori*[105]. Other regulations: Belarus, Romania. or repressive/*a posteriori*[106]. Constitutional Court legislative initiatives: Adigea/Russia, Bashkiria/Russia, Buryatia/Russia, Dagestan/Russia, the Kabardino-Balkar Republic/Russia, Karelia/Russia, Koma/Russia, Northern Ossetia/Russia, Tatarstan/Russia, Tuba/Russia Yakutia/Russia.;
- the nature of review: abstract reviews, concrete reviews (requested by ordinary courts), reviews based on an individuals' petition;

[105] Preventive reviews by subject and country:
1. Constitutional provisions: Moldavia;
2. International agreements: Albania, Armenia, Azerbaijan, Belarus, Bulgaria, Buryatia/Russia, Dagestan/Russia, Estonia, Georgia, Hungary, Karelia/Russia, Kazakhstan, Lithuania, Moldavia, PolandRussia, Slovenia, Tadjikistan, Ukraine;
3. Statutes: Belarus, Estonia, Hungary, Kazakhstan, Northern Ossetia/Russia, Poland, Romania, Russia;
4. Regulations: Belarus, Northern Ossetia/Russia;

[106] Repressive (a posteriori) reviews by type, subject, and country:
1. Abstract reviews:
- Constitutional provisions: Dagestan/Russia, the FRY, Kyrgyzstan, Russia, Ukraine, Uzbekistan;
- International agreements: Adigea/Russia, Azerbaijan, Bashkiria/Russia, the Kabardino-Balkar Republic/Russia, Latvia, Lithuania, Moldavia, Russia, Tatarstan/Russia, Tuba/Russia, Uzbekistan, Yakutia/Russia;
- Statutes: Adigea/Russia, Albania, Armenia, Azerbaijan, Bashkiria/Russia, Bosnia and Herzegovina, Bulgaria, Buryatia/Russia, Croatia, the Czech Republic (as well as the subsidiary power of the Supreme Court), Dagestan/Russia, Estonia, the FRY, the FYROM, Georgia, Hungary, Irkutska Oblast/Russia, the Kabardino Balkar Republic/Russia, Karelia/Russia, Koma/Russia, Kyrgyzstan, Latvia, Lithuania, Moldavia, Mongolia, Montenegro/the FRY, Northern Ossetia/Russia, Poland, Russia, Serbia/ the FRY, the Serbian Republic of Bosnia and Herzegovina, Slovakia, Slovenia, Tadjikistan, Tatarstan/Russia, Tuba/Russia, Ukraine, Uzbekistan, Yakutia/Russia;
- Resolutions of the Parliament: Latvia;
- Regulations: Adigea/Russia, Albania, Armenia, Azerbaijan, Buryatia/Russia, the Czech Republic, Dagestan/Russia, the FRY, Georgia, Hungary, Irkutska Oblast/Russia, the Kabardino-Balkar Republic/Russia, Karelia/Russia, Koma/Russia, Latvia, Lithuania, Moldavia, Montenegro/the FRY, Northern Ossetia/Russia, Poland, Russia, Serbia/the FRY, the Serbian Republic of Bosnia and Herzegovina, Slovakia, Slovenia, Tadjikistan, Tatarstan/Russia, Ukraine, Uzbekistan, Yakutia/Russia;
- Acts of the President of the State: Adigea/Russia, Armenia, Azerbaijan, Bashkiria/Russia, Bulgaria, Buryatia/Russia, Georgia, Latvia, Lithuania, Moldavia, Northern Ossetia/Russia, Russia, Tadjikistan, Tatarstan/Russia, Ukraine, Uzbekistan, Yakutia/Russia;
- Rules and other acts of national administrative units: Azerbaijan, Bashkiria/Russia, Buryatia/Russia, Dagestan/Russia, the FRY, Georgia, Irkutska Oblast/Russia, Karelia/Russia, Koma/Russia, Latvia, Northern Ossetia/Russia, Serbia/the FRY, Slovakia, Slovenia, Russia, Tadjikistan, Ukraine, Uzbekistan, Yakutia/Russia;
- Proclaimed regulatory measures of statutory authorities: Slovenia;
- Other rules: Croatia, the FYROM, Hungary, the Kabardino-Balkar Republic/Russia, Northern Ossetia/Russia, Poland, Serbia/ the FRY, Slovakia, Slovenia, Tadjikistan;
- The conformity of national legal norms with (usually ratified) international agreements: Albania, Bulgaria, the Czech Republic, the FRY, Hungary, Latvia, Slovakia, Slovenia, Poland;
- Regional agreements/agreements of member states closed with the Federal State: Buryatia/Russia, Dagestan/Russia, Irkutska Oblast/Russia, the Kabardino-Balkar Republic/Russia, Karelia/Russia, Koma/Russia;

2. Concrete reviews, requested by regular courts: Adigea/Russia, Azerbaijan, Bashkiria/Russia, Bulgaria, Buryatia/Russia, Croatia, the Czech Republic, Dagestan/Russia, Estonia, Georgia, Hungary, Karelia/Russia, Kazakhstan, Koma/Russia, Kyrgyzstan, Lithuania, Poland (by a request presented by a government body), Romania, Russia, Slovenia, Yakutia/Russia;

3. Interpretation of rules:
- Constitution: Albania, Adigea/Russia, Azerbaijan, Bashkiria/Russia, Bulgaria, Buryatia/Russia, Dagestan/Russia, Hungary, Irkutska Oblast/Russia, Kazakhstan, Koma/Russia Kyrgyzstan, Moldavia, Russia, Slovakia, Uzbekistan, Yakutia/Russia;
- Statutes and other rules: Azerbaijan, Dagestan/Russia, Poland, Uzbekistan;

4. Implementation of rules: Bashkiria/Russia, Irkutska Oblast/Russia, the Kabardino-Balkar Republic/Russia, Russia, Tuba/Russia;

5. Citizens' legislative initiatives: Hungary, Romania;

- the object of reviews: positive acts, omissions[107], jurisdictional disputes[108]- Between the Constitutional Courts of the Member states: the FRY., political parties[109], referendums[110], elections[111]- Confirming the election of deputies: Bulgaria, Georgia, Kazakhstan, Mongolia, Slovakia, Slovenia, Ukraine., constitutional complaints[112]- (Constitutional) complaints requested by municipalities: the Czech Republic, Hungary, Slovenia., capacity for offices[113]- Other state representatives: Bulgaria, Russia, Yakutia/Russia., impeachment proceedings[114]- Other State representatives: Bulgaria, Dagestan/Russia, Georgia, Lithuania, Karelia/Russia, Koma/Russia, Mongolia, Slovenia, Ukraine., powers of a special character - Violations of international law, decisions on matters relating to the appointment of constitutional court judges and their immunities, opinions relating to declarations of martial law, the implementation of decisions issued by international Courts, proposals for the amendment of the Constitution, consultative functions, etc.: Armenia, Bulgaria, the Czech Republic, Moldavia, Russia, Uzbekistan., other tasks[115];

Concerning the intensity of the role of the Constitutional Court and tradition, systems (*i.e.* Hungary, Slovenia, Poland, the Czech Republic, Slovakia) most similar to the German Constitutional Court Model, have strong constitutional courts, whereas certain systems keep the powers of the Constitutional Court within certain limits to prevent it from assuming the role of a "negative Legislature"[116].

---

[107] The omission of (statutory) regulations: Hungary.

[108]
- Between top government bodies: Adigea/Russia, Albania, Azerbaijan, Baskhiria/Russia, Bulgaria, Buryatia/Russia, Dagestan/Russia, the FRY, the FYROM, Georgia, Irkutska Oblast/Russia, the Kabardino-Balkar Republic/Russia, Karelia/Russia, Kazakhstan, Latvia, Mongolia, Poland, Russia, the Serbian Republic of Bosnia and Herzegovina, Slovakia, Slovenia, Tadjikistan, Tatarstan/Russia, Ukraine;
- Between the State and regional or local units: Adigea/Russia, Albania, Bosnia and Herzegovina, Bulgaria, Buryatia/Russia, the Czech Republic (as well as subsidiary power of the Supreme Court), Dagestan/Russia, the FRY, the FYROM, Hungary, Irkutska Oblast/Russia, Karelia/Russia, Koma/Russia, Montenegro/the FRY, Russia, the Serbian Republic of Bosnia and Herzegovina, Slovenia, Tatarstan/Russia, Ukraine;
- Between local or regional units: Bashkiria/Russia, Bosnia and Herzegovina, Buryatia/Russia, the FRY, Irkutska Oblast/Russia, Karelia/Russia, Koma/Russia, Montenegro/the FRY, Russia, Slovenia, Tatarstan/Russia, Ukraine;
- Between courts and other government bodies: Montenegro/the FRY, Serbia/the FRY, Slovenia;
- Other jurisdictional disputes: Croatia, Hungary, Ukraine, Yakutia/Russia;

[109] Albania, Armenia, Azerbaijan, Bashkiria/Russia, Bulgaria, Croatia, the Czech Republic, the FRY, the FYROM, Georgia, Moldavia, Montenegro/the FRY, Poland, Romania, Russia, Serbia/the FRY, the Serbian Republic of Bosnia and Herzegovina, Slovakia, Slovenia, Yakutia/Russia.

[110] Armenia, Croatia, Georgia, Hungary, Kazakhstan, Moldavia, Mongolia, Montenegro/the FRY, Romania, Slovakia, Slovenia.

[111] Elections: Albania, Armenia, Bulgaria, Croatia, the Czech Republic, the FRY, Georgia, Kazakhstan, Kyrgyzstan, Lithuania, Moldavia, Mongolia, Montenegro/the FRY, Romania, Serbia/the FRY, Slovakia;

[112] Constitutional complaints of individuals: Adigea/Russia, Albania, Azerbaijan, Bashkiria/Russia, Buryatia/Russia, Croatia, the Czech Republic, Dagestan/Russia, the FRY, the FYROM, Georgia, Hungary, the Kabardino-Balkar Republic/Russia, Karelia/Russia, Koma/Russia, Kyrgyzstan, Mongolia, Montenegro/the FRY, Poland, Slovakia, Slovenia, Ukraine, Uzbekistan;

[113] The President of the State: Adigea/Russia, Armenia, Azerbaijan, Bashkiria/Russia, Bulgaria, Croatia, Kazakhstan, Kyrgyzstan, Lithuania, Moldavia, Poland, Romania, Yakutia/Russia;

[114] The President of the State: Adigea/Russia, Albania, Armenia, Azerbaijan, Bashkiria/Russia, Bulgaria, Buryatia/Russia, Croatia, the Czech Republic, Dagestan/Russia, the FYROM, Georgia, Hungary, Irkutska Oblast/Russia, Karelia/Russia, Koma/Russia, Mongolia, Montenegro/the FRY, Russia, Slovakia, Slovenia, Tatarstan/Russia, Ukraine, Yakutia/Russia;

[115] Tasks which the Court is charged with by the Constitution or Statute: Adigea/Russia, Azerbaijan, Bashkiria/Russia, Croatia, Dagestan/Russia, the FYROM, Georgia, Koma/Russia, Montenegro/the FRY, Slovenia, Tadjikistan, Tuba/Russia, Ukraine, Uzbekistan.

[116] *e.g.* Bulgaria, Romania, Uzbekistan.

1.6. Some other specific features of particular New Democracy countries are as follows:

- in comparison with other "traditional" systems, the Constitutional Court's interventions on its own initiative (*ex officio*) are more present in some New Democracy systems[117];
- the explicit review of the omission of statutorial regulation (Hungary);
- special constitutional complaints filed by municipalities, similar to the German constitutional review system (the Czech Republic);
- the constitutional review of the implementation of the decisions of International Courts (the Czech Republic);
- the jurisdiction of the Constitutional Courts over the interpretation of legal rules, mostly on the constitutional level,[118] or even of statutes[119];
- in some systems the status of legitimate petitioner (standing) is awarded exclusively to government bodies[120], elsewhere, however, the individual citizen may also have access to the Constitutional Court[121];
- despite the final and binding effect of decisions issued by Constitutional Courts, some systems have been trying to explicitly assure the implementation of constitutional court decisions by the subjects involved (*e.g.* Georgia, by special provision of the *Constitutional Court Act*).

1.7. Different national systems specify different terms of office[122]. The term of office of a member of the Serbian/the FRY Constitutional Court as well as of the Constitutional Court of Tatarstan/Russia is permanent. A term of office that is too long may be dangerous for the evolution of the legal process, whereas too short a term of office could be detrimental for the continuity and the authority of the institution, as well as for the balance of the constitutional court case-law. To strengthen the principle of the independence of constitutional court judges, most systems forbid their re-election[123]. The reappointment of Constitutional Courts and the appointment of constitutional court judges do not always coincide; in some countries the term of office of constitutional court judges expires successively, which results in the successive (re)appointment of a portion of the Constitutional Court[124]. Some systems

[117] Albania, Hungary, Moldavia, Poland, Romania, Uzbekistan, sometimes even in the form of legislative initiatives by the Constitutional Court (the Member States of the Russian Federation: Adigea, Bashkiria, Buryatia, Dagestan, the Kabardino-Balkar Republic, Karelia, Koma, Northern Ossetia, Tatarstan, Tuba, Yakutia).

[118] Albania, Azerbaijan, Bulgaria, Hungary, Kazakhstan, Kyrgyzstan, Moldavia, Russia, Slovakia, Uzbekistan, some Member Sates of the Russian Federation (Adigea, Bashkiria, Buryatia, Dagestan, Irkutska Oblast, Koma, Yakutia).

[119] Azerbaijan, Dagestan/Russia, Poland, Uzbekistan.

[120] Armenia, Azerbaijan, Belarus, Bulgaria, Latvia, Lithuania, Romania, Tadjikistan.

[121] Albania, Azerbaijan, Croatia, the Czech Republic, the FRY, the FYROM, Georgia, Hungary, Kyrgyzstan, Mongolia, Montenegro/the FRY, Poland, Slovakia, Slovenia, Ukraine, Uzbekistan, some Member States of the Russian Federation (Adigea, Bashkiria, Buryatia, Dagestan, the Kabardino-Balkar Republic, Karelia, Koma).

[122] In years: 7 (Slovakia), 8 (Croatia, Poland), 9 (Slovenia, the FYROM, Lithuania, Romania, Hungary), 10 (Ukraine), 11 (Belarus), 12 (Bulgaria), 15 (Kyrgyzstan).

[123] Hungary, Lithuania, Poland and Slovenia do allow the re-election of (constitutional) court judges.

[124] *e.g.* Albania, Bulgaria, Poland, Romania.

specify the minimum age required for appointment as a constitutional court judge[125], while some systems specify the maximum age acceptable for appointment[126].

1.8. As mentioned above in general, in the New Democracy countries the influence of government bodies upon the appointment or elections of constitutional court judges differs from system to system. The varieties applicable to elections or appointments of constitutional court judges are as follows:

1.8.1. Appointment Based Systems (without the Participation of a Representative Body): Slovakia, Burundi, where constitutional court judges are exclusively appointed by the Head of State.

1.8.2. Election Based Systems: As a rule Parliaments exercise greater influence on the elections of constitutional court judges as compared to the elections of judges of ordinary courts[127].

1.8.3. Mixed Systems (Appointment and Election) are systems where one part of constitutional court judges are elected by the Parliament or are appointed by the Head of State or by the President of the Parliament, and the rest by the executive branch[128].

The independent position of the Constitutional Court is further symbolized by the mode of appointment of the President of the Constitutional Court. Its independence is even greater if the President is appointed by the constitutional court judges themselves[129], otherwise, the President is appointed by a qualified body outside the Constitutional Court[130].

1.9. Nearly everywhere the qualifications and the required professional experience of constitutional court judges are subject to high standards. The candidates must not only have more than average legal expertise but also a high degree of sensibility for the political effects of their decisions. Some systems regulate the rules of ethical conduct compulsory for judges of the Constitutional Court by a special *Code*[131].

Most systems recognise the immunity of constitutional court judges and certain systems recognise explicit parliamentary immunity[132]. The independent position of constitutional court judges also implies recognition of the corresponding material independence, *i.e.* sufficient resources, funding and remuneration.

A special feature of the office of constitutional court judge is its incompatibility with certain activities. In almost all systems the office of constitutional court judge is

---

[125] *e.g.* Tadjikistan (30), Kyrgyzstan and Georgia (35), Slovenia, Slovakia, Ukraine (40), Hungary (45).

[126] *e.g.* Belarus and in Tadjikistan (60) as well as in Kyrgyzstan, Russia, Bosnia and Herzegovina, Tatarstan/Russia and Hungary (70).

[127] In Adigea/Russia, Azerbaijan, Bashkiria/Russia, Buryatia/Russia, Croatia, Dagestan/Russia, Estonia, the FRY, Hungary, Irkutska Oblast/Russia, the Kabardino-Balkar Republic/Russia, Karelia/Russia, Koma/Russia, Lithuania, Montenegro/the FRY, Northern Ossetia/Russia, Poland, Serbia/the FRY, the Serbian Republic of Bosnia, Slovenia, Tatarstan/Russia, Tuba/Russia, Uzbekistan and Yakutia/Russia constitutional court judges are exclusively appointed by the legislative body.

[128] In Albania, Armenia, Belarus, Bosnia and Herzegovina, Bulgaria, the Czech Republic, Georgia, Kazakhstan, Romania and Slovakia.

[129] *e.g.* the FRY, Slovenia, Tuba/Russia, Yakutia/Russia.

[130] *e.g.* Bashkiria/Russia, Belarus, the Kabardino-Balkar Republic/Russia, Karelia/Russia, Koma/Russia, Montenegro/the FRY, Northern Ossetia/Russia, Poland, Serbia/the FRY, the Serbian Republic of Bosnia, Tatarstan/Russia.

[131] *e.g.* Uzbekistan.

[132] *e.g.* Bulgaria, the Czech Republic, Slovenia.

compatible with scientific and artistic activity, but incompatible with political and commercial activity. With reference to political activity, there may be various grades of restriction, ranging from the absolute prohibition of membership in political parties[133] to the explicit prohibition of membership in the bodies (only) of political parties (Slovenia).

1.10. The decision-making process may be organised in different ways:

- at plenary court level;
- at the level of a plenary court and chambers[134], where deciding in chambers involves mostly constitutional complaints; however, in these systems, too, important decisions are made by the plenary principle.

The dissenting/concurring opinion has also become gradually accepted in the New Democracy countries[135].

Most constitutional/judicial review systems allow for the organizational autonomy of the institution. This means they authorize the respective constitutional/judicial review bodies to follow their own rules regarding their internal organization. Most constitutional/judicial review bodies also have an independent budget as a separate part of the whole State budget, and they are fully independent in its control. Professional services of the Constitutional Courts are organised in a similar way: they consist of clerks and clerical staff, whereby the head of the professional services generally holds the status of secretary general.

B. The Arab Countries

The Arab countries have introduced some forms of constitutional/judicial review, primarily following the concentrated model (Egypt, former Iraq, Lebanon[136], Syria[137] Should the Court decide that a statute or a decree is contrary to the *Constitution*, whatever is contrary to the text of the *Constitution* is considered null and void with retroactive effect and has no consequence (Article 145) The Court has no right to look into statutes which the President of the Republic submits to public referendum and are

[133] *e.g.* Bulgaria, Croatia, Hungary, Russia, Slovakia, Ukraine.

[134] *e.g.* the Czech Republic, Georgia, Slovenia.

[135] *e.g.* Croatia, Hungary, Slovenia.

[136] Under the *Lebanese Constitution of 23 May 1926*, amended on 19 October 1995, a Constitutional Council was established to review the constitutionality of statutes, and to decide on disputes and protests resulting from presidential and representative elections (Article 19). The right to resort to the Council, with respect to determining the constitutionality of statutes, is enjoyed by the President of the Republic, the President of the Chamber of deputies, and the Prime Minister, or the members of the Chamber of Deputies, and heads of the legally recognized religious groups, with respect to personal affairs, freedom of belief and the exercise of religious rituals, and freedom of religious education.

[137] Under the *Constitution* of 13 March 1973, the Supreme Constitutional Court is composed of five members, of whom one is the President, and all of whom are appointed by the President of the State by decree (Article 139). It is not permissible to combine membership of the Court with a ministerial post or membership in the Parliament (Article 140). The term of office of Court members is 4 years subject to renewal (Article 141). Court members cannot be dismissed from the Court except in accordance with the provisions of statute (Article 142). The Court determines the validity of the special appeals regarding the election of members of parliament and submits a report on its finding (Article 144). In addition, the Court has the following powers:
- the preventive constitutional review of statutes and legislative decrees before their promulgation (Article 145);
- a consultative function at the request of the President of the Republic (Article 147).

approved by the people (Article 146)., Yemen[138] - the trial of the President of the Republic, the Vice-President, the Prime Minister, his deputies, ministers and their deputies in pursuance of statute (Article 151).), the French model (Algeria, Morocco) or particular forms (Tunisia, Kuwait[139], Oman[140], Bahrain).

C. Africa

African constitutionalism shows certain specific features. Some countries declared a new constitutional system on gaining independence, others started their independent development without any (written) Constitution and they adopted one subsequently. The political development of constitutionality in Africa often proves to be less stable, mostly due to the influence of many *coups d'état* and the decisions of the supreme political and military bodies. Sometimes the decisions by these bodies have brought about the suspension of the constitutional system or at least a disrespect for the *Constitution* in practice. Accordingly, many African constitutional systems include the following characteristics: the relatively short duration of the *Constitution* and its temporary nature; frequent and material changes in the constitution; the temporary suspension of normal constitutional institutions, and, in turn, of human rights in view of declarations of martial law , which is in many cases anticipated by the *Constitutions* themselves; and a disparity between the constitutional text and actual legal and constitutional practice. Modern African legal theory states that in comparison with civil constitutional systems, in practice, military regimes are often more intolerant of the judicial protection of constitutional rights.

From the constitutional review point of view, Africa is interesting because of the large variety of systems.

With reference to the influences of foreign legal systems, African constitutional review systems can be classified as follows:

1. Francophone Africa

In this area constitutional review was most often introduced under the influence of the French model of 1958 (*Conseil Constitutionnel* - Constitutional Council). In accordance with the French legal tradition, constitutional review is under the jurisdiction of special Constitutional chambers (of the Supreme Court) - *chambres Constitutionnelles*. On the other hand, a certain number of systems were developed under

[138] The *Constitution of Yemen* of 28 September 1994 extended the powers of the Supreme Court of the Republic particularly to cases of:
- charges and counter charges with respect to the unconstitutionality of statutes, regulations and resolutions;
- controversies over jurisdiction among the judicial authorities;
- the impeachment of any of members of the Parliament as may be decided or referred to the Supreme Court by the Parliament;

[139] Under the *Constitution of 11 November 1962*, a statute specifies the judicial body competent to decide upon disputes relating to the constitutionality of statutes and regulations and determines its jurisdiction and proceedings (Article 173). A statute ensures the right of both the Government and the interested parties to challenge the constitutionality of statutes and regulations before the said body. If the said body decides that a statute or a regulation is unconstitutional, it is considered null and void.

[140] Under the *Constitution* (the *Basic Statute of the State*) of 6 November 1996, the statute defines the judicial body entrusted with the settlement of disputes pertaining to the extent of the conformity of statutes and regulations with the *Basic Statute of the State* and that the said statutes and regulations do not contradict its provisions. The statute also specifies the powers of such judicial body and the procedures which it may follow (Article 70).

the influence of the so-called European model (the Austrian Constitutional Court of 1919 and the German Constitutional Court of 1951).

A few countries established their first constitutional review systems immediately after achieving independence in 1959[141]. Many countries assumed (or introduced anew) the same or similar systems into their recent Constitutions[142]. Cameroon formerly entrusted the implementation of the protection of constitutionality to the Constitutional Council. These countries were followed by Morocco, which, with the *Constitution of 7 March 1962*, introduced the Constitutional Chamber of the Supreme Court, while the then *Tunisian* and *Algerian Constitutions* did not feature any constitutional review.

Numerous Francophone countries developed their constitutional review in a concentrated form, and assigned this function to a single body (although in certain cases at the beginning of the independent development of the relevant legal system this review did not exist).

In certain Francophone countries constitutional review was practiced by the ordinary courts as one of their specialized jurisdictions, or by the Supreme Court as an integral institution, or through a special chamber, or through a Constitutional Department of the Supreme Court, or through a Constitutional Council after the European model. In individual cases this function was performed jointly by the united supreme instance of ordinary justice - by the Supreme Court and the Court of Appeals. Some of these countries initially introduced autonomous and special institutions for constitutional review; subsequently this was replaced by a corresponding new power exercised of the highest ordinary court in the State.

Another group of Francophone African countries covers jurisdictions where constitutional review has always been institutionally separated from ordinary justice and falls accordingly under the power of the Constitutional Court as an independent institution (*e.g.* Madagascar).

2. Anglophone Africa

It is characteristic of Anglophone African countries that they have not assumed the British system with no written Constitution and without constitutional review, but rather followed the American system of judicial review. As a matter of fact, upon independence, many Anglophone countries adopted written Constitutions[143].

Some of these countries, *e.g.* Zambia[144] and Malawi, have adopted the American system of judicial review (the so-called system of diffuse review), which means that review falls

[141] Dahomey - now Benin, Upper Volta - now Burkina Faso, Chad, Gabon, Mali, Mauritania, Niger, Sudan.

[142] Dahomey - now Benin, Upper Volta - now Burkina Faso, the Central African Republic, Chad, Congo, Gabon, the Ivory Coast, Madagascar, Mali, Senegal, Togo.

[143] *e.g.*: Botswana, Gambia, Ghana, Kenya, Lesotho, Malawi, Mauritius, Nigeria, Uganda, Seychelles, Sierra Leone, Swazi, Tanzania, Zambia and Zimbabwe.

[144] However, the *Zambian Constitution* of 1991, amended in 1996 established a Special Tribunal empowered to exercise constitutional review.

under the jurisdiction of each judge and each court - and it is only in the hierarchy of adjudicating that a uniform interpretation of the *Constitution* is secured by the authority of the national Supreme Court.

On the other hand, there are other countries who, in spite of the adopted tradition of the Common Law system, have authorized a single government body to carry out constitutional review (a concentrated system of constitutional review in agreement with the Common Law system). This seems to show that in principle the concentrated system of constitutional review (contrary to the American diffuse system) is not incompatible with the Common Law system. This is the state of affairs in Uganda, in which the *1966 Constitution* gave the Supreme Court exclusive jurisdiction over constitutional matters[145].

Most of the above countries have also followed the American model and have adopted their Bills of Rights. In particular the former African countries of the British Commonwealth - Tanzania and Kenya have adopted the American system of constitutional review, with its special emphasis on the protection of constitutional rights and freedoms. They reduced the possibility of the abuse of human rights through appeals to the Supreme Court[146]. According to the data available, it is not possible to establish how this legal protection was enforced in practice, although the mere existence of this possibility represents an important fact, depending on the respect for the independence of the judiciary in the particular State, and the particular legal system to the extent of which it preserves the "Rule of Law."

It is less known that in these countries human rights' protection systems, resulting from the *European Convention for the Protection of Human Rights and Fundamental Freedoms* of 4 November 1950, had been established prior to their independence. The provisions of the above Convention were in force in numerous African countries due to the fact that Great Britain decided to implement the Extension Clause of Article 63 of the *European Convention for the Protection of Human Rights and Fundamental Freedoms* and since 23 October 1953 enforced the validity of the Convention including its first Protocol of 20 March 1953 also in the African territories under British sovereignty, among others, in particular in Tanganyika and Zanzibar. Upon acquiring independence some of these African countries included the list of rights from the *European Convention for the Protection of Human Rights and Fundamental Freedoms* directly into their Constitutions, such as Nigeria with its *Constitutional Act on the Proclamation of Independence* (1 October 1960).

A special phenomenon is evident in the constitutional review system in Mauritius. It is the so-called New (British) Commonwealth model (Mauritius) and it cannot be classified either under the American or under the European model. This model is characterized by concentrated constitutional review under the jurisdiction of the

---

[145] (Article 95); similarly in Ghana and its 1960 and 1969 *Constitutions* (Article 42 and Article 106 respectively). In Article 2 of the 1969 Constitution it even gave standing to individuals to address the Supreme Court and request constitutional reviews, and pursuant to the modifications of the *1979 Constitution*, it explicitly specified that the Supreme Court should have original and exclusive power to carry out constitutional review.

[146] Article 84 of the *Constitution of Kenya*, Article 42 of the *Constitution of Nigeria* , Para. 4 of Article 30 of the *Constitution of Tanzania* and Article 29 of the *Constitution of Zambia*.

Supreme Court consisting of ordinary judges regularly appointed. The system of Mauritius mainly involves preventive review and the consultative function of the Supreme Court, although repressive review is also possible. Another special feature is that decisions have an *erga omnes* effect.

3. Lusophone Africa

Upon acquiring independence, Mozambique and Angola did not introduce constitutional review after the Portuguese model (also due to the then socialist political system supposedly not compatible with the institution of constitutional review), although the then *Constitution of Mozambique* specified the Supreme Court as the guarantor of respect for the *Constitution*, statutes and other legislative acts. The new *Constitution of Mozambique of 2 November 1990* established an independent body for constitutional review, the Constitutional Council (Articles 180 through 184), with broad powers, whereby the circle of petitioners for constitutional review (standing) was limited to the highest government bodies only. Further, the new *Constitution of Angola* (draft of April 1990) anticipates the foundation of the Constitutional Court with jurisdiction to discuss and to assess the constitutionality and legality of statutes and other legal measures if they do not accord with constitutional principles (Para. 2 of Article 65).

The *Portuguese Constitution of 2 April 1976* only partly served as a model for the *Constitutions of Cape Verde, Guinea Bissao* and *Sao Tome and Principe*[147]. All three countries introduced a particular system similar to the constitutional review[148]. In principle the (ordinary) courts are empowered to not apply unconstitutional statutes. In addition, an ordinary court, the attorney general or some other government body is entitled to submit to the Parliament a request for the constitutional review of a particular law allegedly in violation of the *Constitution*; accordingly, constitutional review is performed by a political (legislative) body. The decisions of the Parliament have an *erga omnes* effect and are published in the official gazette. However, subsequently, in some countries of the respective group the Supreme Court of Justice became empowered to exercise constitutional review (*e.g.* the *Constitution of the Republic of Cape Verde of 25 September 1992*).

4. Hispanophone Africa

The *Constitution of Equatorial Guinea*, in force up to 1991, specified that the National Council as the supreme collective government body had jurisdiction to deal with constitutional matters, including: deciding on the constitutionality of statutes and measures taken for their implementation; the authentic interpretation of respective

[147] Republica Cape Verde (*Constitution of 7 October 1980*, amended 2 February 1981, as well as the *Constitution* of 25 September 1992), Republica Guinea Bissao (*Constitution* of 16 May 1984, as well as the *Constitution* of 11 May 1991) and Republica Sao Tome and Principe (*Constitution of 5 November 1975*, amended for the last time by *Constitutional Statute No. 7/90 of October 1990*).

[148] Articles 90 through 92 of the *Constitution of Cape Verde*; Article 98 of the *Constitution of Guinea Bissao*; Article 11 of the *Constitution of Sao Tome and Principe*.

laws; the review of presidential elections; and the review of the (in)capacity of the President of the Republic to perform their office.

The *Fundamental Law of Equatorial Guinea* of 16 November 1991 introduced the Constitutional Court, which is created within the Supreme Court of Justice (Article 94).

5. Some Countries with the Longest State Tradition

Although Liberia ranks among the oldest independent African countries, it has not introduced any constitutional review despite its State and constitutional tradition. The *Liberian Constitution of 26 July 1847* (with *Amendments of 1955*) does not anticipate any constitutional review of statutes. Neither did the *Ethiopian Constitution of 4 November 1955* feature any constitutional review, whereas the new *Constitution of 21 August 1995* introduced the constitutional review, following a model of specialized State body, although in specific circumstances concerning the supremacy of the Parliament, the decisions by the Ethiopian Council of Constitutional Inquiry must be approved by the Parliament.

D. The Composition of Bodies Empowered to Carry Out Constitutional Review

Particularly in systems where such bodies were established as independent and specialized, their composition has been highly influenced by the executive branch - primarily by the Head of State. The same branch has influenced the composition of such courts even in some countries where constitutional review is carried out by the Supreme Court. The constitutional chambers or departments of supreme courts are composed mainly of professional judges, but also in such cases the executive branch always assists in their appointment.

All the systems feature the principle of the independence of judges who exercise constitutional review. The incompatibility of the office of constitutional court judge with particular activities is considered as well. At the same time, constitutional court judges are entitled to some privileges, *e.g.* they are irremovable. During their term of office, their immunity is equal to representative' immunity.

E. The Powers of Constitutional Review Bodies

1. General

These systems mostly adopted the constitutional review of statutes. Some systems also adopted the preventive review of statutes and/or the so-called consultative function of bodies exercising constitutional review concerning the drafting of statutes, executive regulations or presidential acts. Several systems introduced the constitutional review of presidential and representative elections.

The African systems primarily adopted two systems concerning the effects of constitutional court decisions: the Francophone systems feature *erga omnes* effects, while the Anglophone systems do not feature such effect. The exception is the American rule of *stare decisis*, which is not implemented often by the African Anglophone systems.

In only a few countries is the constitutional complaint guaranteed: e.g. Benin, Congo. In addition, constitutional courts are rarely empowered to exercise *ex officio* review (*e.g.* in Mali, under the Law of 1965).

Concerning systems of concentrated constitutional review the powers are similar: review of the constitutionality of statutes, review of the constitutionality of international agreements (mostly preventive), review of elections *etc.* Often the role of the Head of State as a petitioner before the constitutional court is emphasised, especially concerning the preventive constitutional review of statutes and international agreements. Sometimes the Head of State is a favoured petitioner together with the President of the Parliament. In some countries the government also has the status of legitimate petitioner. On the other hand, quite rarely a group of representatives has the status of legitimate petitioner.

2. The Particular Systems of Constitutional Review

Algeria:

Algeria introduced the constitutional review by the *Constitution* of 10 September 1963. Under Article 64 of the *Constitution*, the Constitutional Council (*conseil constitutionnel*) was empowered to review the constitutionality of statutes passed by the National Assembly as well as the constitutionality of regulations having the force of statute issued by the Head of State (decrees having the force of statute).

By the constitutional reform of 28 February 1989, the Constitutional Council as an independent body was established. Its activities are regulated by the *President's Decree* of 7 August 1989 concerning its internal organization (*Decret presidentiel et reglement interieur*) as well as the presidential decree of 4 April 1989 concerning the appointment and the composition of the Constitutional Council (*Decret presidentiel relatif a la publication de la composition des membres du Conseil constitutionnel*). The Council is composed of 7 members. 3 members are appointed by the President of the Republic, 2 are appointed by the Parliament, 2 are appointed by the Supreme Court from among its members (Article 145 of the *Constitution*). The President of the Council is appointed by the Head of State. The members of the Council (including the President) are appointed for six years. The Council is reappointed in three year intervals. Under the *Decree on the Organization*, new members of the Council have to be appointed within 15 days from when the term of office of previous members has expired. In accordance with the President's directions, the administration is managed by a Secretary General with two assistant-directors for research matters. The budget of the Council is a part of the general State budget.

The office of a member of the Constitutional Council is incompatible with all other offices; the only exceptions are artistic and scientific activities (Article 154). Members of the Constitutional Council are not allowed to hold any other public office; in case of violation, the Council decides on the termination of office of the offender. The decisions of the Constitutional Council are passed by a majority of its members. In case of a deadlock, the president's vote is decisive. A quorum consists of at least 5 members of the Council.

The Council has the following powers:

- the abstract review of acts issued by the President of the Republic or by the Parliament, which entails constitutional review *a posteriori* with *ex nunc* effect. The decisions are binding;
- the preventive review (*a priori*) of acts of the President of the Republic and the Parliament;
- impeachment (Article 84 of the *Constitution*);
- the review of parliamentary and presidential elections;
- the review of the capacity of the President to perform the office of the President;
- the review of the results of referendums:
- the preventive review (*a priori*) of international agreements before their ratification;
- on the proposal of the President of the Republic, a consultative function concerning urgent measures, a State of Emergency (Articles 85, 86 and 87 of the *Constitution*), amnesty (Article 90 of the *Constitution*), as well as in cases of constitutional amendments.

The case-law of the Algerian Constitutional Council is characterised by the great influence of the French Constitutional Council. The decisions of the Algerian Council are published in the Official Gazette. They are signed by the President and Vice-President of the Council. The reporting judge remains anonymous. The decisions are passed by anonymous voting.

The *Constitution* of 28 November 1996 reintroduced the Constitutional Council. The Council is established to guard the respect for the *Constitution* (Article 163). The Council monitors, among other matters, the regularity of referendum operations, the election of the President of the Republic and legislative actions. It announces the result of its operations. The Council consists of nine members (Article 164). Three are appointed by the President of the Republic, two are elected by the National People's Assembly, two are elected by the Council of the Nation, one is elected by the Supreme Court, and one is elected by the Council of State. As soon as they are elected or designated, the members of the Council cease any other mandate, function charge or mission. The President of the Republic designates the President of the Constitutional Council for a single six year term. The other members of the Constitutional Council serve a single term of six years and one half are appointed every three years. In addition, the Council rules on the constitutionality of treaties, laws and negotiations, either by an opinion, if these are not rendered executory, or by a decision otherwise (Article 165). The Council when called upon by the President of the Republic issues an obligatory opinion on the constitutionality of organic laws after their adoption by the Parliament (Article 165). It also rules on the conformity with the *Constitution* of the internal regulation of each of the two chambers of Parliament. When the Council rules that a treaty, accord or convention is unconstitutional. its ratification cannot take place (Article 168). When it rules that a legislative or regulatory provision is unconstitutional, it loses all effect from the day of the decision of the Council (Article 169).

ANGOLA

The new draft Constitution of Angola of April 1990 adopted the principles of the supremacy of the *Constitution* and the independence of the judiciary.

Under Para. 2 of Article 65 the establishment of the Constitutional Court is foreseen, which is empowered to decide on the unconstitutionality and illegality of provisions of statutes and other regulations that violate the principles determined by the *Constitution* of the State.

BENIN (THE FORMER REPUBLIC OF DAHOMEY)

The Constitutional Chamber of the State (Supreme) Court is empowered to carry out constitutional review, and was introduced by Article 47 of the *Constitution* of 14 February 1959. Such regulation was reintroduced by Article 58 of the *Constitution* of 26 November 1960.

The *Constitution* of 8 April 1968 in the last sub-paragraph of Article 62 as well as in sub-para. 1 of Article 85, introduced the constitutional review of basic statutes. Under Article 43 of the same *Constitution*, the Supreme Court of the State was empowered to exercise such powers. Under Article 44 of the *Constitution*, the composition, the organization and activities of the Court are to be regulated by special statute.

The *Constitution* of the Republic of Dahomey of 11 April 1978 (Article 3) introduced the popular complaint before the Supreme Court containing a request for the constitutional review of all statutes.

The new *Constitution* of the Republic of Benin, adopted in December 1990, introduced the Constitutional Court as an independent body of constitutional review, which was then established on 7 June 1993. The Constitutional Court assumed the powers of the now superseded Supreme Court. It is composed of seven members. Four are appointed by a special Council of the Parliament, three are appointed by the Head of State. It is empowered to review the constitutionality of statutes as well as to protect constitutional rights and freedoms. There is no remedy against the decisions of the Constitutional Court, which are binding on all State bodies.

Botswana

The *Constitution* of 30 September 1966, amended of 1987 specifies that where any question as to the interpretation of the *Constitution* arises in any proceedings in a subordinate court and the court is of the opinion that the question involves a substantial question of law, the court may, and shall if any party to the proceedings so requests, refer the question to the High Court (Article 105). The High Court issues its decision upon the question and the court in which the question, subject to any appeal, then disposes of the case in accordance with that decision.

Burkina Faso

The Constitutional Chamber and /or the Constitutional Council of the Supreme Court of the Republic of Burkina Faso (until 1984 the Republic of Upper Volta) was empowered to carry out constitutional review under Article 66 of the *Constitution* of 15 March 1959 as well as under Article 57 of the *Constitution* of 30 November 1960.

The *Constitution* of 14 June 1970 newly empowered the Constitutional Council of the Supreme Court (sub-para. 3 of Article 3 and Article 88).

It has the following powers:

- the preventive constitutional review of statutes (Article 87); - the preventive review of the constitutionality of international agreements (Article 102);
- the constitutional review of the results of referendums (Article 4);
- the constitutional review of elections of the President of the Republic (Sub-para. 7 of Article 25);
- the impeachment of the President of the Republic (Sub-para. 2 of Article 28);
- the constitutional review of elections of representatives (Article 44).

The judges of the Supreme Court are appointed by the President of the Republic (Article 33).

The constitutional amendment of 1977 granted citizens the right to the popular complaint, involving a request for the review of the constitutionality of statutes.

Under the new *Constitution* of 11 June 1991 amended on 27 January 1997, the constitutional review of statutes is exercised also by the Constitutional Chamber of the Supreme Court, which is presided over by the President of the Supreme Court (Article 152). The Constitutional Chamber is composed of (Article 153): the President of the Supreme Court; three judges appointed by the Head of State, following the proposal of the Minister of Justice; three judges appointed directly by the Head of State; as well as three judges appointed by the President of the Parliament. The term of office of members of the Constitutional Chamber is 9 years. The Court is reappointed every three years in proceedings determined by statute. The office of constitutional court judge is incompatible with the office of representative of the Parliament. Other cases of incompatibility are determined by a statute.

The Constitutional Chamber has the following powers: the review of Presidential elections, the review of parliamentary elections, the review of the results of referendums (Article 154); the preventive constitutional review of basic and other statutes before their promulgation (Article 155), the constitutional review of international agreements before their ratification (Articles 150 and 155); the review of the constitutionality of the activities of political parties (Article 156 in connection with Sub-para. 5 of Article 13). The legitimate petitioners for (preventive) constitutional review are the President of the Republic, the Prime Minister, the presidents of both Chambers of the Parliament, and 1/5 of the representatives of the Parliament (Article 157). The decisions of the Constitutional Chamber are generally binding (Article 159). The organization and work of the Constitutional Chamber are determined by statute (Article 160 of the *Constitution*). The new Constitution does not contain an explicitly regulation concerning the popular complaint.

Burundi

The *Constitution* of the Kingdom of Burundi of 16 October 1962 empowered the Constitutional Chamber of the Supreme Court to exercise constitutional review (Article 95). The next *Constitutions* of 11 July 1974 and of 18 November 1980 adopted the same institution, after the civil *Constitution* was suspended in 1981.

The new *Constitution* of the Republic of Burundi was adopted on 18 January 1992. The jurisdiction of the Constitutional Court comprises actions of the State in constitutional matters. It judges the constitutionality of laws and interprets the *Constitution* (Article 149). The Court is composed of an odd number of at least five members appointed by the President of the Republic for a term of six years, with the possibility of reappointment (Article 150). Members of the Court must be jurists of high standing, having at least eight years of professional experience. They are chosen from among individuals recognized for their moral integrity, impartiality and independence. Half the members of the Constitutional Court are career magistrates.

The Constitutional Court is empowered to (Article 151):

- decide on the constitutionality of statutes and regulatory acts adopted in matters other than those related to the domain of the law at the request of the President of the Republic, the Prime Minister, the President of the National Assembly, one quarter of the Representatives, or any individual;
- interpret the *Constitution* at the request of the President of the Republic, the Prime Minister, the President of the National Assembly, or one quarter of the Representatives;
- decide on the propriety of presidential and legislative elections and referenda, and to proclaim their results;
- accept the oath of the President of the Republic marking his entry into office;
- verify the vacancy of the office of President of the Republic.

Organic statutes before their promulgation and internal regulations of the National Assembly before their application, are necessarily subject to constitutional review (Para. 2 of Article 151).

The Constitutional Court is consulted concerning measures issued during the exercise of emergency powers (Para. 3 of Article 79). Any text of a legislative nature may be modified on entering into force by presidential decree or by legislative enactment upon the recommendation of the Constitutional Court (Articles 113 and 114). Unless unforeseeable circumstances intervene as verified by the Constitutional Court, the meetings of the National Assembly are not valid unless they are held at the ordinary site of its sessions (Para. 1 of Article 122).

When the Constitutional Court, upon the request of the President of the Republic, the Prime Minister, the President of the National Assembly, or a quarter of the representatives, declares that an international obligation contravenes the Constitution, such accord may only be ratified after amendment of the Constitution (Article 176).

Every individual interested, as well as the Public Prosecutor, may request that the Constitutional Court rule on the constitutionality of statutes, either directly by means of an action or by exceptional proceedings for claiming unconstitutionality raised in a matter which concerns that person before an authority. Such authority suspends judgment until a decision is reached by the Constitutional Court, which must rule within thirty days (Para. 2 of Article 153).

An act declared unconstitutional may not be promulgated or applied (Article 154). The decisions of the Constitutional Court may not be appealed (Para. 2 of Article 154).

An organic statute determines the organization and operation of the Constitutional Court, as well as the proceedings to be followed before it (Article 155).

The High Court of Justice composed of the Supreme Court and the Constitutional Court, jointly are empowered to hear cases involving the impeachment of the President of the Republic, the Prime Minister, or the President of the National Assembly (Article 157).

Cameroon

The first *Constitution of 1960* did not introduce any constitutional review. The later *Constitution of the Federal Republic of Cameroon* (after the union of its Francophone and Anglophone territories) of 1 September 1961, established the Federal Court (Article 33), which was, as a protector of the constitutional order, empowered only to decide on jurisdictional disputes between State bodies, but not to decide cases concerning the constitutional review of statutes.

By the centralised *Constitution* of 20 May 1972, the country reintroduced the Supreme Court (Articles 7, 10 and 27 of the *Constitution*). Its organization and work was regulated by the *Constitutional Act* of 9 May 1975. Despite further amendments of this

Act (*Act No. 79-02 of 1979, Act No. 83-10 of 21 July 1983*, and *Act No. 83-25 of 29 November 1983*), these regulations did not reinforce the functions of the Supreme Court concerning constitutional review. This function was exercised by the Constitutional Chamber of the Supreme Court (Article 32 of the *Constitution* of 2 June 1972). The legitimate petitioners for the constitutional review of statutes were the President of the Republic or the President of the Parliament.

The new *Law No. 96-06 of 18 January 1996 to Amend the Constitution of 2 June 1972* introduced the Constitutional Council. The Council has jurisdiction in matters pertaining to the *Constitution*. It rules on the constitutionality of statutes (Article 46).

The Constitutional Council issues final rulings (Article 47) on:

- the constitutionality of statutes, treaties and international agreements;
- the constitutionality of rules of procedure of the National Assembly and the Senate prior to their implementation;
- conflicts of powers between State institutions, between the State and the Regions, and between the Regions.

Matters may be referred to the Council by the President of the Republic, the President of the National Assembly, the President of the Senate, one-third of the members of the National Assembly or one-third of the Senators (Para. 2 of Article 47). The presidents of regional executive branches may refer matters to the Constitutional Council whenever the interests of their Regions are at stake.

Statutes, as well as treaties and international agreements may, prior to their enactment, be referred to the Constitutional Council by the President of the Republic, the President of the National Assembly, the President of the Senate, one third of the members of the National Assembly, one-third of the Senators, or the presidents of regional executive branches (Para. 3 of Article 47). Enactment deadlines cease to apply once the relevant matter has been referred to the Constitutional Council. The Constitutional Council advises in matters falling under its jurisdiction.

The Constitutional Council ensures the regularity of presidential elections, parliamentary elections and referendum operations. It proclaims the results thereof (Article 48).

In any case, the Council gives a ruling within a period of fifteen days, once a matter has been referred to it (Article 49). However, at the request of the President of the Republic, such a time-limit may be reduced to eight days.

Rulings of the Constitutional Council are not a subject to appeal. They are binding on all public, administrative, military and judicial authorities, as well as on all individuals and corporate bodies (Article 50). A provision that has been declared unconstitutional may not be enacted or implemented.

The Council is composed of eleven members appointed to a non-renewable nine year term of office (Article 51). These members are chosen from among individuals of established professional reputation. They must be of high moral integrity and proven competence. Members of the Council are appointed by the President of the Republic. They are appointed as follows:

- three, including the President of the Council, by the President of the Republic;
- three by the President of the National Assembly after consultation with the national *Bureau*;
- three by the President of the Senate after consultation with the national *Bureau*;
- two by the High Judicial Council.

Besides the eleven members, former presidents of the Republic are *ex officio* members of the Constitutional Council for life.

In case of a deadlock, the President of the Constitutional Council has the deciding vote.

In the event of the death or resignation or any other cause of incapacity or inability duly established by the competent bodies provided by law, a replacement shall be designated by the competent authority or body concerned and appointed to complete the term of office (Para. 3 of Article 51). Members of the Council take the oath of office as laid down by statute, before a Parliamentary session (Para. 4 of Article 51). The office of member of the Council is incompatible with that of member of the Government, member of Parliament, or of the Supreme Court. Other incompatibilities and matters relating to the status of members, namely obligations, immunities and privileges, are laid down by statute (Para. 5 of Article 51).

A statute regulates the organization and functioning of the Constitutional Council, the conditions for referring matters to it, as well as the proceedings applicable before it (Article 52).

Cape Verde

By the *Constitution of 25 September 1992*, the Supreme Court of Justice became empowered to exercise constitutional review. Its powers are as follows (Articles 300 to 305):

- the preventive review of international treaties when requested by the President of the Republic;
- the abstract review of the constitutionality of any laws or resolutions of general or specific content;
- the abstract review of the illegality of resolutions;
- the concrete review of constitutionality where unconstitutionality has been claimed in a trial;
- the deciding on individual appeals filed by any individual or the Public Prosecutor's Office after the exhaustion of the process established by law by which the original decision was issued.

In cases of the preventive review of international treaties, rulings of the Supreme Court of Justice have the form of an opinion (Para. 1 of Article 306). In other cases, decisions of the Supreme Court have the form of a ruling (Para. 2 of Article 306).

Decisions of the Supreme Court which deal with constitutionality or illegality are published in their entirety in the official journal (Para. 3 of Article 306). Rulings of the Supreme Court which deal with constitutionality or illegality, whatever the process by which they are issued, have general legal force (Article 307). A declaration of unconstitutionality or illegality with general legal force takes effect from the effective date of the law which has been judged unconstitutional or illegal and the removal of the laws which have been revoked (Article 308).

The Central African Republic

Constitutional review was exercised by the Constitutional Council as an independent and special body with such powers as were determined by the *Constitutional Act* No. 60-163 of 12 December 1960 (Article 32). Such regulations were adopted by *Basic Act* No. 61-238 of 1961, as well as by the later *Constitution* of 26 November 1964.

Under the *Constitution* of 4 December 1976 the power of constitutional review was granted to the Constitutional Chamber of the Supreme Court.

After the period when the civil constitutional order was suspended, the Constitutional Council was newly introduced by the *Constitution* of 5 February 1981. The Council was composed of 6 members, which were appointed by the President of the Republic and by the Presidency of the Parliament.

Under the *Constitution* of 21 November 1986, constitutional review is exercised by the Constitutional Council. Its members are appointed by the President of the Republic. The Council is only partially empowered to evaluate the constitutionality of statutes, similar to the so-called French model as follows: the preventive review of statutes before they have been promulgated by the President of the Republic and/or the President of the Parliament.

Under the new *Constitution* of 28 December 1994, the Constitutional Court was established. It is instituted and charged with (Article 70; Articles 24, 26, 27, 28, 29, 30, 31, 32, 61, 64, 68):

- striving for the regularity of presidential, legislative, regional, and municipal elections, and with examining and proclaiming the results of balloting;
- resolving any electoral disagreements;
- resolving conflicts of competence between the executive power, the legislative power, and the territorial authorities;
- exercising a consultative function concerning constitutional amendments;
- the preventive review of international agreements;
- exercising the preventive review of statutes;

- exercising the preventive review of ordinances;
- exercising the preventive review of the rules of procedure of the National Assembly;
- deciding on disagreements concerning amendments during the course of the legislative procedure;
- exercising a consultative function in the circumstances of a State of Emergency;
- deciding on the definitive incapacity or illness of the President of the Republic.

Any person who considers himself wronged may request that the Constitutional Court rule on the constitutionality of statutes, either directly or by the proceedings on unconstitutionality brought before an authority in an affair which concerns them (Para. 3 of Article 70).

The Court is composed of 9 members who carry the title of Counsellors (Article 71). The non-renewable mandate is 9 years. The Court members are appointed as follows:

- 3 by the President of the Republic, of which at least two are jurists;
- 3 by the President of the National Assembly, of which at least two are jurists;
- 3 magistrates elected by their peers.

The Court members are chosen from among law professors, advocates and magistrates having at least 15 years of experience as well as qualifications recognised by the State. The nine members of the Court are appointed concurrently. In addition, the former Presidents of the Republic are honorary members of the Constitutional Court with a consultative voice. The Court members are irremovable during the duration of their mandate. They may not be investigated nor arrested without the authorisation of the Court. The functions of a Court member are incompatible with any political or administrative function, or any salaried employment (Article 72).

The Court decisions are not susceptible to any recourse. They impose themselves upon public powers, all administrative and judicial authorities, and all individuals (Article 74). Any text declared unconstitutional is null and of no effect; it may not be promulgated, nor applied (Article 71).

Chad

The Constitutional Court as an independent body was established under Article 51 of the *Constitution* of 31 March 1959. Under the constitutional amendments of 1960 and 1962, the function of constitutional review was granted to the Supreme Court in a plenary session (Article 64 of the *Constitution* of 16 April 1962).

The *Constitution* (the "*National Charter*") dates from 20 December 1989, and was amended on 28 February 1991. It introduced the Supreme Court as the highest body of the judicial hierarchy, composed of the Constitutional Council, the Judicial Council, as well as the Administrative and Financial Council. Constitutional review is exercised by the Constitutional Council. The system of constitutional review was established under American and European influences, primarily under the influence of the model of the French Constitutional Council. The Supreme Court has 8 permanent members (Article 172), who are appointed by the President of the Republic upon his proposal and the proposal of the Parliament. They are appointed for 8 years (Article 173). The President of the Supreme Court is appointed by the Head of State; the President of the Supreme Court is at the same time the President of the Constitutional Council (Article 174). The powers of the Constitutional Council are (Article 175): the preventive review of the constitutionality of statutes, the constitutional review of international agreements (before the promulgation of statutes, before the promulgation of international agreements, as requested by the President of the Republic, the President of the Parliament or 1/4 of the members of the Parliament), and the review of the constitutionality of elections. The Constitutional Council may propose the issuance of new statutes or the amending of current statutes (Article 155).

The *Constitution of the Republic of Chad* of 14 April 1996 introduced the Constitutional Council as a special independent State body (Article 164). The Council is composed of nine members including three magistrates and six jurists of a high level appointed in the following manner (Article 165):

- one magistrate and two jurists by the President of the Republic;
- one magistrate and two jurists by the President of the National Assembly;
- one magistrate and two jurists by the President of the Senate.

The mandate of the members of the Council is of nine years and not renewable. The Council is appointed by thirds every three years. The members are irremovable during their mandate. They must have recognized professional competence, good morals and high probity. The President of the Council is elected by his peers for a term of three years and is re-electable (Article 168).

The Council powers are as follows (Article 166):

- to judge the constitutionality of laws, treaties and international agreements;
- to review presidential, legislative and senatorial elections;
- to review the results of referendums;
- to exercise the preventive review of statutes;
- to exercise the preventive review of the rules of procedure of the Parliamentary chambers;
- to adjudicate jurisdictional disputes between State bodies.

The office of a member of the Council is incompatible with the office of a member of the Government, the exercise of any elective mandate, of any public function, and any other for-profit activity (Article 167).

Every citizen may request a review of the unconstitutionality of a matter before any jurisdiction regarding a matter that concerns him (Article 171). Council decisions are not susceptible to any recourse (Article 174). They bind public powers, and all administrative, military and judicial authorities.

Comoros

The Constitutional Council as a special body empowered to exercise constitutional review was established by the *Constitution* of 1 October 1978 (Article 33). In practice the Constitutional Council is represented by the Supreme Court, which works as a constitutional council if appropriate regarding constitutional matters.

It has the following powers:

- the review of presidential and parliamentary elections;
- the repressive review of the constitutionality of statutes and executive regulations;
- the preventive review of the constitutionality of statutes and executive regulations;
- impeachment concerning the liability of the highest State officials.

The *Constitution* of 30 October 1996 introduced the High Council of the Republic, which among other matters also adjudicates constitutional matters (Article 49). It is composed of:

- four members appointed by the President of the Republic;
- three members elected by the Federal Assembly upon the proposal of the President of the Federal Assembly;
- one member elected by the council of each island, upon the proposal of the president of the council of the island.

The members are chosen by reason of their honour, and their judicial, financial and economic expertise. They are appointed for a seven year renewable mandate. Their office is incompatible with any other elected mandate, any political function and any private professional activity (Article 50). The President of the Council is elected by his peers for seven years (Article 51). The Council is empowered:

- to review the regularity of presidential and legislative elections;
- to review the regularity of the holding of referendums and proclaim the results;
- to exercise the preventive and repressive review of the constitutionality of laws, ordinances, treaties or international agreements, and any normative provision having the force of statute (Article 53).

The decisions of the Council are not susceptible to any recourse.

Congo

Constitutional review was introduced by the establishment of the Constitutional Chamber of the Supreme Court of Congo (Congo Brazzaville) under Article 58 of the *Constitution* of 2 March 1961.

The *Constitution* of 8 December 1963 in Sub-para. 3 of Article 72 and in Article 73 determined that the Constitutional court is composed of all chambers of the Supreme Court. This Constitutional Court was empowered to exercise the constitutional review of statutes and international agreements. Subsequently, by the *Reorganisation of the Judiciary Act* No. 83-53 of 21 April 1983, this body was remodelled into only one Constitutional Chamber of the Supreme Court.

On the basis of the *Constitution* of 8 July 1979 (Article 86 through 93) the Constitutional Council was established as a constitutional review body by *Ordinance No. 019/84* of 23 August 1984 . Its activities were regulated in detail by *Act No. 074-84* of 7 November 1984, instituting the following powers: the preventive constitutional review of statutes and international agreements, the review of parliamentary elections, the review of the legality of referendums and the preventive constitutional review of internal acts of the Parliament. The President of the Republic appoints eight members of the Council, the other eight members are appointed by the Parliament. The President of the Republic also appoints the President and Vice-President of the Council. The office of a member of the Constitutional Council is incompatible with any other public office. The decisions of the Constitutional Council are indisputable and bind all State bodies.

It should be noted that the *Constitution of Congo* of 21 April 1983 introduced the popular complaint (Article 69).

The *Constitution of the Republic of the Congo* of 15 March 1992 instituted the Constitutional Council (Article 138). The Council consists of nine members:

- two magistrates elected by the High Council of the Magistrate;
- two Law Professors from the University, elected by their peers,
- two Lawyers elected by their peers;
- three members, one each named by the President of the Republic, the President of the National Assembly, and the President of the Senate (Article 139). The members must have professional experience of a least 15 years. The Council is appointed by thirds every two years. The President of the Council is elected by his peers for a duration of two years, and is re-electable (Article 40). The functions of a member of the Council are incompatible with those of a Minister or a Member of Parliament (Article 141). The Council is empowered:
- to exercise the preventive and repressive review of the constitutionality of laws, regulations and international agreements;
- to ensure the regularity of the election of the President of the Republic;
- to ensure the regularity of legislative elections;
- to ensure the regularity of referendums.

Any person can petition the Constitutional Council on the constitutionality of statutes, either directly, or in proceedings initiated before the proper body in an matter which concerns them (Article 148). The decisions of the Constitutional Council are not susceptible to any recourse and bind all public powers, public authorities, judiciaries and individuals (Article 149).

Djibouti

The Constitutional Court (*Cour constitutionnelle*) was introduced by *Constitutional Act* No. L.R./77-002 of 27 June 1977 (Article 2).

Under the *Constitution* of 1981, the empowered body exercising constitutional review is the Constitutional Council.

The *Constitution of the Republic of Djibouti* of 4 September 1992 reintroduced the Constitutional Council as an independent body exercising constitutional review. It consists of six members, whose term of office lasts eight years and is not renewable. They are appointed as follows (Article 76):

- two by the President of the Republic;
- two by the President of the National Assembly;
- two by the High Council of the Judiciary.

One half of the membership of the Constitutional Council is renewed every four years. The President of the Council is appointed by the President of the Republic from among its members. Former Presidents of the Republic are *de jure* members of the Council. The members of the Council enjoy the immunity accorded to members of the National Assembly. Members of the Council must be at least thirty years of age and be selected primarily from among experienced jurists. The Council is empowered (Articles 77 to 80):

- to ensure the regularity of all election;
- to ensure the regularity of all referendums;
- to exercise the preventive review of statutes and the rules of procedure of the National Assembly.

Legislative provisions relating to the fundamental rights of any person as recognized under the *Constitution* may be referred to the Constitutional Council, by special proceedings, in connection with any proceedings that are under way before a court (Article 80). The claim of unconstitutionality may be entered by any plaintiff before any authority or court (Article 80). Decisions of the Constitutional Council have the authority of *res judicata* They may not be appealed and must be recognized by all Governmental authorities, administrative and judicial authorities and by all individuals (Article 81).

Egypt

The Supreme Constitutional Court of Egypt was empowered by of the *Constitution* of 11 September 1971(Articles 174 to 178 of the *Constitution*), amended on 22 May 1980, as well as by the *Supreme Constitutional Court Act* No. 48/1979 of 29 August 1979.

The Court is composed of the President and an "appropriate number" of judges appointed by the President of the Republic. The Court decides in chambers. Each chamber is composed of 7 judges. The President of the Constitutional Court is appointed by the President of the Republic by a special decree. Candidates applying for the office of judge of the constitutional court must fulfil the conditions necessary for office within the judiciary. The minimum age is 45 years. Constitutional court judges are chosen from among members of the Supreme Court, State officers, State employees or former State employees who have carried out the function of adviser for at least five years, from among professors of law with at least eight years experience, as well as from among lawyers with at least ten years experience. The office of constitutional court judge in incompatible with other offices; the exceptions are legal activities within international organisations, foreign countries, as well as scientific activity. Constitutional court judges are irremovable.

The Constitutional Court is exclusively empowered to:

- review the constitutionality of statutes and executive regulations;
- decide on jurisdictional disputes between judicial bodies;
- decide on disputes concerning the enforcement of judgments of judicial bodies or other authorities exercising judicial power;
- interpret statutes and decrees of the President of the Republic concerning the constitution in case of a different interpretation when it is necessary to assure the unity of the constitution.

In a plenary session the Court decides by an absolute majority of members present. The Court decisions are final and indisputable, and binding for all State bodies and for every individual. They are published in the Official Gazette 15 days after promulgation. Unconstitutional statutes and other regulations may not be implemented from the day onwards when Court decisions are published. In order to petition, a fee has to be paid. The Court has its own independent budget created following the model of the general State budget.

Equatorial Guinea

The *Constitution* of 15 August 1982 established the State Council (Articles 99 to 103) as the highest State body specialized to review constitutional matters including the constitutionality of basic statutes as well as measures for their implementation. The State Council is also empowered to officially interpret such statutes, review presidential elections, as well as to determine the Presidents capacity to hold office. The Council is composed of 11 members. 8 of them are appointed by the President of the Republic, two (of three remaining) are members by means of their current office, *i.e.* the President of the Supreme Court and the Minister of National Defence (which are practically appointed by the President of the Republic). In addition, the President of the Republic also appoints the President of the State Council.

The system of Equatorial Guinea also features also *habeas corpus* proceedings.

The *Fundamental Law of Equatorial Guinea* of 16 November 1991 introduced the Constitutional Court, which is created within the Supreme Court of Justice (Article 94). The Constitutional Court is composed of the President of the Supreme Court of Justice, as president, and four members appointed by the President of the Republic, of which two are nominated by the Chamber of People's Representatives.

The Court members are elected for four years.

The Court has jurisdiction in the following matters:

- the constitutionality of laws;
- the determination of the respective limits of statutes and regulations;
- provisions and judicial acts which violate fundamental rights and liberties recognized in the Fundamental Law;
- other matters vested in it by the Organic statutes:
- the regularity of Presidential and legislative elections and referenda (Article 95).

Members of the Court may not be members of the Government, the Chamber of People's Representatives, nor hold the office of Attorney General, nor any elective office (Article 96).

Eritrea

The *Constitution* of 23 May 1997 empowered the Supreme Court as the court of last resort to exercise:

- sole jurisdiction to interpret the *Constitution* and the constitutionality of any statute enacted or any measure undertaken by the Government;
- sole jurisdiction to try and adjudicate charges against a President who has been impeached by the National Assembly pursuant to the *Constitution*.

The organization, operation and the tenure of justices of the Supreme Court are determined by statute.

Ethiopia

The *Constitution of 21 August 1995* established the Council of Constitutional Inquiry as a State body exercising constitutional review (Article 82). The Council has eleven members comprising:

- the President of the Federal Supreme Court, who serves as its President;
- the Vice-President of the Federal Supreme Court, who serves as its Vice-President;

- six legal experts, appointed by the President of the Republic on the recommendation of the Parliament, who have proven professional competence and high moral standing;
- three persons designated by the Parliament from among its members.

The Council establishes the organizational structure which ensures the expeditious execution of its responsibilities.

In principle, all constitutional disputes are decided by the Parliament (Article 83). The Parliament may, within thirty days of receipt, decide a constitutional dispute submitted to it by the Council.

The Council is empowered to investigate constitutional disputes (Article 84). Should the Council, upon consideration of the matter, find it necessary to interpret the *Constitution*, it shall submit its recommendations thereon to the parliament. Where any federal or State statute is contested as being unconstitutional and such a dispute is submitted to it by any court or interested party, the Council considers the matter and submits it to the Parliament for a final decision. When issues of constitutional interpretation arise in the courts, the Council:

- Remands the case to the concerned court if it finds there is no need for constitutional interpretation; the interested party, if dissatisfied with the decision of the Council, may appeal to the Parliament.
- Submits its recommendation to the Parliament for a final decision if it believes there is a need for constitutional interpretation.

The Council drafts its *Rules of Procedure* and submits them to the Parliament, as well as implements them upon approval (Article 84).

Gabon

At first constitutional review was exercised by the Judicial Council (Article 37 of the *Constitution* of 19 February 1959). Subsequently these functions were exercised by the Supreme Court in a plenary session (Article 66 of the *Constitution* of 14 November 1960).

The *Constitution* of 21 February 1961 (amended on 17 February 1967, on 13 December 1967 and on 29 May 1968) determined in Article 59 that the Constitutional Chamber of the Supreme Court was empowered to exercise constitutional review.

The Constitutional Chamber was empowered to perform the:

- preventive review of draft statutes;
- constitutional review of statutes;
- preventive constitutional review of international treaties entered into by the State.

On the basis of Article 36 of the *Constitution*, the organization of the Court was regulated by statute (the *Act of 20 November 1962*, amended by *Act No. 41-70 of 5 August 1970*). Subsequently such matters were similarly regulated by *Act No. 6-78 of 1 June 1978*.

The Constitutional Chamber was composed of: the President of the Supreme Court, the President of the Judicial Chamber, the President of the Administrative Chamber and by the President of the Chamber of Auditors. The above mentioned members were appointed by the Head of State by a decree. Other members were also appointed by the Head of State, but only after previous consultation with political parties.

The new *Constitution* of 26 March 1991 (*Constitutional Act No. 03/91*, amended by *Act No. 01/94* of 18 March 1994, and *Act No. 001/97* of 22 April 1997) established the Constitutional Court as a special and independent body of constitutional review (Chapter IV of the *Constitution*). It is a body exclusively empowered to exercise constitutional review (Article 83) with following powers:

- the preventive review of the constitutionality of basic (on the request of the Prime Minister) and other statutes (on the request of the President of the Republic, the Prime Minister, the President of the Parliament, a group of representatives, the President of the Supreme Court, or any citizen or person affected by such a statute or act) before their promulgation;
- the preventive review of the constitutionality of other regulations of State bodies;
- the adjudication of jurisdictional disputes between State bodies;
- the review of the constitutionality or legality of all electoral procedures (on the request of any voter, candidate, or any political party);
- the review of referendums;
- the concrete review of norms on the request of a court, concerning a particular case (Article 86);
- the preventive review of the constitutionality of international agreements before their ratification (Article 87);
- the interpretation of the Constitution, on the request of the President of the Republic, the Prime Minister, the President of the Parliament or a group of representatives (Article 88).

The Constitutional Court is composed of 9 members, with a mandate of 7 years; one re-election is possible (Article 89). Three judges are appointed by the President of the Republic, three are appointed by the President of the Parliament, and three are appointed by the Judicial Council. The conditions that need to be met to be elected constitutional court judge are as follows: one must be a professor of law; a member of a bar; have carried out of activities in the legal field at least 15 years, and one must have the personal qualities necessary for the honourable performance of this office. The President of the Court is elected from among constitutional court judges; in case of his absence, he is replaced by the oldest judge. The office of constitutional court judge is incompatible with any other public office or any other private or professional activity (Article 90).

Each year the Constitutional Court (Article 91) reports on its activities to the President of the Republic, the President of the Parliament, as well as to the President of the Supreme Court.

There is no legal remedy against Constitutional Court decisions (Article 92). The decisions bind all State bodies and individuals.

The organization and activities of the Constitutional Court are regulated by statute (Article 93).

Gambia

Under the *Constitution* of 1965 the Supreme Court was empowered to exercise constitutional review.

The regulation introduced by the *Constitution* of 24 April 1970, as well as by the *Constitution* of 7 August 1996, generally adopted the American system of a diffuse constitutional/judicial review.

Ghana

The first *Constitution* of 1957 (the *Independence Constitution* of 1957) determined under Para. 5 of Article 31 that the Supreme Court has original and explicit jurisdiction in all proceedings that concern the validity of a statute. A similar regulation was adopted by the next *Constitution* of 1960 (the *Republican Constitution* of 1960) in Para. 2 of Article 42.

The *Constitution* of 1969 (the *1969 Second Republican Constitution of Ghana*) determined in Para. 1 of Article 106 that the Supreme Court has original jurisdiction concerning:

- all cases which concern the validity or interpretation of the *Constitution*;
- the constitutional review of any regulations (issued by the Parliament or other State bodies);
- the concrete review of norms on the request of an ordinary court.

By Article 2 of the *Constitution* of 1969 Ghana introduced the popular complaint before the Supreme Court, including the request for a constitutional review.

The new Constitution of Ghana of 28 April 1992 adopted the American system of judicial review, including human rights protection proceedings *i.e.: habeas corpus, certiorari, mandamus, prohibition* and *quo warranto*.

Guinea

The *Fundamental Law of the Second Republic of Guinea* of 23 December 1990 empowered the Supreme Court to exercise constitutional review. The Supreme Court has the authority to determine the constitutionality of laws and international agreements (Articles 64, 67, 78 and 83). It also has the authority to determine in first and last resort any recourse against the acts of the President of the Republic (Articles 38, 60, 74 and 83), as well as recourse against ordinances, before their ratification (Articles 66 and 83).

The Supreme Court also has the authority to determine in first and last resort any recourse against the elections to the National Assembly and to local assemblies.

The Ivory Coast

The *Constitution* of 3 November 1960 and *Constitutional Act No. 60-356* (amended on 11 January 1963, 22 October 1975, 1 September 1980, 26 November 1980, 12 October 1985, 31 January 1986 and 6 November 1990, 2 July 1998) introduced by Article 57 the Constitutional Chamber of the Supreme Court as the empowered constitutional review body. The activities of the Constitutional Chamber are regulated in detail by *Act No. 61-201* of 2 June 1961 (later amended by *Act No. 78-663* of 5 August 1978).

The Constitutional Chamber is presided over by the President of the Supreme Court. In addition, it s also composed of the Vice-President of the Supreme Court and four members appointed for five years. Two members are appointed by the President of the Republic, two by the President of the National Assembly. Candidates for the Constitutional Chamber must be persons with high reputation and experience in the field of constitutional matters.

Generally speaking, the system was established following the French system and/or the model of the French Constitutional Council. The Council has the following powers:

- the preventive constitutional review of international agreements (Article 55);
- the preventive constitutional review of statutes (Article 23). A preventive review may be requested by the President of the Republic or by the President of the Parliament. The possibility of *ex officio* proceedings is excluded;
- the review of presidential elections (Article 10);
- the review of parliamentary elections (Article 29);
- the review of referendums (Article 4);
- impeachment against the President of the Republic (Article 11).

The Constitutional Chamber also has a consultative function, i.e. facultative (concerning draft statutes, ordinances and decrees) or obligatory (when a statute has to be amended by decree).

The decisions of the Constitutional Chamber are final.

Madagascar

Madagascar is one of the African countries with the oldest and relatively continuously developed system of constitutional review.

Under the *Constitution* of 29 April 1959 (amended on 1 July 1969), the Supreme Council *(conseil superieur (supreme) des institutions)* was empowered to exercise constitutional review (Article 45) with the following powers:

- the preventive and repressive review of statutes (Article 47);
- the preventive and repressive constitutional review of ordinances (Article 45);
- the preventive and repressive constitutional review of decrees (Article 33);
- the preventive constitutional review of international agreements (Sub-para. 4 of Article 14 as well as Sub-para 1 and 3 of Article 48).

Under *Ordinance No. 73-041* of 7 August 1973 adopted by the constitutional referendum of 7 November 1972, this body was remodelled into the Supreme Constitutional Court.

The next *Constitution of Madagascar* of 31 December 1975 reintroduced the Supreme Constitutional Court *(Haut Cour Constitutionnelle)* composed of seven members. Two among them were appointed by the President of the Republic, two by the Supreme Revolutionary Council, two by the National Assembly and one by the Government. As a body with some political characteristics (Article 88 of the *Constitution*), it was empowered to exercise: the repressive constitutional review of statutes, ordinances and autonomous charters, to adjudicate jurisdictional disputes between State bodies and decentralized institutions (Article 88), to review presidential elections, to appoint members of the Supreme Revolutionary Council, as well as to review representatives' elections (Article 91). In addition, the Court was empowered to exercise some kind of preventive constitutional review: the President of the Republic could consult the Constitutional Court concerning all draft statutes (bills) or draft decrees. The organization and work of the Constitutional Court were regulated by executive statute.

Under the new *Constitution* of 18 September 1992 (amended on 16 August 1995), the Constitutional Court decides on the constitutionality of international agreements, statutes, ordinances and autonomous regulations, adjudicates jurisdictional disputes between State bodies as well as between central and decentralised collective bodies (Article 106). The Court reviews presidential and representatives' elections as well as the results of referendums (Article 109). It is empowered to exercise the preventive constitutional review of statutes at the request of the President of the Republic (Articles 110, 111 and 112). The Constitutional Court also decides on impeachment motions against the President of the Republic resulting from alleged violations of the *Constitution* (Article 50). It is empowered to exercise the concrete review of norms at the request of an ordinary court concerning concrete proceedings (Article 113).

The Court is composed of nine members (Article 107) appointed for six years. Re-election is not allowed. Three members of the Court are appointed by the President of the Republic following the proposal of the Council of Ministries, two are appointed by the Parliament, one by the Senate, three by the Supreme Council of the Magistracy. The President of the Court is elected by the members of the Court from among themselves; the election is confirmed by presidential decree. The office of constitutional court judge is incompatible with the office of a member of the Government, the Parliament, with elected public office, with paid professional activity, as well as with membership in a political party or in trade union (Article 108).

MALI

In the former Federal Republic of Mali, the Constitutional Chamber of the Federal Court was empowered to carry out constitutional review (Article 48 of the *Constitution* of 17 January 1959).

By the Constitution of 22 September 1960, the Constitutional Chamber of the State Court became empowered to review the constitutionality of statutes (Article 42).

Instead of the Constitutional Chamber of the State Court, constitutional review was later carried out by the Constitutional Chamber of the Supreme Court (*Act No. 65-1 and No. 65-2/A.N.R.M.* of 13 March 1965). It is characteristic of the regulation of this period that the Constitutional Chamber of the Supreme court was empowered to act *ex officio*. The institution of the Constitutional Chamber as a specialized chamber of the Supreme Court empowered to exercise constitutional review was also adopted by the subsequent *Ordinance No. 1/CM L.N.* of 28 November 1968 as well as by the later *Constitution* of 2 June 1974 (Article 66). The members of the Constitutional Chamber were appointed by the President of the Republic following the proposal of the Minister of Justice.

By the new *Constitution* of 25 February 1992, the Constitutional Court was established as a completely independent body concerning its relationship to the legislative branch (Article 85). It has the following powers (Article 86):

- the preventive constitutional review of statutes (following the proposal of the President of the Republic, the Prime Minister, the President of the Parliament, 1/10 of the representatives, or some other of the highest State bodies);
- the preventive constitutional review of international agreements following the proposal of the above legitimate petitioners;
- the constitutional review of administrative acts which concern constitutional rights and freedoms;
- the preventive constitutional review of the internal rules (*i.e.* rules of procedure) of the Parliament and other highest State bodies;
- the adjudication of jurisdictional disputes between State bodies;
- the review of elections;
- the review of the legality of referendums.

The Constitutional Court is composed of nine members elected for seven years (Article 91). Three members are appointed by the President of the Republic (among them, at least two candidates must be lawyers), three are appointed by the President of the Parliament (among them, at least two candidates must be lawyers), three are appointed by the Judicial Council. The candidates are recruited from among professors of law, barristers or lawyers with at least 15 years experience, as well as also from among qualified persons from State posts. The president is elected from among the members of the Constitutional Court (Article 92). The office of constitutional court judge is incompatible with any public, political or administrative office, or with any private or professional activity (Article 93).

The decisions of the Constitutional Court are indisputable and binding on all State bodies and individuals. The organization, work and proceedings of the Constitutional Court are regulated by statute (Article 94).

Morocco

The *Constitution* of 1962 followed by the *Constitution* of 31 July 1970 (amended in 1972) introduced the Constitutional Chamber of the Supreme Court as a constitutional review body (*Chambre Constitutionnelle de la Cour Supreme du Maroc,* Articles 93 and/or 96).

On the basis of Article 95 of the *Constitution,* the organization and work of the Constitutional Chamber was regulated by the *Act* of 9 May 1977. The Chamber was composed of six members empowered first of all to exercise the preventive constitutional review of statutes. Three members were appointed by the King, including the President), and three members were appointed by the President of the Chamber following consultation with political parties.

By the *Constitution* of 7 October 1996, the Constitutional Council was established. The Council comprises six members appointed by the King for a period of nine years and six members appointed for the same period, one-half by the President of the Chamber of Representatives, one-half by the President of the Chamber of Counsellors, after consultation with political parties. Each category of membership is renewable by thirds every three years (Article 79). The President of the Council is chosen by the King from among the members he appoints. The term of the President and of the members of the Council is not renewable.

The Council has the following powers (Article 81):

- to review the legality of parliamentary elections;
- to review the legality of referendums;
- to exercise the preventive review of statutes and the rules of each parliamentary chamber.

Council decisions are not susceptible to any appeal. They are binding on public powers, and all administrative and jurisdictional authorities.

Mauritania

The *Constitution* of 22 March 1959 (amended on 20 May 1961, 24 April 1964, 12 February 1965, 12 July 1966 and 4 March 1968) introduced the Supreme court as a constitutional review body (Article 41).

The Supreme Court was empowered to exercise:

- the preventive constitutional review of statutes (Article 45);
- the preventive constitutional review of international agreements (Article 45).

Such regulations were adopted also by the later *Constitutional Charter* of 1978.

The new *Constitution* of 12 July 1991 introduced the Constitutional Council as the constitutional review body. The Council is composed of six members, whose mandate is nine years and is not renewable (Article 81). One third of the Council is chosen every three years. Three of the members are appointed by the President of the Republic, two by the President of the National Assembly and one by the President of the Senate. The members of the Council must be at least 35 years old. They may not belong to the leadership of any political party. The enjoy parliamentary immunity. The President of the Council is appointed by the President of the Republic from among the members whom he names. The office of a member of the Council is incompatible with that of a member of the Government or of Parliament (Article 82).

The Council has the following powers (Articles 83 to 86):

- to evaluate the legality of presidential and parliamentary elections;
- to evaluate the legality of referendums;
- to exercise the preventive review of statutes and regulations.

Council decisions are not subject to appeal. They must be complied with by public authorities and by all administrative and jurisdictional authorities (Article 87).

Mauritius

The *Constitution* of 12 March 1968 (amended in 1982, 1983, 1986, 1990, 1991, 1992, 1994, 1995, 1996, 1997) determines that the Supreme Court is empowered to decide on the complaints of individuals concerning violations of their constitutional rights (Article 17). The current constitutional review model, similar to the Indian system, is called the New (British) Commonwealth Model. It cannot be classified either under the American or the European model. It is characterized by a concentrated constitutional review under the jurisdiction of the Supreme Court consisting of ordinary judges without political nomination; it focuses on preventive (*a priori*) review and the consultative function of the Supreme Court, although repressive (*a posteriori*) review is also possible; decisions take an *erga omnes* effect (Articles 83 and 84).

Mozambique

Under the *Constitution* of 2 November 1990 the Constitutional Council as a constitutional review body is empowered to exercise the following powers (Articles 180 through 184):

- the constitutional review of statutes and executive regulations of State bodies;
- the adjudication of jurisdictional disputes between State bodies;
- the review of the legality of referendums;
- the review of electoral procedures;
- the verification of statutorial conditions applying to candidates for the office of the President of the Republic.

The circle of legitimate petitioners is relatively limited: the President of the Republic, the President of the Parliament, the Prime Minister and the Public Prosecutor of the Republic.

The decisions of the Constitutional Council are indisputable and are published in the Official Gazette of the Republic.

The composition, organization and work of the Constitutional Council and its proceedings are regulated by statute.

Namibia

The *Constitution* of 9 February 1990 introduced the American system of a diffuse constitutional review. Such review is exercised by all courts. Furthermore, the Constitution determines the principle of the independence of courts.

The Supreme Court is the highest constitutional review body (Article 79). It is composed of the President of the Court and by such number of judges as appointed by the President of the Republic following the recommendation of the Judicial Commission.

The Court is empowered to interpret the *Constitution*, to review the implementation of the *Constitution* and to protect basic rights and freedoms.

The decisions of the Supreme Court have an *erga omnes* effect (Article 81).

Niger

The *Constitution* of 29 July and 3 November 1991 adopted the elements of the former *Constitutions* of 18 December 1958, 12 March 1959 (*i.e.* the Constitutional Department of the State Court under Article 48 of the Constitution) and of 3 August 1968.

Constitutional review is exercise by the Constitutional Chamber of the Supreme Court, which is composed of the Judicial Chamber, the Administrative Chamber, the Chamber of Auditors and the Budgetary Chamber (Para. 1 and 2 of Article 104).

The composition, organization, proceedings and work of the Supreme Court are regulated by statute (Para. 3 of Article 104 of the *Constitution*). The Budget of the Supreme Court is a part of the State budget (Para. 2 of Article 97).

The powers of the Constitutional Chamber are as follows (Article 98):

- the preventive constitutional review of statutes, on the request of the President of the Republic, the President of the Parliament, the Prime Minister or one tenth of the representatives (Para. 1 through 4 of Article 98, Para. 2 of Article 84, Para. 3 of Article 87, Article 92);
- the popular complaint concerning the constitutional review of statutes (Para. 5 of Article 98);
- the review of presidential elections (Para. 3 of Article 40);
- impeachment (Article 44):
- the review of representatives' elections (Article 64).

Decisions have an *erga omnes* effect. Decisions on the determination of the unconstitutionality of a statute are published in the Official Gazette as soon as possible.

The new *Constitution* of 26 December 1992, extensively amended on 22 May 1996, adopted the former regulation and also introduced a special chamber of the Supreme Court empowered to exercise constitutional review. The Supreme Court has the following powers (Articles 94, 95, 102, 103):

- the preventive constitutional review of organic statutes and internal regulations of the highest State bodies;
- the concrete constitutional review of statutes;
- the adjudication of jurisdictional disputes between State institutions;
- the review of the legality of presidential, legislative and local elections;
- the review of the legality of referendums;
- the interpretation of the *Constitution*.

The decisions of the Supreme Court are not susceptible to any recourse. They bind all public powers and all administrative, civil, military and judicial authorities (Article 104).

Nigeria

The *Constitution* (Decree of 3 May 1989, enforced on 1 October 1992) empowers the Supreme Court as a constitutional review body (Article 228). It is composed of its President and by such number of judges as determined by statute, but the number may not exceed 15 judges. The members of the Supreme Court are appointed by the Head of State (Article 229). The candidates should have at least 15 years of experience in the country.

The Supreme Court is empowered:

- to adjudicate jurisdictional disputes between the Federation and member states or between member states themselves (Article 230). In such proceedings the decision making process of the Court is exercised in a plenary session (Article 233);
- to review presidential and vice-presidential elections (Article 232).

The decisions of the Supreme Court are final. Otherwise, the Nigerian system of constitutional review has all the characteristics of the American diffuse system of judicial review (Article 6 of the *Constitution*), in which this function is exercised by all courts.

Rwanda

Initially, Rwanda introduced a constitutional review exercised by the Constitutional Chamber of the Supreme Court (Article 102 of the *Constitution* of 24 November 1962).

By the *Constitution* of 20 November 1978, the Constitutional Court was established as an independent body with special jurisdiction. The Supreme Cassation Court and the State (National) Council together form the Constitutional Court. By introducing such a system, Rwanda placed itself among the countries which separate constitutional review from the ordinary judiciary.

The *Constitution* of 10 June 1991 re-established the Constitutional Court, composed of the Court of Cassation and the Council of State assembled, which is in charge of reviewing the constitutionality of statutes and statutory orders. It alone is competent to order the forced resignation of the President of the Republic (Article 90).

Senegal

Under the *Constitution* of 1960, the Supreme Court was not empowered to carry out constitutional review.

However, the *Constitution* of 7 March 1963 (amended on 20 June 1967, 14 March 1968 and 26 February 1970) introduced the Supreme Court as a constitutional review body (the last Subparagraph of Article 47). The powers of the then Supreme Court were as follows:

- the preventive constitutional review of statutes (Article 63);
- the preventive constitutional review of international agreements (Article 78).

Subsequently the organization and work of the Supreme Court of Senegal was regulated by *Ordinance No. 60.17* of 3 September 1960. Further amendments which generally adopted the previous regulation were included in *Act No. L.O. 43/86* of 29 December 1986, primarily concerning the composition of the Supreme Court. The essential amendments were adopted by *Act No. 87-09* of 2 February 1987.

The constitutional basis for the system of constitutional review can be found in the Constitution of 7 March 1963, amended on 20 June 1967, 14 March 1968, 26 February 1970, 19 March 1976, 6 April 1976, 28 December 1978, 6 May 1981, 1 May 1983 and 24 March 1984, as well as on 3 September 1992 and on 13 June 1994. Under the regulation in force, the Court is composed of: its President, three presidents of chambers, the public prosecutor, the State legal officer, 14 judges and 15 advisers. The members of the Supreme Court are appointed by decree, and their office is for life. The Court has the following powers: the review of presidential elections, the review of the organization of referendums, the preventive constitutional review of basic and other statutes, the preventive constitutional review of international agreements (generally, on the request of the President of the Republic), impeachment against the President of the Republic, the protection of the constitutional rights of individuals, the review of the implementation of the budget, and a cassatory power above the ordinary courts.

Under the regulation in force, the Constitutional Council was introduced (Article 80). The Council is comprised of five members: a President, a Vice-President and three judges. The duration of their mandates is six years. The Court is partially renewable every two years starting with the President or two members other than the President, in an order based on the date of the end of their mandates (Article 80 bis). The members of the Council are appointed by the Head of State. The mandate of Council members cannot be renewable. It is only possible to terminate the office of Council members before the expiration of their mandate due to their physical incapacity, and under conditions specified by organic statute.

The Council is the guardian of the rights and freedoms defined by the *Constitution* and statute (Article 82).

The Council reviews the constitutionality of statutes and international obligations, and jurisdictional disputes between the executive and the legislative branches, conflicts of competence between the Council of State and the Court of Cassation, as well as of claims of unconstitutionality raised before the Council of State or the Court of Cassation (Article 82).

Except in cases of flagrant offence, Council members can only be prosecuted, arrested, detained or judged in a criminal matter with the authorisation of the Council and under the same conditions as the magistrates of the Council of State and the Court of Cassation (Article 83).

Organic statute determines the other powers of the Constitutional Council, as well as its organization, the regulations for appointing its members and the proceedings to be followed before it (Article 84).

The Seychelles

The *Constitution (Third Republic)* of 21 June 1993 introduced the function of the Supreme Court as Constitutional Court (Article 129). Such jurisdiction and powers are exercised by not less than two judges sitting together.

Constitutional questions before the Constitutional Court may be initiated by any affected individual (Article 130). Upon hearing an application, the Constitutional Court may:

- declare any act or omission which is the subject of the application to be a contravention of the *Constitution*;
- declare any statute or the provision of any statute which contravenes the *Constitution* to be void;
- grant any remedy available to the Supreme Court against any person or authority which is the subject of the application or which is a party to any proceedings before the Constitutional Court, as the Court considers appropriate.

When in the course of any proceedings in any court, other than the Court of Appeal of the Supreme Court sitting as the Constitutional Court, or tribunal, a question arises with regard to whether there has been or is likely to be a contravention of the *Constitution*, the court or tribunal shall, if it is satisfied that the question is not frivolous or vexatious or has not already been the subject of a decision of the Constitutional Court, immediately adjourn the proceedings and refer the determination of the question to the Constitutional Court.

Sierra Leone

Under the *Constitution* of 1 October 1991, the Supreme Court is empowered to perform constitutional review. It is composed of its president, at least four permanent judges and an appropriate number of other judges (Article 121 of the *Constitution*).

The Supreme Court has original and exclusive jurisdiction in all matters concerning the implementation of the *Constitution* as well as the power of constitutional review following the model of the American system of diffuse review (Article 124 of the *Constitution*). The following proceedings may be initiated before the Supreme court: *habeas corpus*, *certiorari*, *mandamus* and *prohibition* (Article 125 of the *Constitution*). The Constitution also allows the popular complaint (Para. 1 of Article 127 of the *Constitution*).

The Court decisions are final and indisputable (Article 122 of the *Constitution*).

South Africa

The country was established in 1910 by the unification of former British colonies under the *South Africa Act 1909,9 Edward VII, Ch.9*. The further constitutional documents are the *British Statute of Westminster 1931 (22 Geo. V, Ch.4)* as well as the *South African Status of the Union Act 1934 (the Act No. 69, 1934)* and the *Republic of South Africa Constitution Act 1961 (the Act No. 32, 1961)*. From the beginning, the country adopted the British legal system with all its elements, which meant that the constitutional review was not included. Following such regulation, the Supreme Court functioning under the *Constitution of 1961* and the Supreme Court of 1969 were not empowered to exercise constitutional review.

The Court was established in 1994 by South Africa's first democratic constitution - the *interim Constitution of 1993*. By the *1996 Constitution*, the Court established in 1994 continues to hold office. The eleven member Court held its first session in February 1995. The Court members may serve for a non-re-appointable term of 12 years, and must retire at the age of 70. They are all independent. Their duty is to uphold the law and the *Constitution*, which they must apply impartially and without fear, favour or prejudice.

The Constitutional Court consists of a President, a Deputy President and nine other judges. A matter before the Constitutional Court must be heard by at least eight judges. The Constitutional Court (Article 167 of the *Constitution*) is the highest court in all constitutional matters. The Court:

- may only decide constitutional matters and issues connected with decisions on constitutional matters;
- issues the final decision on whether a matter is a constitutional matter or whether an issue is connected with a decision on a constitutional matter.

Only the Constitutional Court may:

- decide disputes between State bodies in the national or provincial sphere concerning the constitutional status, powers or functions of any of those State bodies;
- decide on the constitutionality of any parliamentary or provincial Bill;
- decide on applications by members of National Assembly or members of a provincial legislature to the Constitutional Court for an order declaring that all or part of an Act of Parliament or an Act of a provincial legislature is unconstitutional;
- decide on the constitutionality of any amendment to the *Constitution*;
- decide that the Parliament or the President has failed to fulfil a constitutional obligation; or
- certify a provincial constitution.

The Constitutional Court makes the final decision on whether an Act of Parliament, a provincial Act or the conduct of the President is constitutional, and must confirm any order of invalidity made by the Supreme Court of Appeal, a High Court, or a court of similar status, before that order has any force.

The national legislation and the *Rules of the Constitutional Court* allow a person, when it is in the interest of justice and with leave of the Constitutional Court:

- to bring a matter directly to the Constitutional Court; or
- to appeal directly to the Constitutional Court from any other court.

A constitutional matter includes any issue involving the interpretation, protection or enforcement of the *Constitution*.

The Constitution requires that a matter before the Court is heard by at least eight judges. In practice, all eleven judges hear every case. If any judge is absent for a long period or a vacancy arises, an acting judge may be appointed by the President of the Republic on a temporary basis. Decisions of the Court are reached by a majority vote of the judges sitting in that case. Each judge must indicate his or her decision. The reasons for the decision are published in a written judgment.

The Court played an important role in the adoption of the *1996 Constitution*. Concerning the *Interim Constitution*, the Parliament sitting as the Constitutional Assembly was required to produce a new constitutional text. In turn, the Court was required to certify that the new text complied with the 34 Constitutional Principles agreed upon in advance by the negotiators of the *Interim Constitution*. In its decision on the *Certification of the Constitution of the Republic of South Africa 1996 (4) SA 744 (CC) (6 September 1996)* the Court ruled that the constitutional text adopted by the Constitutional Assembly in May 1996 could not be certified. The Court identified the features of the new text that did not in its view comply with the Constitutional Principles and gave its reasons for that view. The Constitutional Assembly then had to reconsider the text, taking the Court's reasons for non-certification into account. The Constitutional Assembly reconvened and on 11 October 1996 adopted an amended constitutional text containing many changes from the previous text, some dealing with the Court's reasons for non-certification and others tightening up the text. The amended text was then sent to the Constitutional Court for certification. In its judgment in its *Certification of the Amended Text of the Constitution of the Republic of South Africa, 1996 (4 December 1996)* the Court held that all of the grounds for the non-certification of the earlier text had been eliminated in the new draft, and accordingly certified that the text complied with the requirements of the Constitutional Principles. The text duly became the *Constitution of the Republic of South Africa, 1996* and came into effect in February 1997.

The judgments of the Court are based on the *Constitution*, which is the supreme law of the land. They guarantee the basic rights and freedoms of all persons. They are binding on all organs of government, including Parliament, the Presidency, the police force, the army, the public service and all courts. This means that the Court has the power to declare an Act of Parliament null and void if it conflicts with the *Constitution* and to review executive actions in the same way.

When interpreting the *Constitution*, the Court is required to consider international human rights laws and may consider the law of other democratic countries. The Constitutional Court is the highest court in the land for all constitutional matters.

KwaZulu-Natal/The Federal Republic of South Africa

The position of the Constitutional Court was regulated by the *Resolution of the Legislative Assembly* of 1 December 1992. The Constitutional Court had original and exclusive powers concerning the following matters:

- the constitutional review of State legislation;
- the constitutional review of regional legislation;
- deciding on non-conformity between State and regional legislation;
- deciding on jurisdictional disputes between regions within the State;
- the constitutional review of federal legislation;
- deciding on jurisdictional disputes between federal and State bodies;
- impeachment against the governor and ministers;
- the validity and legality of collective agreements;
- the constitutional review of the statutes of political parties;
- other matters as determined by the *Constitution* or the *Constitutional Act*.

The circle of petitioners before the Constitutional Court was limited to State bodies, and under certain conditions, also political parties. The decisions of the Constitutional Court had *erga omnes* effect.

The Constitutional Court was composed of 15 members. Three were appointed by the governor, six by the Parliament, three by the Judicial Council and three by the Bar Chamber. When deciding on impeachment, the Constitutional Court was able to extend its composition with additional members. Their qualifications and powers were determined by the Constitutional Court. Constitutional Court Judges were appointed from among lawyers and attorneys at law with more than 20 years of professional practice, professors of law and from among judges of the highest courts. Even foreign citizens were entitled to apply for the position of Constitutional Court Judge. They were appointed for 10 years; re-election was not possible. The office of constitutional court judge was incompatible with any other public office or with any professional activity on the territory of South Africa. After retirement, Constitutional Court Judges were not allowed to hold any public office. The Constitutional Court worked also in chambers composed of four or more judges. The members of the Constitutional Court appointed their president from among themselves for three years. The Constitutional Court was empowered to regulate its own organization and work by its own internal regulation. Members of the Constitutional Court enjoyed immunity; however, they could be charged with a crime by 3/4 of the representatives of both parliamentary chambers. The salaries of Constitutional Court Judges were determined by statute, and they could not be lower than the salaries of ministers. The Constitutional Court created and proposed its own budget to the Parliament directly.

SUDAN

Originally constitutional review was exercised by the Constitutional Chamber of the State Court (Article 44 of the *Constitution* of 23 January 1959).

Under the *Constitution* of 10 October 1985, the protector of the *Constitution* and statutes is the Supreme Court (Articles 125 through 128), with the following powers:

- the interpretation of the *Constitution* and statutes;
- the constitutional review of statutes;
- the protection of basic rights and freedoms.

Concerning constitutional matters, the Supreme Court and Court of Appeals act together provided that the composition of this body is not less than three judges. They are appointed by the Head of State.

Under the (Federal) *Constitution* of 24 December 1995, the constitutionality of any statute passed by the (Federal) National Assembly or a provisional decree issued by the President of the Republic, or a member state law passed by the member state Assembly, or a provisional decree issued by the member state Government, may be challenged before the Supreme Court, on the basis that such a statute or decree is in conflict with the federal constitutional system or contravenes any of the human rights enshrined in the *Constitution* (Article 68).

TOGO

Constitutional review was introduced by the establishment of the Constitutional Chamber of the Supreme Court (Article 70 of the *Constitution* of 11 May 1963). The same institution was reintroduced by the *Constitution* of 30 December 1979 (Article 44). The Constitutional Chamber of the Supreme Court was composed of: the President of the Supreme Court and five members, who were appointed by the Council of Ministers following the proposals of political parties.

Under the new *Constitution* of 14 October 1992, constitutional review is exercised by the Constitutional Court as the highest jurisdiction of the State regarding constitutional matters (Article 99). The Court is composed of seven members, of which two are elected by the National Assembly upon the proposal of the President of the Assembly, one member appointed by the president of the Republic, one member appointed by the Prime Minister, one magistrate elected by his peers, one lawyer elected by his peers, and one professor of law elected by his peers, for a non-renewable term of seven years (Article 100). During the first term, two members of the Court are elected by the Parliament for three years and one member is appointed by the President of the Republic for three years. The Court President is elected by his peers for a renewable term of three years (Article 101). Court members enjoy immunities (Article

102); their office is incompatible with other government office, any elected office, public employment or with any professional activity (Article 103). The organization and functioning of the Court, the proceedings, and the disciplinary codes relating to Court members, are established by an organic statute (Article 103). The Court has the following powers:

- to exercise the preventive constitutional review of statutes and the rules of procedure of the highest State bodies;
- to exercise the concrete (repressive) constitutional review of statutes requested by an ordinary court;
- to exercise a consultative function.

Court decisions are not be susceptible to any other authority. These decisions apply to all public bodies and to all civil, military and judicial authorities (Article 106).

Tunisia

Constitutional review is exercised by the State Council (Article 69 of the *Constitution* of 1 June 1959, amended in 1965, 1967, 1969, 1975, 1976, 1981, 1988 1993), which was established in 1987. It is composed of professors of law and judges. Its powers are very limited; generally, it has only a consultative power.

Uganda

Under the *Constitution* of 27 September 1995, any question as to the interpretation of the *Constitution* is determined by the Court of Appeals sitting as the Constitutional Court (Article 137). When sitting as a Constitutional Court, the Court of Appeals consists of a bench of five members of that Court. A person who alleges that an act of Parliament or any other law or anything in or done under the authority of any law, or an act or omission by any person or authority, is inconsistent with or in contravention of a provision of the *Constitution*, may petition the Constitutional Court for a declaration to that effect, and for redress where appropriate.

Where any question as to the interpretation of the *Constitution* arises in any proceedings in a court of law other than a Field Court Martial, the court may, if it is of opinion that the question involves a substantial question of law, and, if any party to the proceedings requests it to do so, refer the question to the Constitutional Court for a decision.

Zaire

The Constitutional Court of Zaire (the Belgian Congo, the Democratic Republic of Congo) was established as an independent constitutional review body by the *Basic Act* of 19 May 1960 as well by the *Constitution* of 1 August 1964. By the *Constitution* of 24 June 1967, the same constitutional review system was adopted (Para. 4. of Article 19). The Constitutional Court had the following powers (Article 71 of the *Constitution*):

- the constitutional review of statutes and other acts having the force of statute;
- the adjudication of jurisdictional disputes between the highest State bodies;
- the interpretation of the *Constitution*;
- the preventive constitutional review of international agreements (Sub-para. 4 of Article 68 of the Constitution).

The organization and work of the Constitutional Court was regulated by its *Rules of Procedure* (Article 45). Constitutional Court judges were appointed by the President of the Republic, one third of them on his own proposal, one third of them on the proposal of the National Assembly, and one third of them on the proposal of the Judicial Council (*conseil de la magistrature*).

The mentioned system was amended by *Act No.* 74-020 of 15 August 1974, which gave constitutional review power to the Supreme Court. This new power of the Supreme Court was adopted by the subsequent *Act* of 15 February 1978, as well as by the *Constitutional Act* of 19 February 1980.

The further *Constitution* of 27 June 1988 established in Article 103 the following powers of the Supreme Court (*Cour Supreme de Justice*): determining the constitutionality of statutes and other acts having the force of statute, the interpretation of the *Constitution* as well as the constitutional review of other acts issued by other State bodies.

The new *Constitution* of 5 July 1990 again vested in the Supreme Court the constitutional review function with the following powers: the constitutional review of statutes and other acts having the force of statute, the interpretation of the *Constitution*, the review of presidential and parliamentary elections, as well as the review of the legality of referendums (Article 103 of the *Constitution*).

ZAMBIA

The *Constitution* of 1991 (amended in 1996) introduced a special Tribunal, which may be appointed by the Chief Justice (Article 27). The Tribunal consists of two persons selected by the Chief Justice from among persons who hold or have held the office of a judge of the Supreme Court or the High Court. The Tribunal is empowered to exercise:

- the preventive review of the constitutionality of bills (within three days after the final reading of the bill in the Assembly);
- the repressive review of the constitutionality of statutory instruments (within fourteen days of the publication of the instrument in the official gazette);
- the concrete review of constitutionality when requested by an ordinary court .

ZIMBABWE

The *Constitution of Zimbabwe Amendment (No. 9) Act*, 1989, introduced the parliamentary review of constitutionality. For this purpose the Parliamentary Legal Committee was established (Article 40A). The Parliamentary Legal Committee consists of such number of members of Parliament, other than Ministers, being not less than three, as the Committee on Standing Rules and Orders may from time to time determine, the majority of whom must be legally qualified as follows: they must have been a judge of the Supreme Court or the High Court; or qualified to practice law in Zimbabwe for not less than five years, whether continuously or not; or have been a magistrate in Zimbabwe for not less than five years; or possess such legal qualifications and such legal experience as the Committee on Standing Rules and Orders considers suitable and adequate for their appointment to the Parliamentary Legal Committee.

The Parliamentary Legal Committee examines (Article 40B):

- every bill, other than a constitutional bill, which has been introduced in Parliament;
- every bill, other than a Constitutional bill, which is amended after its examination by the Committee, before the bill is given its final reading in Parliament;
- every draft bill transmitted by a Minister to the Secretary to Parliament for reference to the Committee;
- every statutory instrument published in the official gazette;
- every draft statutory instrument transmitted by the authority empowered to do so to the Secretary of the Parliament for reference to the Committee.

In addition, the Committee reports to Parliament or the Minister or authority, as the case may be, whether in its opinion any provision of a bill, draft bill, statutory instrument or draft statutory instrument would, if enacted, be, as the case may be, in conflict with the *Declaration of Rights* or any other provision of the *Constitution*.

It is the duty of the Parliament to consider any report presented to it which states that, in the opinion of the Parliamentary Legal Committee, a provision of a bill would, if enacted, be in conflict with the *Declaration of Rights* or any other provision of the *Constitution*.

F. Asia

1. General

Despite politically unstable constitutional systems in Asian countries, the institution of constitutional/judicial review has been or is a feature of the systems of the following countries: Bangladesh, Brunei, China, Hong Kong, India, Indonesia, Japan, Laos, Malaysia, Mongolia, Nepal, North Korea, Pakistan, Papua New Guinea, the Philippines, Singapore, South Korea, Sri Lanka, Taiwan, Thailand and Vietnam.

The constitutional systems of the above countries were influenced by various foreign legal systems. The Soviet model influenced China, Laos, North Korea and Vietnam. Certain countries reflect the influence of the American system (*e.g.* India, Japan, Papua New Guinea). Individual legal systems contain elements of the German, Swiss and French systems (*e.g.* Japan, South Korea, Taiwan, Thailand), and in some systems, the elements of the Dutch system (Indonesia, Sri Lanka). The greatest contribution of the American system to the development of legal systems in Asian countries is, however, evident in the adoption of the principle of the independence of the judiciary in many of these systems, as relating to the constitutional review of statutes and other legal measures. The constitutional review function is most developed in India, Japan, the Philippines and in South Korea. The development of individual systems was also influenced by the Indian system; under its effect constitutional review developed in Malaysia, Singapore and in Sri Lanka.

Asian countries include the following main models of constitutional review:

- THE AMERICAN MODEL has been adopted for appellate reviews in specific proceedings relating to the constitutionality of statutes and administrative measures within the scope of the general rules of proceedings; such a model of a diffuse judicial review was above all adopted by the former and by the existing British Commonwealth countries (Bangladesh, Hong Kong (until 1 July 1997), India, the Philippines), Malaysia, Nepal, Pakistan, and Singapore). This system has also been adopted by Japan;
- the so-called EUROPEAN OR AUSTRIAN MODEL, used for the review of the constitutionality of statutes in special proceedings of special constitutional courts is less widespread in Asia (Mongolia, South Korea, Sri Lanka, Thailand);
- the MIXED SYSTEMS, with elements of the Continental and Common Law systems (Indonesia, Taiwan);
- SPECIAL SYSTEMS OF CONSTITUTIONAL REVIEW (Brunei, Burma/Myanmar, China, Hong Kong as a special Administrative Territory of China (after 1 July 1997), North Korea, Laos, Vietnam), where the function of constitutional review is performed predominantly by the Parliament or certain parliamentary bodies.

2. The Particular Systems of Constitutional Review

Bangladesh

The *Constitution* of 4 January 1972 was temporarily suspended in 1974 because a State of Emergency was declared. This *Constitution* was created following such models as the *Magna Carta* of 1215, the *Petition of Rights* of 1628 and the *Bill of Rights*, as well as the *American Constitution*, but in the form of a written *Constitution*. It established a catalogue of constitutional rights. A diffuse constitutional review was introduced following the American model. The *Constitution* was essentially amended on 15 August 1975. This constitutional amendment introduced the independence of the judiciary and two courts as the highest State courts were established: the Supreme Court and the High Court. The Supreme Court has the role of Appeal Court in relationship to the High Court. However, the High Court has original power to exercise constitutional review following the American model: *i.e. mandamus, prohibition, quo warranto, certiorari, and habeas corpus*. The same order was reintroduced by the *Constitution* of 10 October 1991.

Brunei

The *Constitution* of 1959 with its amendments (which is still in force) introduced the principle of the supremacy of the *Constitution*.

The constitutional review body is the Interpretation Tribunal, which also performs a consultative function for the Head of State (the *sultan*). Court decisions are issued in written form, are published in the Official Gazette, and are final and binding on all State bodies. The Court is composed of the president and two members appointed by the Head of State. The Court President may be a person who has held a high judicial office or who has been a judge for the last ten years in any part of the British Commonwealth (Article 86 of the *Constitution*).

Cambodia

Under the *Constitution* of 21 September 1993, the Constitutional Council has a duty to safeguard respect for the *Constitution*, to interpret the *Constitution*, and the laws passed by the Assembly (Article 117). The Constitutional Council has the right to examine and decide on contested cases involving the election of assembly members.

The Constitutional Council is composed of nine members with nine year mandates (Article 118). 1/3 of the members of the Council are replaced every three years. 3 members are appointed by the King, 3 members by the Assembly and 3 others by the Supreme Council of the Magistracy. The President is elected by the members of the Constitutional Council. He/she has a deciding vote in case of a deadlock. Council members are elected from among individuals with degrees in Law, Administration, Diplomacy or Economics and who have considerable professional experience (Article 119). The office of Council member is incompatible with that of a member of the

Government, member of the Assembly, President or Vice-President of a political party, or President or Vice-President of a trade-union or sitting judges.

The King, the Prime Minister, the President of the Assembly, or 1/10 of the Assembly members may forward draft bills to the Constitutional Council before their promulgation (Article 121). The Assembly Rules of Procedure and various organisational statutes must be forwarded to the Constitutional Council before their promulgation. The Constitutional Council decides within no more than thirty days whether the statutes and the Internal Rules of Procedure are constitutional.

After a statute is promulgated, the King, the Prime Minister, the President of the Assembly, 1/10 of the Assembly members or a court, may request that the Constitutional Council examine the Constitutionality of that statute (Article 122). Citizens have the right to appeal against the constitutionality of statutes through their representatives or the President of the Assembly.

Provisions in any article ruled by the Constitutional Council as unconstitutional may not be promulgated or implemented (Article 123). Council decisions are final.

The King consults with the Constitutional Council on all proposals to amend the Constitution (Article 124).

An organic statute specifies the organization and operation of the Constitutional Council (Article 125).

China

The Chinese legal system in force has not adopted the judicial review of constitutionality. The current body exercising constitutional review is the National People's Congress and its Standing Committee. The National People's Congress is the highest body of State authority and as such it is empowered to decide on the most important State matters. According to Chinese legal theory, the establishment of a special constitutional review body would be in conflict with the system of "democratic centralism and the integration of the decision-making process". Chinese legal theory notes many failings of the western systems of constitutional review where such review is exercised by a judicial body. They note that courts do not have review power as long as statutes and other regulations prejudice the rights of citizens and require citizens to lodge an application before a court. Another failing Chinese theorists note is the situation in those western systems in which the constitutional court can not abrogate a statute (an active role), but merely issue a decision that such a statute not be implemented (a passive role). In addition, they claim that in western systems it is difficult to find a completely independent constitutional review body.

The mentioned review of constitutionality was introduced by the Chinese Constitution of 1954 as well as by the Constitution of 1978 (but the Constitution of 1975 did not specify which State body is empowered to exercise such review). The new Chinese Constitution regulates the matter more precisely because it determines explicitly that both bodies, the National People's Congress as well as its Standing Committee are empowered to exercise the review of constitutionality. When the Congress is in session (once a year) it is not possible to also discuss constitutional matters, however such matters should be followed continuously. Such a role is performed by the Standing Committee, which is a permanent committee and meets every two months. The committee works under the supervision of the National People's Congress. The activities of the Standing Committee are supported by some special working bodies, *e.g.* the National Council, the Judicial Council, the Financial and Economic Council, *etc.* (whose responsibilities are divided concerning particular fields of activities). Their work is regulated by the National People's Congress Basic Act; they study the constitutionality and legality of statutes and other regulations of central, local and autonomous authorities. Their reports are presented before the Standing Committee. The Councils operate following the directives of the Standing Committee and/or the National People's Congress. In addition, all other State bodies, public organisations and citizens are obliged by statute to inform these Councils of eventual cases of unconstitutionality or illegality. However, these Councils are not empowered to decide a matter, but they may only submit proposals and commentaries in the form of reports to the Congress or the Standing Committee. The working committees also study draft statutes and other regulations for the Standing Committee and the Congress. In such a manner a certain form of the preventive review of constitutionality and legality has been exercised. Legal theory has stated that there certainly also exists real violations of the Constitution and statutes in the form of unconstitutional and illegal activities which are impossible to follow.

Chinese legal theory emphasizes that the western system of the review of constitutionality and legality exercised by one specialized body is not acceptable for their system of democratic centralism and for the structure of the Chinese State. Despite this official statement, there are some proposals to establish a special body under the supervision of the National People's Congress specialised only in the review of constitutionality and legality. Such a body may be called the Constitutional Council of the National People's Congress. It would be elected by the National People's Congress and composed of 50% representatives and 50% legal advisers (of the appropriate age, qualifications, and experience *etc.*). The powers of the Constitutional Council would be as follows:

- reporting on the unconstitutionality or illegality of regulations issued by the supreme legislative body (the National People's Congress and the Standing Committee);
- deciding on the unconstitutionality and illegality of other regulations issued by other State bodies;
- proposing that the National People's Congress or its Standing Committee establish an Investigation Council for discovering unconstitutionality;
- reviewing any other regulations;

- evaluating the implementation of the Constitution in the country and submitting appropriate reports to the National People's Congress and its Standing Committee;
- submitting opinions and proposals to the National People's Congress and its Standing Committee;
- deciding on jurisdictional disputes between State bodies.

Under the Constitution in force, the local People's Congresses and standing councils as local bodies of State authority for particular local administrative territories, are empowered to exercise constitutional review. The jurisdictions between both central bodies and local bodies in the respective fields are separated. The central bodies exercise the review of constitutionality and legality on the level of cases and/or regulations which are important for the whole country, while local bodies exercise such function on their appropriate local level. The central bodies are empowered to review decisions passed by local bodies exercising the review of constitutionality and legality, i.e. the central bodies may abrogate the decisions of local bodies if such decisions are issued in conflict with the spirit of the Constitution.

Hong Kong

Until 1 July 1997 the constitutional review existed in Hong Kong as an evaluation of the conformity of ordinances with local constitutional acts; in such a framework the then local Legislature was limited concerning its legislative activities.

Hong Kong had a written *Constitution* based on two acts of the British Queen:

- the *Letters Patent* of 5 April 1843;
- the *Royal Instructions* of 6 April 1843.

The texts of both documents were valid from 14 February 1917, and were amended by later amendments and changes. Since 1 July 1997 onwards the basic constitutional act of Hong Kong has been the *Basic Law of the Hong Kong Special Administrative Region of the People's Republic of China*. Following the new legal order it is expected that the institution of constitutional review will be implemented in the same form on the basis of the mentioned constitutional act, i.e. the evaluation of local ordinances with the *Basic Law*.

Generally speaking, the American diffuse system of judicial review is in force, which means that all courts may deal with such matters, with the Supreme Court providing an appropriate supervisory role. The Supreme Court of Hong Kong in current form dates from 1976. It operates in senates composed of three or five judges. The Supreme Court includes its component parts: the High Court and the Court of Appeals. Constitutional review is of great importance, primarily from the point of view of limiting of the competencies of the Legislature. Delegated legislation (local ordinances) must not be in conflict with either basic acts.

The legal protection of constitutional rights is guaranteed by the following proceedings: *habeas corpus*, *mandamus*, *prohibition* and *certiorari*.

India

In general, India adopted the American system of diffuse judicial review, which means that such review is exercised by all courts, however, the Supreme Court, as well as some other high courts, are empowered to decide in several special proceedings on human rights protection, e.g. *habeas corpus*, *mandamus* and *certioari*.

Under the first system introduced by the *Basic Constitutional Act* in 1949, the Supreme Court was exclusively empowered to carry out constitutional review. The system in force, based in particular on *Constitutional Amendment No. 42* from 1976, as well as on *Constitutional Amendments No. 43 and 44* from 1977 and 1978, empowers the Supreme Court and all the highest courts in the country to exercise judicial review in different forms of proceedings (*e.g. habeas corpus etc.*). However, in accordance with the constitutional system in force, the powers of the Indian Supreme Court are limited. It is exclusively empowered to exercise the constitutional review of central statutes. There is also a quorum required for the unconstitutionality of a statute to be declared, *i.e.* no less than 7 judges or no less than two thirds of Court members.

The forms of human rights protection proceedings in the jurisdiction of the Supreme Court are listed in Article 32 of the *Indian Constitution* (adopted following the American model): *habeas corpus, mandamus, prohibition, certiorari, quo-warranto*. As adopted from English law, in India the last remedy is a decision of the Supreme Court.

In addition, the Indian system also features the constitutional review of legislation following the American model: the courts are authorized to declare null and void acts issued by the Legislature and the Executive which are determined to be unconstitutional. However, the Indian system of constitutional review differs from the American: in India such review is not based on judicial dogma as in the USA, but constitutional review is explicitly determined by a written *Constitution* (Article 13 - basic rights protection; Articles 32, 131, 131a, 132, 132a, 133, 134, 135, 136, 137 and Article 226 of the *Constitution*). Furthermore, the system in force is described as a system containing elements of the American system of judicial supremacy as well as elements of the English system of parliamentary supremacy.

Indonesia

The first *Constitution* dated from 1945, and the second one from 1950. Subsequently a new *Constitution* was adopted in 1955, but in July 1959 the 1945 *Constitution* was adopted again.

The *Constitution* in force is based on the following principles: the recognition of constitutional rights, legality concerning all statutes in all their possible forms, the independence of the judiciary.

Concerning constitutional review, the Indonesian Supreme Court only has the power to interpret statutes, but not to review them in the sense of an American judicial review. However, the Indonesian Supreme Court is empowered to exercise a certain preventive review concerning cases relating to the organization of the Government (the review of draft statutes and other regulations). The courts are independent and free when exercising their judicial function. The Supreme Court has exclusive cassatory jurisdiction concerning all cases. Indonesia does not have any constitutional council (as in France) nor any constitutional court (of the European type). The system in force is a certain mixed European- Common Law system.

Habeas corpus proceedings were introduced in December 1981 by the new *Criminal Code*.

JAPAN

Under the *Constitution* of 1947, which was created under American influence, the Japanese system of constitutional review differs substantially from the American diffuse system. Para. 1 and 2 of Article 76 of the *Constitution* determines that constitutional review is concentrated within the Supreme Court. In addition, under Article 81 of the *Constitution*, the Supreme Court is empowered to carry out the constitutional review of any statute, order, executive regulation or administrative act. All the courts, the Supreme Court at the top, may determine the constitutionality of laws, orders, regulations or official acts only when the determination of constitutionality is required in the course of making a ruling in concrete cases. They do not have the power to determine the constitutionality of laws, orders, regulations or official acts which are not related to concrete cases. Such characteristics are similar to the European model of constitutional review. The Japanese system also has a particular form of the popular complaint, which is, however, limited to a dispute of the validity of elections (the so-called people's action-*minshu sosho* or objective action-*kyakken sosho*). However, it differs from the European system because the proceedings entail the decision-making process *in concreto* (concerning a concrete case) under Article 76 of the *Constitution*; but at the same time Article 81 of the *Constitution* grants to the Supreme Court the authority of the court of last instance. On the other hand, the Supreme Court is not empowered to exercise the abstract review of norms because it does not have an appropriate legal basis in the *Constitution*.

The determination of unconstitutionality in Japanese system (as in the American system) has the two following two forms:

- a statute itself may be declared unconstitutional. In practice, the Japanese Supreme Court had issued until 1991 4 decisions concerning such matters which have *erga omnes* effect;
- on the other hand, the Court may decide that the implementation of a statue is unconstitutional in a concrete case. Such cases are most frequent in Japanese constitutional case-law. Therefore court decisions in principle have an *inter partes* effect.

The Japanese system also allows the dissenting or concurring opinion of judges. Subsequent discussion concerning the suitability of the dissenting opinions of supreme court judges resulted in the expansion of such dissenting opinions.

Japanese Supreme Court judges are appointed by the Government. In addition, there is a particularity that Supreme Court judges may be recalled by electors within a general electoral procedure in the House of Commons. Up to the present, such proceedings have not led to a recall in practice.

Malaysia

The first *Constitution* was adopted on 31 August 1957 (the *Federation of Malaya Agreement*). Diffuse constitutional review was possible even before independence (carried out by all ordinary courts as well the highest courts and the Supreme Court). However, the influence of the American system was only indirect. The *Constitution* in force (subsequently introduced as the *Constitution of Malaysia* of 16 September 1963, amended in 1992, 1993, and 1994) explicitly declares the principle of the supremacy of the *Constitution* (Article 4).

At present constitutional review is regulated separately by a written constitutional act. The subject of such a review can be any executive regulation, and under certain conditions the constitutional review of statutes is also possible. In addition, the courts also have the function of interpreting the *Constitution*.

The conditions for being appointed a judge of a higher court are as follows: citizenship; and ten years of practice as an attorney at law or judicial experience in the public administration. Judges are independent. Concerning their number, a directive declares that any court must be composed of no less than 5 judges (for the Supreme Court of Malaya 12 judges are determined, for Borneo 8 judges; however the Parliament can change this number; so for the Supreme Court of Malaya, the Parliament determined in practice 15 judges). The judges are appointed by the Parliament following their proposal by the Government. The maximum age limit for appointment is 65 years.

The Supreme Court (the Federal Court) has original jurisdiction to carry out constitutional review (Articles 128 to 130). With the introduction of constitutional review, Malaysian case-law has been absorbing American constitutional case-law; however, in the past, their case-law was more influenced by the English or Indian systems. The Federal Court may also exercise the constitutional review of statutes issued by the legislature: in such situations, the Court is explicitly empowered to exercise the constitutional review of such statutes. In addition, the court is also explicitly empowered to adjudicate jurisdictional disputes between the Federation and its constituent entities. Concerning constitutional disputes relating to other kinds of legislation, other (ordinary) courts are empowered to initiate such proceedings by requesting such before the Federal Court (the "concrete review").

It is possible to initiate *habeas corpus* proceedings before the High Court.

A real diffuse review was introduced by the constitutional amendment of 1981.

Mongolia

The new Mongolian *Constitution* was adopted on 12 February 1992.

This *Constitution* introduced the Constitutional Court as an independent body with exclusive power to carry out constitutional review - *Undsen Huuliin Tsets* (Articles 64 to 67 of the Constitution). The Court is composed of nine members appointed for six years. They are appointed by the Parliament: three by itself, three on the proposal of the Head of State, and three on the proposal of the Supreme Court. The members of *Tsets* elect the President for three years from among themselves; one re-election is possible. The dismissal of a judge of the Constitutional Court prior to the expiration of their term of office is possible as determined by Para.4 of Article 65 of the *Constitution* if a judge violates statute. Such judge is dismissed by the Parliament following the decision of the *Tsets* and the body which proposed that the judge be elected.

Proceedings before the *Tsets* may be requested by the following petitioners (Para.1 of Article 66 of the *Constitution*): the Parliament, the Supreme Court and the Public Prosecutor. It is not clearly defined by the *Constitution* if the proceedings can be initiated by an individual petitioner. However, following a list of *Tsets* powers, it is possible to state that this body deals also with the constitutional complaints of citizens. It is foreseen that a *Tsets Act* will regulate this matter in detail. The *Tsets* is empowered to adjudicate jurisdictional disputes between different State bodies. It is only empowered to issue an opinion, which then has to be finally approved by the Parliament; but in some cases the decision of the *Tsets* can be final (Para. 2 of Article 66). Furthermore, the *Tsets* is empowered to decide finally on the constitutionality of regulations issued by the Parliament, the President of the Republic or by the Government. The *Tsets* also decides on the constitutionality of referendums as well as on the constitutionality of presidential and parliamentary elections. In addition, the *Tsets* deals with the impeachment of the Head of State, the President of the Parliament as well as the Prime Minister. The *Tsets* also decides on the dismissal of representatives; the result of such proceedings may only be an opinion, the final decision has to be issued by the Parliament.

Nepal

The *Constitution* in force was adopted in December 1981 and is based on the *Constitutional Amendments* of 25 January 1967, 12 December 1975 and of 15 December 1980.

The right to legal remedies for the protection of human rights before the Supreme Court is regulated by Article 16 in connection with Article 71 of the *Constitution*.

The Supreme Court is composed of the President and a limited number of judges determined by statute, but not more than six (Article 68 of the *Constitution*). The Court has statutory autonomy: it may issue its own internal rules. The Court President is appointed by the King following consultations with the highest State officials (the *raj sabha*, similar to the State Council); other judges are appointed by the King following consultation with the Court President. Judges are appointed for ten years, one reappointment is possible for a term of office as determined by the King himself (Article 69). The maximum age limit for judicial office is 65 years, the minimum is 45 years. Other conditions are as follows: candidates must be lawyers; have no less than five years of recent judicial experience; and no less than seven years experience in government service or as an attorney at law. The dismissal of a judge of the Constitutional Court prior to the expiration of their term of office is possible on the request of the affected judge or as a consequence of inappropriate professional performance.

The Court has the following powers:

- jurisdiction above other courts;
- special powers:
  - the evaluation of the implementation of the *Constitution*;
  - the power to decide in cases of *habeas corpus, mandamus, prohibition, quo warranto* and *certiorari* concerning human rights protection (Article 71).

Generally speaking, the American system of judicial review was adopted. Within the scope of this system, the constitutional review of statutes is also possible, because the Constitution explicitly determines that statutorial principles as determined by the Supreme Court in matters of its jurisdiction are binding on all other courts (*stare decisis*). However, the Supreme court may change its decisions (Article 73 of the *Constitution*).

The *Constitution* of 9 November 1990 reintroduced the Supreme Court as the highest court in the judicial hierarchy (Article 86). Judges may hold office until they attain the age of sixty-five. The term of office of the Chief Justice is seven years from the date of appointment (Article 87). Any Nepali citizen may file a petition in the Court to have any statute or any part thereof declared void on the grounds of inconsistency with the *Constitution* because it imposes an unreasonable restriction on the enjoyment of the fundamental rights conferred by the *Constitution* or on any other grounds. Furthermore, extraordinary power rests with the Supreme Court to declare that statute as void either *ab intio* or from the date of its decision if it appears that the statute in question is inconsistent with the *Constitution* (Article 88).

In addition, the Court may, with a view to imparting full justice and providing the appropriate remedy, issue appropriate orders and writs including *habeas corpus, mandamus, certiorari,* prohibition and *quo warranto*.

North Korea

The first *Constitution* was adopted on 8 September 1948, the current *Constitution* was adopted on 27 December 1972, and revised on 9 April 1992.

A certain form of constitutional review falls under the jurisdiction of:

- the Standing Committee of the Supreme People's Assembly,[149] which, following Article 101 of the *Constitution*, examines and adopts bills raised in the intervals between sessions of the Assembly, abrogates old laws and regulations when new bills and amendments to laws are adopted, and interprets current laws and ordinances. The Standing Committee issues decisions and instructions (Article 102);
- the Public Prosecutor's Office, which is responsible under Para. 2 of Article 165 of the *Constitution*, for deciding if acts of State bodies are in conflict with the *Constitution* and other regulations issued by the National Assembly, the Head of State and other State bodies of the highest level.

Pakistan

The first *Constitution*, adopted in 1956 and amended in March 1962, was followed by the first democratic *Constitution* after the establishment of the State, adopted in 1973 (amended by *Amendment No.2* on 16 October 1979, as well as by *Presidential Order No.1* on 27 May 1980), which included constitutional rights guarantees. It also determined the jurisdiction of the Supreme Court for particular forms of the constitutional review of statutes, both preventive and repressive. Furthermore, *habeas corpus* proceedings were introduced.

The *Provisional Constitution Order* of 24 March 1981 granted the President of State the right to amend the *Constitution*, which resulted in the suspension of the *Constitution* in 1973. This entailed a termination of the independent judiciary (Articles 175 to 212 of the *Constitution* of 1973) and the developed judicial review system exercised by the Supreme and High Court concerning human rights protection (which was guaranteed by Articles 8 to 28 of the *Constitution* of 1973). In the meantime, the *Constitution* was amended by *Amendment No. 4* of 1975 and by *Amendment No. 5* of 1976. Both amendments limited the jurisdiction of higher courts in the field of human rights protection, which had been introduced by the *Constitution* of 1973. Following such tendencies, the executive branch ignored directions issued by the then Supreme Court in 1977 concerning conditions for the reestablishment of the system of legality. Under the *Constitution* of 1973, Pakistan also had *habeas corpus* proceedings, which were finally abrogated by an *Act* in 1981.

149 Similar to such bodies established in Laos and in Myanmar.

The Philippines

The first *Constitutions* dated from 1935 and from 1973. The *Constitution* of 1935 first introduced constitutional review (the Supreme Court and/or all ordinary courts - the American system of diffuse review). The then existing *habeas corpus* proceedings were suspended from 1973 to 1986.

The second *Constitution* of 1973 (amended in 1981) adopted the same system.

Under the *Constitution* of 15 October 1986, the Supreme Court is empowered to perform constitutional review (Item 2 of Para. 4 of Article 8 of the *Constitution*). Diffuse proceedings were adopted following the American model, which means that all ordinary courts are obliged to protect human rights and freedoms (sentence 2 of Para. 1 of Article 8 of the *Constitution*). The courts instituted a number of standards concerning the constitutional review as well as the appropriate conditions for such a review, *e.g.*:

- the existence of a concrete case;
- the personal and essential interest of any party that initiates a constitutional review;
- the need that the constitutional question be decided before the issuance of a decision in a particular case.

The judiciary enjoys financial autonomy and independence. The Supreme Court is composed of the President and 14 members (Item 1 of Para. 4 of Article 8 of the *Constitution*). The Court may also act in chambers composed of three, five or seven members. Questions concerning the constitutional review of statutes and international agreements are decided by the Court in principle in a plenary session; cases concerning the constitutionality of presidential decrees, the promulgation of decrees, ordinances and other regulations are decided by two thirds of Court members present and voting. The Court's powers include the following (Para. 5 of Article 8): *certioari, habeas corpus, mandamus,* (similar to the Indian system), as an Appeals Court decides in cases in lower courts concerning constitutional review.

Members of the Supreme Court must be citizens of the Philippines of no less than 40 years of age and with no less than 15 years of legal experience. The office of judge is incompatible with any other quasi-judicial or administrative office. Judges of the Supreme Court are appointed by the President of the Republic.

Dissenting or concurring opinions are welcomed, but must be supported.

Singapore

The first *Constitution* of the independent State was adopted on 16 September 1963 (revised in 1992, amended in 1993, 1994, 1995).

It is characteristic of Singapore that the country does not have a single constitutional text, but rather that three texts are still in force:

- the State Constitution of Singapore of 1963;
- the Constitution of the Federation of Malaysia of 1963
- the Singapore Independence Act No. 9 of 7 August 1965.

The principle of the supremacy of the *Constitution* was introduced (Article 4 and Para. 2 of Article 5 of the *Constitution* of 1963).

Singapore introduced the American system of diffuse constitutional/judicial review, but the American principle of *stare decisis* is implemented less in practice. However, in the *Constitution* of Singapore, the American system is in use only indirectly because of the many adopted elements of the Malaysian and Indian *Constitutions*. In general, the case-law, and primarily the constitutional case-law, is closer to British conservativism than American activism.

The highest body carrying out constitutional review is the Supreme Court. Singapore also has *habeas corpus* proceedings and *mandamus, prohibition, quo warranto* and *certiorari*. The practice of Singapore courts is influenced not so much by American jurisprudence, as by the English, Malaysian, and mainly the Indian Supreme Courts. Such a situation is a consequence of their similar constitutional systems, in the framework of which, Singapore courts have tried to adapt foreign jurisprudence to their concrete circumstances.

South Korea

Since its foundation, South Korea has survived six major State structure changes and nine constitutional changes. The first *Constitution* was adopted on 17 July 1948, later amended in July 1952, November 1954, July 1960, November 1960, November 1962, October 1969, December 1972, October 1980 and in October 1987. Constitutional review was introduced by the first *Constitution* (during the First Republic from 1948 to 1960), however, constitutional review in a proper sense following the German model, was actually introduced by the so-called *Constitution of the Second Republic* (1960-1961). The Third Republic (1962-1972) adopted the American system of constitutional review, which was exercised by the Korean Supreme Court. The Fourth Republic (1972-1980) as well as the Fifth Republic survived a period of regression concerning constitutional review. Only a constitutional commission was active in that period because the principle of constitutional review was not compatible with the then ruling military regime. By the special *Declaration of 29 June 1987*, democracy was re-established and the principle of the separation of powers was introduced: the legislature, the executive as well as the judicial branch. This was an appropriate basis for the introduction of constitutional review, which was re-established following the German model.

The *Constitution* of the Sixth Republic regulated the Constitutional Court (*heonbeop jaep'anso*) in Chapter VI by Articles 111 to 113. The position and work were regulated in detail by *Constitutional Court Act No. 4017* of 5 August 1988, which came in to force on 1 September 1988.

The Constitutional Court is composed of nine members. All members are appointed by the President of the Republic for six years. Members may be reappointed; three of the Court members are proposed by the Parliament, the other three by the President of the Supreme Court. The President of the Constitutional Court is appointed by the President of the Republic on the basis of the previous approval of the Parliament. The heads of the legislative, executive and judicial branches are associated members of the Constitutional Court on the basis of their office. Members of the Constitutional Court are appointed from among candidates who are no less than 40 years old, have no less than 15 years of legal experience practicing law (as judges, prosecutors, attorneys at law, lawyers), or who have held a high office in a public enterprise or who have been a professor of law. The upper age limit is fixed at 65 for Court members and 70 years for the Court President. The independence of Constitutional Court judges is ensured by three factors: their irremovability, unless they receive a sentence for a criminal offence; their political neutrality, which means that Constitutional Court judges may not be members of any political party; their incompatibility which means that the office of Constitutional Court judge is not compatible with any parliamentary office, membership in any local assembly, or the position of employee, administrative clerk or adviser in any special interest group. In practice only six judges are permanent. The others hold honorary offices. They are mainly professors of public law.

The Constitutional Court has its own administrative services and a body which carries out research in the field of constitutional review and which prepares draft decisions. Concerning its status as a constitutional institution, the Constitutional Court has its own independent budget. Funds are granted to the Court from the State budget on the basis of statute. The Constitutional Court also has administrative autonomy concerning its internal rules, proceedings and administration.

The powers of the Constitutional Court are divided into the five following areas:

- the constitutional review of statutes;
- impeachment;
- deciding constitutional complaints of individuals;
- determining the constitutionality of political parties;
- the adjudication of jurisdictional disputes between State bodies.

Decisions are issued by a majority of six votes. The petitioners before the Constitutional Court are required to have legal representation. The review of the constitutionality of statutes is based on rules of civil proceedings; impeachment is based on rules of criminal proceedings; concerning other matters, mainly administrative proceedings rules are applied.

The constitutional review of statutes is regulated by Article 107 of the *Constitution*, the petitioners are ordinary courts. The Korean Constitutional Court features only the concrete review of statutes and the abstract review. Such reviews also existed in the period of the Second Republic. In the period of the Sixth Republic the abstract review was not practiced, however as a certain form of compensation, the individual constitutional complaint was introduced. Korean constitutional review applies to statutes issued by the Parliament as well as acts of the Head of State having the force of statute.

Under Article 65 of the *Constitution*, impeachment proceedings may be initiated against the highest State officers due to a violation of the *Constitution*: e.g. against the Head of State, the Prime Minister, members of the Government, judges, Constitutional Court judges, the central electoral commission, and members of the Office of Financial Inspection.

Under Article 68 of the *Constitutional Court Act* of 1988, following a violation of constitutional rights by a public authority body, citizens may lodge a constitutional complaint before the Constitutional Court. A complaint is a subsidiary legal remedy for individuals, whose introduction was influenced by the Swiss, German and Austrian experiences. The object of such a complaint may be any act of State and local authorities. All acts of the legislative and executive branch are included. However, it is necessary, before lodging a complaint, to exhaust all possible legal remedies. The judgments of ordinary courts are excluded from the constitutional complaint; however, the Supreme Court is empowered to carry out their review.

The review of the constitutionality of political party activities is determined in Sub-para. 4 of Article 8 of the *Constitution* ; such activities which violate the democratic order may be disputed.

The adjudication of jurisdictional disputes between public authority bodies is regulated by Article 61 of the *Constitutional Court Act* of 1988. There are three kinds of jurisdictional disputes:

- disputes between State bodies;
- disputes between State bodies and local communities;
- disputes between local communities.

The South Korean constitutional review system also includes the issuance of dissenting/concurring opinions.

Constitutional Court decisions are binding on all State bodies.

Sri Lanka

The Constitutional Court was introduced by the *Constitution* of May 1972 (Articles 54 and 55 of the *Constitution*). The Constitutional Court was empowered to carry out the constitutional review of legislation. It also was able to exercise the preventive review of legislation following special proceedings. In addition, the constitutional review also included *certioari* and *mandamus* proceedings.

The *Constitution* of 1972 was repealed and a new *Constitution* was adopted in February 1978 (Amended on 20 November 1978, 26 February 1979, 27 August 1982, 25 February 1983 , 8 August 1983, 4 October 1983, 6 March 1984, 24 August 1984, 6 August 1986, 17 February 1987, 14 September 1987, 14 November 1987, 24 May 1988, 17 December 1988 and 17 December 1988). By the mentioned *Constitution*, the constitutional review jurisdiction of the Supreme Court was introduced (Article 118). The Supreme Court exercises:

- the preventive constitutional review of statutes (Articles 119 to 124);
- the interpretation of the *Constitution* (Article 125);
- to hear and determine any question relating to the infringement or imminent infringement by executive or administrative action of any fundamental right (Article 126);
- a consultative function (Article 129);
- jurisdiction in election petitions (Article 130).

The Supreme Court is composed of the Chief Justice and of not less than six and not more than ten other judges. The members of the Court are appointed by the President of the Republic (Article 107).

Taiwan (the Republic of China)

The constitutional basis is the Constitution of the Chinese Republic of Taiwan promulgated on of 1 January 1947 and finally officially enacted on 25 December 1947. Transforming along with the Constitution through the years later on, the Grand Justices authority as well as its interpretation have reflect the development of the constitutional process itself.

On Taiwan constitutional review is exercised by the Republic of China Constitutional Court (Grand Justices Council), with special regard to the interpretation of the *Constitution*. The Grand Justices power to interpret the *Constitution* is not limited to the letter of the *Constitution* per se, the essence, spirit and historical background of the *Constitution* must also be factored into deliberation. The system also includes the dissenting or concurring opinions of judges. The jurisprudence is published in a special collection, together with the dissenting and concurring opinions of judges added to the appropriate decision or interpretation.

The Grand Justices is empowered:

- to protect the individual's rights as provided in the *Constitution*;
- to decide disputes arising from the application of the *Constitution*;
- to decide disputes concerning division of power among particular governmental authorities;
- to declare the unconstitutionality of statute or regulation;

- to unify conflicting opinions concerning the interpretation and implementation of statutes and regulations;
- to clarify constitutional ambiguities;
- to provide for social order;
- to decide upon unconstitutional activities of political parties;
- to decide upon unconstitutionality of regulations issued by the provincial self-government.

The interpretation of norms has a long tradition in the Chinese legal system, as it derives from ancient Chinese history. The national doctrine as an interpretative standard based on legal philosophy, has an even higher reputation and authority than the regulation itself. In modern Chinese constitutional history the interpretative function has been held by different institutions (e.g., the Supreme Court in Beijing established on 7 December 1906, the Supreme Court in Nanjing established on 25 October 1927, as well as the Judicial Office established on 20 October 1928). Provisions concerning the interpretative function of the judiciary were included in only a few *Constitutions*, e.g., the *Constitution* of 1 May 1914, which introduced a special consultative court for deciding cases of suspect implementation of the *Constitution* by the President of State. The work of this body was regulated by special statute. Under the *Constitution of the Republic of China* of 10 October 1923, constitutional review was exercised by members of both chambers of the Parliament. The draft *Constitution* of 1 June 1931 empowered the central executive Party Committee to carry out constitutional review, however, under the draft *Constitution* of 5 May 1936, this function was assigned to the Judicial Office.

Under Articles 78 and 173 of the *Constitution of the Republic of China,* the Judicial Yuan (or Judiciary) shall have a number of Grand Justices to be empowered to interpret the *Constitution*, as well as statutes and executive regulations whenever they are in conflict with the Constitution. Para. 4 of Article 5 of the *Amendment of the Constitution* further provides that the Grand Justices shall form a Constitutional Court to adjudicate the matters relating to the dissolution of political parties violating the *Constitution*. Under Article 79 of the *Constitution*, the Judicial Yuan appoints a list of Grand Justices to carry out this function. They are appointed on the proposal of the President of State with the consent of the Control Yuan. The terms and activities of the Grand Justices are regulated by the *Rules Governing the Adjudication of the Grand Justices Council* of 16 September 1948 (1st Term, 7/1948-9/1958), the *Law Governing the Adjudication of the Grand Justices Council* of 21 July 1958 (2nd Term, 9/1958-9/1967; 3rd Term, 10/1967-9/1976, 4th Term, 10/1976-9/1985, 5th Term, 10/1985-) and by the *Law of Constitutional Interpretation Procedure* of 3 February 1993 (5th Term, -9/1994 and 6th Term, 10/1-1994-present).

Under the regulation in force 15 Grand Justices are appointed to the bench.

The regulation in force permits the individual petitioner to file or relief or protection under the *Constitution*. If a person or party, whose constitutional rights have been infringed upon and remedies provided by law have been exhausted and who has doubt as to the constitutionality of a law or regulation as had been applied in the final decision of such person's case by the ordinary court of last instance, may petition to the Grand Justices for interpretation of the *Constitution*. In addition, a lower court judge who, during the trial of a case, opines that the statute at issue is in conflict with the Constitution, may interrupt the proceedings and petition the Grand Justices for constitutional interpretation.

THAILAND

The first *Constitution* was adopted on 27 June 1932, followed by many constitutional amendments.

The subsequent *Constitution* was adopted in 1978 (the *Constitution of the Kingdom of Thailand B.E.2521*), and amended by *Amendment B.E.2528* (of 1985) and *Amendment B.E.2532* (of 1989). The Constitutional Court was regulated in Chapter X (Articles 184 to 193). The court was composed of the President of the Parliament, the President of the Supreme Court, the General Public Prosecutor and four judges appointed by the Parliament from among qualified candidates. The office of the President of the Constitutional Court was exercised by the President of the Parliament. Incompatibilities were determined by Article 185 of the *Constitution*: A member of the Constitutional Court was not able to be a senator, a member of a representative chamber, a member of a local assembly, a local administrator, a permanently paid employee, an employee of a local authority or an employee of a State enterprise. A member of the Constitutional Court enjoyed certain privileges as determined by statute (Article 186). The office of a member of the Constitutional Court could terminate in the following situations (Article 188): death, resignation, acceptance of another office which is incompatible with the office of constitutional court judge, or a sentence of imprisonment. The Constitutional Court was empowered to carry out the preventive review of draft statutes (Article 190 of the *Constitution*) on the request of the Parliament or the Prime Minister. In addition, the Constitutional Court exercised the concrete review of norms on the request of an ordinary court (Article 191 of the *Constitution*). The Constitutional Court also adjudicated jurisdictional disputes between the Supreme Court and other courts, as well as disputes between other courts (Article 179 of the *Constitution*). The decisions issued by the Constitutional Court were final and were published in the Official Gazette (Article 192 of the *Constitution*).

The *Constitution* in force was adopted on 11 October 1997. The Constitutional Court is regulated by Articles 255 to 270. The Court consists of the President and fourteen judges appointed by the King following the proposals of the Senate and the judges of the Supreme Court, judges of the Supreme Administrative Court, qualified lawyers, as well as qualified political scientists (Article 255). The judges elect one from among themselves to be the President of the Court. Special qualifications for the mentioned candidates and their incompatibilities are defined by Articles 256 and 258.

The President and the judges hold their office for nine years from the date of their appointment by the King and they hold office for only one term (Article 259). The outgoing Court members remain in office to perform their duties until the newly appointed President and judges of the Court take office. In addition, the Court members vacate office upon: death, reaching seventy years of age, resignation, being disqualified, committing a violation, being sentenced by a judgment to imprisonment, *etc.* (Article 260). The Court has the following powers (Articles 263 to 266):

- to exercise the preventive constitutional review of statutes and the rules of procedure of the Parliament;
- to exercise the concrete (repressive) review of the constitutionality of statutes requested by an ordinary court; such decisions of the Constitutional Court apply to all cases but do not necessarily determine the final judgments of the courts;
- to adjudicate jurisdictional disputes between State bodies.

The consultative chamber of the Court for hearing a decision consists of not less than nine judges. The decision is arrived at by a majority of votes, unless otherwise determined in the *Constitution*. The Court decisions and all judges thereof are published in the official gazette (Article 267). The Court decision must at least consist of the following: the background of the allegation, a summary of the facts from the hearings, the reasoning of the decision on questions of fact and questions of law, and the provisions of the *Constitution* and the law invoked and resorted to (Article 267). Court decisions are deemed final and binding on the National Assembly, Council of Ministers, courts and other State bodies (Article 268). The proceedings of the Court are prescribed by the Constitutional Court (Article 269). The Court has an independent administrative unit with a Secretary as its head responsible directly to the President of the Court (Article 270). The Court office has autonomy in personnel administration, its budget and other activities as provided by statute (Article 270).

Vietnam

Under the former *Constitution of the Republic of South Vietnam* of 24 October 1956, amended in 1960, the Constitutional Court was introduced by Articles 85 to 88. The Court was empowered to decide on the constitutionality of statutes, decrees having the force of statute, administrative regulations, and to exercise the concrete review of norms (as requested by ordinary courts in concrete cases). Decisions on the unconstitutionality of statutes had an *erga omnes* effect, they were published in the Official Gazette. Similar to South Korea, the amended *Constitution of South Vietnam* of 1 April 1967 granted the function of constitutional review to the Supreme Court (Articles 76 to 83 of the new *Constitution*). This Court was called the *Alta Corte de Justicia*. It was empowered to exercise the constitutional review of statutes, decrees having the force of statute, other decrees, ministerial orders and other regulations issued by administrative bodies (Para. 1 of Article 91 of the *Constitution*).

The former North Vietnam adopted its first *Constitution* in November 1945. The second *Constitution* was adopted on 31 December 1959, the third in July 1976, and a further draft constitutional text was created in December 1980. Under the *North Vietnam Constitution* of 1959, the power to exercise the preventive review of draft statutes was held by the Standing Committee and the National Committee of the National Assembly. The power to interpret the *Constitution* was held by the State Council. Under Article 105 of the *Constitution*, the Supreme People's Supervisory Body was introduced, which had to supervise the implementation of statutes by State bodies and citizens.

The *Constitution of the Socialist Republic of Vietnam* of 15 April 1992 introduced the parliamentary review of constitutionality. The National Assembly Standing Committee has the following duties and powers:

- to supervise enforcement of the *Constitution*, statutes and resolutions of the National Assembly, as well as orders and resolutions of the National Assembly Standing Committee itself;
- to discontinue the implementation of the acts of the Government, the Prime Minister, the Supreme People's Court, and the Supreme People's Organ of Control which are at variance with the *Constitution*, statutes and resolutions of the National Assembly;
- to recommend that the National Assembly rescind these acts as well as the acts of the Government, the Prime Minister, the Supreme People's Court and the Supreme People's Organ of Control which are at variance with the orders and resolutions of the National Assembly Standing Committee itself (Article 81). In addition, the committees of the National Assembly study and review bills, petition statutes, draft regulations, other bills and the reports entrusted to them by the National Assembly. They exercise their right of supervision within the scope of their duties and jurisdiction as prescribed by statute (Article 95).

G. Central and South America

I. General

Constitutional review (with different effects) also developed in the countries of Central and South America. This justice is based on a rather rich tradition of constitutionalism in some countries.

There are the four main systems of constitutional review:

a) THE AMERICAN OR DIFFUSE MODEL, the most widespread model, in which all courts, from the lowest to the highest, review the constitutionality of statutes and administrative measures in specific proceedings using common procedural rules. In the diffuse system decisions generally take effect *inter partes* only. As a rule, court decisions concerning the unconstitutionality of statutes are retroactive, *i.e. ex tunc* (with *pro praeterito* consequences).

The American system of judicial review has influenced numerous countries in Central and South America, where it was adopted even back in the 19th Century by mainly countries with a federal state system.[150] In some countries this system has subsequently been amended and corrected through the parallel introduction of the European model; such cases are referred to here as the "mixed systems," of modern Brazil, Colombia, Ecuador, Guatemala, Peru and Venezuela.

The characteristics of the Central and South American variant of this system are as follows: all judges and courts have constitutional/judicial review jurisdiction; in pure systems standing is reserved for (ordinary) courts only; decisions have *inter partes* effect; the contents of the decision are in fact the finding - a statute may be declared null and void (the principle of the nullity of an unconstitutional State regulation), with *ex tunc* and/or *pro-praeterito* effect.

The systems with the American model of judicial review in Central and South America are further characterized by *amparo* proceedings. In Argentina *amparo* was established in 1853 by the *Federal Constitution*, but in practice the Supreme Court began to exercise its powers as late as in 1860. Mexico was the first to introduce it on 5 February 1857, and readopted it in the *Constitution of 5 February 1917*. *Amparo* proceedings were also introduced by other countries following the Mexican model[151].

b) THE EUROPEAN OR AUSTRIAN (OR CONCENTRATED MODEL), adopted by Constitutional Courts specialized for the review of the constitutionality of statutes in special proceedings, is less widespread. In such a system the decisions of the constitutional review body have an *erga omnes* effect and they may declare unconstitutional statutes to be abrogated. Their decisions have an *ex nunc* effect with *pro futuro* consequences, *i.e.* the abrogation takes effect only at the moment when the decision on abrogation is issued by the Court. There is a characteristic feature that in some countries the concentrated system exists in parallel to the diffuse system (*i.e.* in Brazil, Colombia, Ecuador, Guatemala, Peru and Venezuela). The exclusive power of constitutional review is reserved either for the Supreme Court (Panama, Paraguay, Uruguay) for a special chamber of the Supreme Court (Costa Rica) or for the Constitutional Court (the Argentinean Province of Tucuman, Chile, Surinam[152]). Considering the fact that the introduction of constitutional/judicial review is usually related to the democratisation process in a specific country, it is worth mentioning the example of Argentina, where this transformation process of the social and legal system started on the level of province (as evidenced by the introduction of the constitutional

---

150 Originally this system was adopted by Mexico (1857), Venezuela (1858), Argentina (Constitutions of 1853, 1860 and 1863), Brazil (1890) and subsequently also by the former British colonies of Central America (Barbados, Guyana, Jamaica, Trinidad and Tobago). Furthermore, it was adopted by some states with little federal experience, such as Colombia (1850), or by a few states irrespective of the form of the state system, such as the Dominican Republic (1844), where this system has been preserved to the present day.

151 *e.g.* Guatemala (the *Constitution of 1965* and the *Amparo Act* of 3 May 1966), Honduras (the *Constitution of January 1982* and the *Amparo Act* of 14 April 1936, amended in February 1982) and Nicaragua (the *Constitution of 20 July 1979*), together with the *Statute of Rights and Guarantees* of 21 August 1979 and the *Amparo Act* of 28 May 1980.

152 Under the *Constitution* of 30 October 1987, the Constitutional Court was introduced as a body created by statute which is entrusted with judging the constitutionality of legal rules and measures. The composition, tasks and jurisdiction of this body are regulated by statute (Article 144).

protection of human rights in individual provincial Constitutions or even by the above example of the establishment of a Constitutional Court in the Province of Tucuman).

c) Some countries have a mixed, *i.e.* diffuse and concentrated system of constitutional/judicial review, *e.g.* Brazil, Colombia, Ecuador, Guatemala, Peru and Venezuela. Most often these countries have modified the original diffuse system by adapting it to the respective circumstances (*e.g.* in Argentina, and in particular, Mexico, with its specific *judicio de amparo* as a form of constitutional complaint). Accordingly, the concentrated and diffuse systems of constitutional/judicial review may coexist in the same country.

Mixed systems are characterized by the popular complaint (*actio popularis*) as introduced by certain countries[153].

d) Other Systems of Constitutional Review

A special system of constitutional review is known in Cuba, where according to the *Constitution of 24 February 1976*, the power of constitutional review is held by the National Assembly (legislative body).

2. The Particular Systems of Constitutional Review

Argentina

Generally, the system of *incidenter* review (indirect constitutional review) was adopted. However, some provinces have a double system of constitutional review (direct and indirect). The new regulation in some provinces after 1957 is of main importance (Chaco, Chubut, Formosa, Neuquen, Rio Negro).

The constitutional review system is based on Articles 31 and 100 of the *Constitution* of 1 May 1853 (with *Amendments from 1860, 1866, 1898, 1957 and 1994*). With reference to the prevailing system, each judge is empowered, irrespective of their position, to evaluate the conformity of laws and administrative acts with the *Constitution*. Constitutional review is exclusively reserved for the judiciary. The decisions take effect *ex tunc* and, naturally, *inter partes*.

Habeas corpus proceedings are possible; a complaint of this kind is meant to protect the right to Personal Liberty (Article 18 of the *Constitution*). Exclusive power to decide on such complaints is reserved for criminal judges, however this is limited merely to deciding on acts and facts where a violation of fundamental constitutional rights is involved. The *amparo* is regulated by the *Ley nacional sobre Ley de Amparo* of 18 October 1966.

[153] *e.g.* Colombia (the *Constitution of 1961*; *Act No. 96 of 1936* and *Decree No. 432 of 1969*), Venezuela (the *Constitution of 1961*; the *Supreme Court Act* of 30 July 1976), Panama (the *Constitution of 1972*, as amended in 1983; the *Constitutional Complaint Act* of 24 October 1956), El Salvador (the *Constitution of 8 January 1962*; the *Constitutional Proceedings Act* of 14 January 1960), as well as Brazil (the *Constitution of 1967*, as amended in 1969 and *Act No. 4717 of 21 June 1965*); a certain form of popular complaint (*actio popularis*) exists also in some Argentinean Provinces (Chaco, Neuquen, Santiago del Estero) and Costa Rica (based on the *Civil Proceedings Code* of 25 January 1933, as amended on 23 December 1937).

Another type of proceeding includes specific protection complaints - *recurso de amparo*. This was introduced pursuant to the decisions of the Argentinean Supreme Court of 1957 (the *Angel Siri* Case) and of 1958, on the example of the *amparo* complaint in Mexico and in certain other Central American countries, as well as in Brazil, where such a complaint is referred to as the *mandado de seguranca*. With the *recurso de amparo*, the protection of rights was extended from *habeas corpus* (relating to the right to Personal Liberty) also to all other rights guaranteed by the national *Constitution*. Whether to decide on such complaints is the decision of each judge.

On the federal level the Supreme Court is empowered to settle jurisdictional disputes between judges of different provinces, or judges of federal and provincial levels according to specific proceedings.

The constitutional review in Argentinean Provinces consists of the following:

- the constitutional complaint against laws before the highest provincial court (only in the Provinces of Buenos Aires, La Rioja, Chaco, Neuquen, Entre Rios, Santiago del Estero, and Rio Negro);
- *habeas corpus*, in all provinces, provided that cases are in the jurisdiction of the relevant criminal judge;
- *amparo*, in all provinces, provided that cases are in the jurisdiction of the relevant judge. In such cases the Province of Tucuman, however, anticipates the jurisdiction of the Constitutional Court. With reference to the *amparo*, the Province of Tucuman anticipates the possibility of abstract constitutional review (Para. 4 of Article 22 of the *Constitution*);
- jurisdictional disputes between municipalities in a specific province which are subject to the decisions of the Provincial Supreme Court.

The "abstract" constitutional review only follows the so-called *incidenter* proceedings.

The *Constitution* of the Province of Tucuman of 28 April 1990 established its Constitutional Court on the European model (*Tribunal Consitucional*). Its power is limited to provincial legislation. The Constitutional Court is declared to be the supreme protector of the *Constitution*, in particular in cases of its violation (*e.g.*, impeachment, Article 5, Para. 1 of Article 133 of the *Constitution*). The *Constitution* envisages the *amparo* as a means of protecting constitutional rights before the Constitutional Court (Article 22 of the *Constitution*). The five member Constitutional Court is empowered to carry out repressive abstract constitutional reviews of laws and executive regulations (Para. 1 of Article 134 of the *Constitution*), preventive abstract constitutional reviews of draft laws and draft executive regulations (Para. 2 of Article 134 of the *Constitution*), reviews of elections of members of the Provincial legislative body (Para. 3 of Article 134 of the *Constitution*), to adjudicate charges against State officers in cases concerning violations of the *Constitution* (Article 5 and Para. 4 of Article 134 of the *Constitution*), and to settle jurisdictional disputes between legislative and executive bodies of the Province, between Provincial courts, municipal bodies, between the Province and municipalities, as well as between municipalities themselves (Para. 5 of Article 134 of the *Constitution*).

BELIZE

Under the *Constitution* of 21 September 1981, amended by *Act* No. 26 of 1988, where any question as to the interpretation of the *Constitution* arises in any court and the court is of the opinion that the question involves a substantial question of law, the court has to refer the question to the Supreme Court (Article 96).

BOLIVIA

Under the *Constitution* of 2 February 1967, the Supreme Court of Justice, among other duties, was empowered to decide upon, as the final authority, questions of pure law wherein the decision rests upon the constitutionality or unconstitutionality of a law, decree or resolution of any kind (Article 127). It was also empowered: to decide on charges against the President and Vice-President of the Republic and Ministers for offences committed in the discharge of their office whenever Congress decrees impeachment; to settle jurisdictional disputes between municipalities or between these and political authorities, and between either of these and the municipalities of the provinces; to decide complaints against the resolutions of the legislative branch or one of its chambers, whenever such resolutions may effect one or more concrete rights, either civil or political; to decide disputes between local governments, whether they concern their boundaries or any other rights in such a controversy.

By the *Law of Reform of the Political Constitution of the State* of 12 August 1994, the Constitutional Court was newly re-instituted. The new Constitutional Tribunal is composed of five members elected to ten year terms. Its powers are detailed in Article 120, all of which deal with issues of constitutionality, unconstitutionality, and conflicts of competence. Article 121 specifies that there is no further recourse beyond a decision of the Tribunal, and that statute regulates its organization and functioning as well as the proceedings before the Tribunal.

BRAZIL

In general, the Brazilian system of constitutional review is a mixed system. Similar to the Argentinean, also the Brazilian system follows the American model. However, by the constitutional reform of 1934 the direct request for the determination of unconstitutionality before the Supreme Court of Justice was introduced. Therefore the Brazilian system can be treated as a mixed system.

The diffuse system already existed under the *Constitution* of 1891 and the *Federal Act No. 221* of 1894. All federal judges are empowered to carry out the constitutional review of statutes and federal executive regulations. At the same time, in the Brazilian system *habeas corpus* proceedings have a long tradition as introduced by Para. 22 of Article 73 of the *Constitution* of 1891.

The powers of the Brazilian Supreme Federal Court are as follows (Articles 102, 103, 34 and 36 of the *Constitution*):

- the abstract review of federal and provincial legislation, and its conformity with the *Federal Constitution* as requested by the *acao direta de inconstitucionalidade*. The circle of petitioners of the *acao* was extended by the Constitution of 1988. When deciding on an abstract review, the Supreme Federal Court may by a temporary order temporarily suspend the implementation of certain statute;
- an abstract omissional complaint may be lodged by the same circle of petitioners;
- *representacao interventiva*: the interventionist complaint of the General Public Prosecutor requesting the evaluation of the conformity of provincial law with appropriate principles of federal regulations;
- jurisdictional disputes between the Federation and provinces and between provinces;
- *habeas corpus* proceedings (limited to the protection of personal liberty);
- *habeas data* proceedings, which entails the constitutionally guaranteed implementation of informational self-determination. This was introduced by Article 6 of the *Constitution* of 1988.
- *mandado de seguranca* (from 1934 onwards), a wider legal remedy protecting the constitutional rights which are not protected by *habeas corpus*;
- *mandado de injuncao*, a special individual complaint in case of an omission by the legislature, as introduced by Article 5 of the Constitution of 1988.

Decisions issued by the Supreme Federal Court in abstract review proceedings have *erga omnes* effect - *eficacia general*, and the force of statute (Articles 175 and 178 of the *Rules of Procedure of the Supreme Federal Court*). Decisions concerning the unconstitutionality of statutes issued in *incidenter* proceedings in a concrete case only have *inter partes* effect (with the exception of the *erga omnes* effect granted in 1934).

Decisions and temporary orders are published in the Official Gazette, and simultaneously also in the Official Digest. Generally, the parties are obliged to pay court fees. *Habeas corpus* proceedings and the abstract review are free of charge.

The concentrated system, from 1934 onwards, gives the Supreme Federal Tribunal the power to determine the unconstitutionality of the constitutions of member states and state laws, however only on the request of the Attorney General of the Republic, which entails an element of the abstract review of norms. By the *Constitutional Amendment* of 12 December 1965, such a possibility was extended to include the constitutional review of all state regulations, federal as well as those issued by member states. In such a manner, the abstract review of norms was introduced based primarily on the request of the Attorney General of the Republic as a legitimate petitioner. By Article 103 of the *Constitution* of 1988 the circle of abstract review petitioners was extended. Petitioners may be different federal and provincial bodies, political parties represented in the parliament, and social organisations.

Under the diffuse Brazilian system, all courts of first instance are entitled to not implement any statute which they consider to be unconstitutional, however not *ex officio*, but always on the request of a party in the proceedings. Such decisions have *inter partes* and *ex tunc* effect.

The *Brazilian Constitution* of 1891 also introduced the competence of the Supreme Federal Tribunal to review decisions issued by lower courts in cases of constitutional matters, when requested by a party which has lost such a case. Such a decision has *inter partes* and *ex tunc* effect; the statute is still in force but not applicable in a concrete case. However, the Federal Chamber may declare such a decision issued by the Supreme Federal Tribunal to have *erga omnes* and *ex nunc* effect (from 1934 onwards as well as under the *Constitution* in force).

The concentrated system has been in the jurisdiction of the Supreme Federal Tribunal since 1934, but only the General Public Prosecutor has standing to petition. In this case the court decisions have *erga omnes* effect and they are declaratory.

Indirect constitutional review is possible in complaints concerning the protection of constitutional rights and freedoms (*mandado de seguranca*) which exist in parallel beside *habeas corpus* proceedings. In addition, the Brazilian system also has a certain form of the popular complaint, *i.e.* "popular action for the protection of public assets" (Para. 3 of Article 102 of the *Constitution* in force) which is, in principle, possible against administrative acts, but indirectly also entails the constitutional review of statutes (an administrative act may be based on an unconstitutional statute).

The most recent constitutional revision was adopted in 1988 (which was already amended in 1992, 1993, 1994, 1995, 1996, 1997 and 1998). Under the Brazilian system any court or any judge may declare unconstitutional any statute which could be implemented in a concrete case. This unconstitutional statute is not declared null, however, it may not be implemented. The court decision has only *inter partes* effect. On the other hand, the *Constitution* of 1934 regulated in Para. 4 of Article 90 the possibility that the decision of the Brazilian Supreme Federal Court by which in *incidenter* proceedings a statute is declared unconstitutional, may be granted the force of statute by an act issued by the Federal Chamber (the *Constitution* of 1988 regulates this matters by Para. 10 of Article 52).

The Supreme Federal Court of Brazil (*Supremo Tribunal Federal*) is composed of 11 members (Article 101 of the 1988 *Constitution*). They are appointed by the President of the Republic after confirmation by an absolute majority of the members of the Parliament. There are some conditions determined by the *Constitution* for appointment: Brazilian citizenship, membership in the bar, a minimum age limit of 35 years, and a maximum age limit of 65 years. Under Article 95 of the *Constitution*, Court members are guaranteed permanency of salary, office for life and irremovability. However, Article 93 of the *Constitution* determines the mandatory retirement of age to be 70. The President of the Supreme Federal Court is elected directly (by an absolute majority) from among Court members for two years; re-election is explicitly excluded. Each judge may choose two legal advisers.

The Supreme Federal Court can also act as a proponent of statutes regulating the judiciary (Article 93 of the *Constitution*). Under Articles 99 and 168 of the *Constitution*, the Supreme Federal Court also has administrative and financial autonomy (it may make independent proposals concerning its budget).

The Supreme Federal Court may work in a plenary session; such a session is obligatory in the following situations: determining the unconstitutionality of a statute; issuing a temporary order in abstract review proceedings; impeachment proceedings concerning the President of the Republic, ministers or representatives; or jurisdictional disputes. In addition, the Court also has two chambers composed of five members. Court proceedings were regulated by the *Rules of Procedure* of 16 March 1967, amended on 27 October 1980 in accordance with the explicit constitutional provision on the autonomy of the Supreme Federal Court concerning its internal organization. The new *Constitution* does not contain an explicit authorization granted to the Court to issue rules of procedure. Therefore, until matters are regulated by statute, the provisions of the old *Rules of Procedure* are implemented unless directly contrary to the *Constitution*. A plenum of the Court can decide in the presence of no less than 8 judges. A majority of six judges present and voting is necessary for a decision on the unconstitutionality to be issued. Any judge has always been able to issue a dissenting opinion (*voto vencido*). Such dissenting opinions must be included in the decision where also the *ratio* of votes is indicated in detail. Subsequently, the dissenting opinion is published as a part of the decision in the Official Digest of the Supreme Court (*Revista Trimestral de Jurisprudencia*).

Chile

The *Constitution* of 1925 empowered the Supreme Court to exercise constitutional review, but this constitutional review was of an *incidenter* character (Article 86). By the constitutional reform of 21 January 1970, the Constitutional Court was established, above all with the aim that a special body adjudicate jurisdictional disputes between State bodies. The activities of this Court ceased in 1973. The Constitutional Court was reintroduced by the *Constitution* of 11 September 1980 (Articles 81 and 83). Its work is regulated by the *Basic Constitutional Act* of 12 May 1981. The Court has the following powers: the preventive review of statutes; impeachment; the review of the constitutionality of referendums; the repressive review of the constitutionality of statutes and decrees having the force of statute requested by direct application; other powers as determined by statute.

Colombia

The first *Constitution* of the present Colombia of 30 March 1811 (the *Constitution of Cundinamarca*) introduced the constitutional review of statutes by a special Chamber similar to the *French Constitution* of 1799. Further *Colombian Constitutions* of 1821, 1832 and 1843 did not include any constitutional review of norms. However, the *Constitution* of 1853 determined in Item 6 of Article 42 that the Supreme Court may declare municipal regulations and regulations of provincial assemblies null if they violate the *Constitution* and statutes of the Republic. The *Constitution* of 1858 as the *Constitution of the Federal State of Colombia*, empowered the Supreme Court to suspend the unconstitutional legislative norms of federal member states. The final decision on the validity or invalidity of such norms was in the jurisdiction of the Chamber.

The new centrist *Constitution* of 1886 introduced in Article 90 a real constitutional review, *i.e.* that the Supreme court decided on the constitutionality of statutes on the basis of a veto by the President, but the decision of the Supreme Court had *erga omnes* effect. This *Constitution* is, in general, still in force. The amendments adopted by Articles 40 and 41 of the *Constitutional Act* of 1910, are, in a modified version (the amendment of 1945), still in force. In case of conflict between a statute and the *Constitution*, the provisions of the *Constitution* prevail. The Supreme Court is empowered to protect constitutionality. The Court is empowered to decide finally on the constitutionality of statutes and executive regulations following a (popular) complaint, which may be lodged by any citizen. On the other hand, it is important that the decisions of the Colombian Supreme Court have *erga omnes* effect, and at the same time the effect of *res judicata*. It is not possible to dispute a final Court decision. The *Colombian Constitution* also introduced impeachment but not in such an expressive form. Impeachment proceedings against the President of the Republic, a Minister, the Prosecutor General and the members of the Supreme Court may be initiated by the Parliament. The decision is issued by the Chamber.

Concerning the regulations of 1961, the constitutional review bodies were the Plenum of the Supreme Court and the Administrative Court. Their powers were as follows:

- the *actio popular* before the Supreme court - against a statute or an act having the force of statute; decisions have *erga omnes* effect;
- the *accion de nulidad* before the Administrative Court - against executive regulations; decisions have *erga omnes* effect;
- the *accion de restablecimiente del derecho* before the Administrative Court (in the form of a constitutional complaint); decisions have *inter partes* effect;
- impeachment of the highest State officials.

Since 1910 all Colombian courts have had a constitutional basis (Article 215 of the *Constitution*) for carrying out the constitutional review of statutes (the diffuse system). A legal basis for the diffuse system had already existed (Article 5 of the *Act No. 57* of 1887). However, this system functions in parallel with the concentrated system of constitutional review. The diffuse system has a feature whereby proceedings are not initiated by the Court *ex officio*, but on the basis of a petition of a party with expressed legal interest (standing). The decisions have *inter partes* effect. Similar to other diffuse systems, a judge can not declare an annulment, but only that the unconstitutional statutory provision may not be used. In addition, the *Colombian Constitution* also included the concentrated system of constitutional review (Article 214 of the *Constitution* of 1961), which was in the jurisdiction of the Supreme Court of Justice, and from 1968 onwards, in the jurisdiction of the Constitutional Chamber of the Supreme Court (*Sala Constitucional*). The organization and work of this Chamber is regulated in detail by *Decree No. 432* of 1969. Following this decree, the Chamber is composed of five judges, specialized in public law (*derecho publico*). It is empowered to exercise the direct and general constitutional review of all state regulations (the exceptions are international agreements), which may be initiated by a popular complaint filed by any individual (without the condition of legal interest). The proceedings have an objective character. The Court is not bound by the petition and may work also *ex officio*. The right to the popular complaint is recognised as a constitutional right. The effects of decisions in concentrated systems are *erga omnes, res judicata* and *ex nunc*. Since 1886 it has been possible to carry out a preventive review on the basis of a veto of the President of the Republic before the promulgation of statute.

By the constitutional reform of 1979, the Constitutional Chamber of the Supreme Court received even more autonomy concerning constitutional review as influenced by the European system of constitutional review and tendencies in this field in Chile, Ecuador and Peru.

The new Constitution of 1991 regulates the protection and implementation of rights in the 4th Chapter of part II of the Constitution. It is also important that the system introduced many remedies for constitutional rights protection:

- The right to popular complaint - *accion popular de inconstitucionalidad* - which as a wider right concerning the general protection of constitutional rights is not designed only for the protection of basic rights but for the protection of all constitutionality. Furthermore, Colombia (similar to Venezuela) introduced the popular complaint very early. It was adopted by the *Constitution* of 1910, but later was regulated in detail by *Act No.* 96 of 1936 and *Decree No. 432* of 1969, which were amended by later constitutional amendment in 1979.
- In accordance with the English tradition as well as with the tradition of many Latin American countries, *e.g.* Argentina, Bolivia, Venezuela, Brazil and Peru, the new *Colombian Constitution* also preserved *habeas corpus* proceedings for the protection of the right to personal freedom (Article 30 of the *Constitution*). This is a limited form of the constitutional rights oriented only to personal freedom.
- The new *Constitution* introduced also a specific and direct remedy for the protection of constitutional rights, regulated in Article 86 of the *Constitution* - the so-called *accion de tutela*; this right was primarily introduced into the constitutional text, mainly under the influence of Spanish law. This right includes the right of any individual to dispute a statute or an administrative regulation because of a violation of their constitutional rights. The *Constitution* envisages a detailed statutorial regulation on the exercising of this right (Article 90 of the *Constitution*). At the same time, the new *Constitution* explicitly determines the circle of rights which are protected by the *accion de tutela* (Article 86: the rights

determined in Articles 11 to 31 as well as the rights determined in Articles 33, 34, 37 and 40). It entails the summary regulation of the protection of explicitly determined rights which have to be exercised directly on the basis of the *Constitution*. It is not important which body carries out the protection and on which proceedings the protection is based; what is important is what the subject of protection is. In practice there are rights which can be claimed by an affected individual any time before an ordinary court when such an individual feels affected following any violation due to any action or omission by a body of public authority. This legal remedy can be defined as a certain subsidiary *amparo* proceeding (besides the popular complaint adjudicated by the Constitutional Court and *habeas corpus* proceedings), similar to proceedings concerning constitutional rights protection from the Spanish system as regulated by the *Act* of 26 December 1978. This *Act* regulated the protection of rights in cases when such protection was not covered by the constitutional complaint under the Spanish *Constitutional Court Act*. However, the Spanish Constitutional Court is empowered under the Spanish *Constitutional Court Act* to adjudicate cases relating to *Act No.* 62 of 1978. Such regulation differs from the Colombian *accion de tutela*, whereby ordinary courts are primarily empowered to adjudicate such cases and the Colombian Constitutional Court acts only in a supervisory capacity (Para. 9 of Article 241 of the *Constitution*).

It is important that the new *Constitution* defined the Constitutional Court as an independent institution exercising constitutional review which replaced the former Constitutional Chamber of the Supreme Court. This entails a great change in accordance with the principle of the supremacy of the *Constitution* under the influence of European countries which formed special bodies as protectors of the supremacy of the *Constitution*. However, Colombian legal theory supported the idea of creating an independent constitutional review a long time ago: in 1957, 1959, 1975 and in 1978.

Costa Rica

Under the special *Act* of 1989 (which actually entailed the amendment of the *Constitution* of 8 November 1949, whose most recent amendment was declared by *Law 7347 of 1 July 1993*) the European model of constitutional review was adopted, however with the modification that constitutional review is concentrated within a special chamber of the Supreme Court. This Constitutional Chamber of the Supreme Court is exclusively empowered to adjudicate the following cases concerning constitutional review: popular complaints requesting the constitutional review of a statute (with *erga omnes* effect); preventive reviews of draft statutes (as a consultative function), as well as the constitutional review of legislation in the form of a concrete review.

Ecuador

Under the *Constitution* of 15 January 1978, amended in 1983, the Supreme Court is exclusively empowered to exercise the constitutional review of statutes on the basis of a diffuse system. In addition, by the same *Constitution* of 1978, the Constitutional Court (*Tribunal de Garantias Constitucionales*) was established. Under Article 140 of the *Constitution*, the Court is composed of three members appointed by the Parliament, the President of the Supreme Court, the General Public Prosecutor, the President of the Supreme Electoral Court, a representative of the President of the Republic, a representative of Trade Unions and a representative of the Chamber of Commerce. It exercises the constitutional review of legislation in a concentrated form. In addition, it is also empowered to decide on complaints of citizens concerning violations of the *Constitution*. The new Ecuadorian *Tribunal de Garantias Constitucionales* functions on the basis of the amended *Constitution* of 12 July 1979. It has many similarities to the Austrian model of constitutional review; however the system in Ecuador still preserved *amparo* and *habeas corpus* proceedings.

Subsequently, the *Constitution* was amended in 1993, 1995, 1996 and in 1997. The proceedings of *habeas corpus, habeas data* and *amparo* were reintroduced. In addition, the Constitutional Tribunal (*Tribunal Constitucional*) was introduced. It is composed of nine members and their respective substitutes, who last four years in their functions and may be re-elected (Article 174). The Court members must satisfy the same requirements as the ministers of the Supreme Court of Justice. The National Congress designates the Court members in the following manner:

- two from lists of candidates submitted by the President of the Republic;
- two from lists of candidates submitted by the Supreme Court of Justice, which may not include its own members;
- two elected by the Legislature, who may not be a member of a Legislature;
- one from the list of candidates submitted by the municipal mayors and the provincial prefects;
- one from the list of candidates submitted by the legally registered national workers headquarters and the national indigenous and peasant organisations;
- one from the list of candidates presented by the legally recognized *Production Chambers*.

The members may not be prosecuted for their votes and for the opinions that they formulate in the exercise of the powers attributable to their post. The Court elects a President and a Vice-President from among its members, to a two year renewable term of office. The Court is empowered (Article 175):

- to decide on complaints presented regarding laws, decree-laws, decrees and ordinances, that are fundamentally or procedurally unconstitutional, and totally or partially suspend their effects;
- to decide on the unconstitutionality of administrative acts of all public authorities. The declaration of unconstitutionality brings about the revocation of the act, without prejudice to the administrative body that then adopts the necessary measures to preserve respect for constitutional norms;

- to take cognizance of resolutions that deny recourse to *habeas corpus*, or *habeas data*, and of the cases of obligatory consultation or appeals foreseen in the Recourse of *Amparo*;
- to decide on objections of unconstitutionality made by the President of the Republic in the process of forming statutes (the preventive review);
- to settle jurisdictional disputes as assigned by the Constitution;
- to exercise the other powers conferred on it by the Constitution and statutes.

The declaration of unconstitutionality causes a judgment to be issued which is then promulgated in the official journal, from which date it enters into effect, leaving without effect the disposition and the act declared unconstitutional (Article 176). The Constitutional Tribunal reports annually to the National Congress in writing regarding the performance of its functions (Article 177).

El Salvador

Under the *Constitution* of 15 December 1983, the Supreme Court of Justice has a Constitutional Division, which is empowered to take cognizance of and resolve petitions on the unconstitutionality of statutes, decrees and regulations, cases of *amparo*, *habeas corpus*, and controversies between the Legislature and the Executive branch.

The Constitutional Division is composed of five magistrates appointed by the Legislative Assembly. Its President is elected by the same on each occasion similar to the parliamentary election of Magistrates to the Supreme Court of Justice.

Guatemala

The system of Guatemala can be characterised as a mixed system of constitutional review. The diffuse system was introduced by the *Constitution* of 1921 and was preserved until the *Constitution* of 1965, which is still in force. All courts are empowered to exercise judicial review *ex officio*. Proceedings are *incidenter*, decisions have a declaratory character with *inter partes* and *ex tunc* effect.

Influenced by the European model of constitutional review, the *Constitution* of 1965 introduced a concentrated system of constitutional review (Articles 216 to 265 of the *Constitution*, *i.e.* a tribunal dedicated to deciding constitutional matters - *Corte de Constitucionalidad*). The Constitutional Court has explicit power to determine the unconstitutionality of statutes with *erga omnes* effect. However, this Constitutional Court is not a permanent body, it operates only if constitutional review is necessary. The Court is composed of 12 members. Four members are appointed by the Supreme Court of Justice; the others are appointed also by the Supreme Court but from among members of the Court of Appeals and the Administrative Justice Tribunal. The President of the Constitutional Court is at same time the President of the Supreme Court of Justice. Constitutional review is based on direct requests. However, such requests are not a popular complaint similar to the Venezuelan or Colombian popular complaint, because in Guatemala the circle of petitioners is limited: the National Council, the Public Prosecutor, as well as an individual who is directly affected by an unconstitutional statute or state regulation. In addition, the individuals must have legal counsel. The decisions have *erga omnes* and *ex nunc* effect (in exceptional cases, the Constitutional Court may determine *ex tunc* effect). The Court decisions are published in the Official Gazette (*Diario Official*). The system of Guatemala also includes *amparo* proceedings (following the Mexican model) and *habeas corpus* proceedings. Proceedings before the Constitutional Court are regulated by the *Ley de amparo, habeas corpus y de constitucionalidad* of 3 May 1966.

In general, the *Constitution* of 31 May 1985, amended on 17 November 1993, adopted the same system. In concrete cases, in every proceedings of whatever competence or jurisdiction, in any instance, and in cassation and even before sentence is decreed, the parties are able to lodge as an action, exception, or incident the total or partial unconstitutionality of a statute. The (ordinary) court has to make a determination in that respect (Article 266).

Actions against the statues, regulations or provisions of a general character which contain a partial or total absence of constitutionality are heard directly by the Tribunal or Court of Constitutionality (*Corte de Constitucionalidad*) (Article 267). Under the current system, the Court of Constitutionality is a permanent tribunal of exclusive jurisdiction, whose essential function is the defence of the constitutional order. It acts as a collegiate tribunal with independence from the other State bodies and exercises specific functions assigned to it by the Constitution and the statute in the matter (Article 268). The economic independence of the Court is guaranteed through a percentage of the revenues that correspond to the Judicial branch.

The Court is composed of five members, each of whom has a respective alternate (Article 269). When it is adjudicating matters of unconstitutionality against the Supreme Court of Justice, the Parliament, or the President or Vice-President of the Republic, the number of its members rises to seven, the other two members being selected by lot from among the alternates. The members serve a five year term of office. They are appointed in the following manner:

- one member by the plenary of the Supreme Court of Justice;
- one member by the plenary of the Parliament;
- one member by the President of the Republic;
- one member by the Higher University Council of the State University;
- one member by the Assembly of the Bar Association.

Simultaneously with the appointment of the member, that of the respective alternate occurs before the Parliament.

In order to be a member of the Court, the following requirements must be fulfilled: candidates must be of Guatemalan origin; be a lawyer belonging to the Bar Association; be of recognized integrity; and have at least 15 years of experience (Article 270). The

Court members enjoy the same privileges and immunities as the members of the Supreme Court of Justice.

The Presidency of the Court is filled by the same appointed members on a rotating basis for a term of office of one year, beginning with the eldest member, and following in descending order of age (Article 271).

The Court has the following powers:

- sole jurisdiction to decide charges against statutes or provisions of a general character, and challenges of partial or total unconstitutionality;
- sole jurisdiction to function as Extraordinary Tribunal in *amparo* actions against the Parliament, the Supreme Court of Justice, the President or Vice-President of the Republic;
- to decide on appeal all *amparo* petitions brought before any ordinary court;
- to decide on appeal all petitions against statutes that charge unconstitutionality in concrete cases;
- to issue opinions on the constitutionality of treaties, agreements, and bills, at the request of State bodies;
- to adjudicate any conflict of jurisdiction in matters of constitutionality;
- to compile the doctrine and constitutional principles that have been invoked for the purpose of resolving *amparo* proceedings and the unconstitutionality of statutes, and to keep the legal journal or gazette up to date;
- to issue opinions on the unconstitutionality of statutes vetoed by the executive branch alleging unconstitutionality, and;
- to act, render opinions, dictate, or take cognizance of those matters under its competence established in the *Constitution*.

Honduras

Under the *Constitution of the Republic of Honduras* of 11 January 1982, amended on 30 January 1991, statutes may be declared unconstitutional by reason of form or content (Article 184).

The Supreme Court of Justice has original and exclusive competence over hearing and deciding such matters, and must render its decisions with the requirements of definitive sentences.

Any individual who considers their direct, personal, and legitimate interests affected may request the review of the constitutionality of a statute and its applicability (Article 185):

- by an action filed before the Supreme Court of Justice;
- by a petition which may be asserted in any judicial proceedings;

- a judge or tribunal during any judicial proceedings may directly request a review of the constitutionality of a statute and its applicability before handing down a decision. In such a case, the proceedings are suspended and the case transferred to the Supreme Court of Justice.

In addition, the system of Honduras adopted *habeas corpus* and *amparo* proceedings as forms of constitutional guarantees (Articles 182 and 183).

Mexico

The institution of the constitutional review is firmly grounded in the legal tradition of the country as *amparo*. This institution dates from the draft *Constitution of the State of Yucatan* of 1840. *Amparo* was further adopted by the *Constitution* of 1857 and without many changes by the *Constitution* (in force) of 1917. After the enactment of the *Constitution* of 1917, *amparo* was regulated in detail by the special *Act* of 1919, which was in force until 1936. Since 1936 the present *Amparo Proceedings Act* has been in force.

Amparo (*judicio de amparo*) in Mexico is designed for the review of conformity with the *Constitution*, and was introduced not only for the protection of the supremacy of the *Constitution*, but also for exercising and protecting rights guaranteed by the *Constitution*. The *Constitution* regulated these matters in Article 103. The object of *amparo* proceedings is always high regulations (statutes) which violate the rights guaranteed by the *Constitution*. The review of conformity with the *Constitution* in *amparo* proceedings is in the jurisdiction of the federal judiciary bodies, and takes the form of an *amparo* complaint. Under Article 105 of the *Constitution* in force, the Supreme Court is also empowered to adjudicate jurisdictional disputes between the Federation and federal member states as well as between federal members states and federal member state bodies. The petitioner of such proceedings may be the affected State body.

The *Constitution* of 1847 was adopted under American influence, which resulted in the regulation that federal courts are obliged to protect constitutional rights and freedoms. The same regulation was adopted by the *Constitution* of 1857, which introduced a unique judicial institution, the *judicio de amparo*. At present, the regulation is based on the constitutional text of 1982 (amended from 1989 to 1997), which follows the directives of the 1917 *Constitution*. *Amparo* is based directly on the *Constitution* (Article 103), which completely reserved such proceedings for the federal courts. The effect of an *amparo* decision is *inter partes*; it is only of precedence importance for courts.

Nicaragua

Under the *Constitution* of 19 November 1986, amended on 4 July 1995, the Supreme Court exercises constitutional review. The Court is composed of twelve magistrates elected by the National Assembly (Article 163). The Court is composed of several chambers, among them also the Constitutional Chamber. The organization and membership of chambers is determined by the judges themselves. The full Court takes cognizance of and resolves instances of the unconstitutionality of any law, and conflicts of competence and constitutionality between the powers of the State. The President of the Court is elected from among the judges to a one year term of office with the possibility of re-election.

Among other matters, the Court is empowered to carry out the following functions:

- to take cognizance of and resolve *amparo* proceedings concerning the violation of constitutional rights, in accordance with the *Amparo Act*;
- to take cognizance of and resolve instances of the unconstitutionality of statutes;
- to adjudicate jurisdictional disputes between bodies of the public administration, and between them and individuals;
- to adjudicate jurisdictional disputes between municipalities or between them and bodies of the Central Government;
- to adjudicate jurisdictional disputes between the branches of the State;
- to adjudicate jurisdictional disputes between the central Government and the Municipal Governments and the Autonomous regions of the Atlantic Coast.

Panama

Under the *Constitution* of 11 October 1972, amended in 1972, 1987, 1983, 1993 and 1994, the Supreme Court of Justice guards the integrity of the Constitution (Article 203). The Court in a plenary session tries and rules on cases concerning the unconstitutionality of statutes, decrees, decisions, resolutions and other acts that for reasons of substance or form are challenged before it, by any person.

When during the proceedings of a case, the public official entrusted with the administration of justice considers, or it is observed by one of the parties, that the legal or regulatory provision applicable to the case is unconstitutional, he submits the question to the cognizance of the Court in a plenary session, except when the provision has already been the subject of a decision, and orders a continuance of the case, until the question of constitutionality is decided.

Only the parties are able to formulate such observations at the appropriate moment during the proceedings.

Persons affected by the act, resolution, order or decision in question may request protection by administrative courts; and any individual or legal entity domiciled in the country may file a popular complaint.

The decisions issued by the Supreme Court are final, definitive and binding, and must be published in the official gazette. Neither writ of unconstitutionality, nor constitutional guarantees (*amparo*) can be admitted against Court judgments.

Paraguay

Under the *Constitution* of 20 June 1992, the Supreme Court of Justice has the power to declare any legal provision or Court decision unconstitutional (Article 132). In addition, *habeas corpus*, *amparo* and the *habeas data* proceedings were introduced (Articles 133 to 135).

The Constitutional Chamber of the Supreme Court is empowered to hear and resolve cases involving the unconstitutionality of statutes and other related instruments, declaring inapplicability for each specific case of a legal provision that is contrary to the *Constitution* through rulings that only affect the case in question (Para. 1 of Article 260). Furthermore, the Court is empowered to decide on the unconstitutionality of final or interlocutory decisions, nullifying those that contradict the *Constitution*. Petitions of unconstitutionality may be filed directly before the Constitutional Chamber or by way of defence before any other court and at any moment during a case. In such cases, the respective action is submitted to the Supreme Court.

Peru

Peru has introduced a mixed system. The *Constitution* of 12 July 1979 followed the tradition of the diffuse system (Article 236). All judges were empowered to exercise judicial review in *incidenter* proceedings with decisions having *inter partes* effect. In addition, by the *Constitution* of 1979, also a concentrated system of constitutional review was introduced. The *Tribunal de Garantias Constitucionales* was established (Articles 296 to 305) composed of nine members; three are appointed by the Congress, three by the executive branch and three by the Supreme Court (*La Corte Suprema de la Republica*). Court activities were regulated by the *Court of the Constitutional Guarantees Basic Act No. 23385* of 19 April 1982, amended on 22 August 1985 (*Reforma de la Casacion Constitucional ante el TGC*). This Court was empowered to exercise the constitutional review of legislation and to review decisions decided by lower courts in *habeas corpus* and *amparo* proceedings. These two proceedings had a legal basis in the Constitution. In addition, *habeas corpus* proceedings were regulated by the *La ley de habeas corpus y amparo no 233506*.

Direct petitioning for constitutional review proceedings (*accion de inconstitucionalidad*) was limited to the following petitioners: the President of the Republic, the Supreme Court, the Public Prosecutor of the Republic, a group of 60 members of the Parliament, 20 senators, and 50,000 citizens, whose signatures had to be confirmed by the National Elections Board. The Constitutional Court was not bound by the petition, it was able extend it *ex officio*. The decisions had *erga omnes* effect and only *ex nunc (pro futuro)* effect, however, in exceptional cases an *ex tunc* effect could be determined.

In the past, constitutional review in Peru was exercised based on the constitutional texts in force. At first, such review was exercised by the Central Chamber (1822), the Protective Chamber - *senado conservador* (1823), the Review Sub-Chamber - *camara de censores* (1826), the National Council (1828), and the Congress (1856, 1860, 1867, 1919). In 1931 the American system of diffuse review was adopted. In 1979 the *Tribunal Garantia Constitucionales* was introduced based on the European model. The adoption of the European model was influenced by similar institutions from other Latin American countries: Guatemala (1965), Chile (1970, 1980), and Colombia (1970). A special desire was present to adopt the Austrian model of constitutional review in parallel with the simultaneous existence of the American system of diffuse judicial review. So as a body of concentrated constitutional review, the *Tribunal de Garantias Constitucionales* was established. It was regulated by Articles 296 to 304 of the *Peruvian Constitution* (*Constitucion politica del Peru*) of 28 July 1979. The Tribunal was an independent constitutional body. Its activities were regulated by the *Constitution* and the *Court of the Constitutional Guarantees Basic Act*. The Court was composed of nine members appointed for six years. Three members were appointed by the Congress, three by the executive branch and three by the Supreme Court. Re-election was possible. The candidates had to fulfil the following conditions: 10 years of membership in the Supreme Court or in some other highest court in the country; or 9 years of experience as a law professor; they must have a democratic view of life, and a demonstrated interest in the protection of human rights. The Court had power to decide the following matters: popular complaints containing a request for the constitutional review of statutes; *habeas corpus* and *amparo* proceedings; the constitutional review of all statutorial regulations; jurisdictional disputes between the highest State bodies and between bodies on the level of departments and regions; also the preventive constitutional review of draft statutes. Decisions on unconstitutionality had the force of statute and were published in the Official Gazette.

By the *Constitution* of 29 December 1993 the following constitutional guarantees were introduced (Article 200): the action of *habeas corpus*; the action of *amparo*, the action of *habeas data*; the action of unconstitutionality; the popular action; the *accion de cumplimiento*.

The Constitutional Court is the body that reviews adherence to the Constitution (Article 201). It is autonomous and independent. It is composed of seven members elected for a five-year term.

For membership in the Court, the candidate must meet the same requirements as those mandated for a member of the Supreme Court. The Court members enjoy the same immunities and the same prerogatives as congressmen. They are subject to the same incompatibilities. No immediate re-election to membership is possible. The Court members are elected by the National Congress with affirmative votes of two-thirds of the legal number of its members. Judges of the Constitutional Court, and judges or prosecutors who have not relinquished their position for a year prior, cannot be voted into membership.

The Constitutional Court has the power (Article 202):

- to determine with sole jurisdiction the constitutionality of laws;

- to adjudicate, as the court of last instance, decisions denying *habeas corpus*, *amparo*, *habeas data*, or an executory order;
- to adjudicate jurisdictional disputes.

The following are authorized to initiate a constitutional review: the President of the Republic; the Public Prosecutor; the Defender of the People; 25% of congressmen; a petition by 5,000 citizens whose signatures are confirmed by the National Elections Board; the Presidents of Regions in agreement with the Council of Regional Coordination or provincial mayors in agreement with the Council in matters of their competence; or professional colleges in the fields of their specialty (Article 203).

Decisions of the Constitutional Court which declare the unconstitutionality of a norm are published in the official gazette. On the day following publication, said norm becomes null and void (Article 204). A decision of the Constitutional Court declaring a legal norm unconstitutional in whole or in part does not have retroactive effect. Once domestic remedies have been exhausted, whoever feels that their constitutional rights have been violated in his constitutional rights may resort to international tribunals or organizations established according to treaties or agreements to which Peru is a party (Article 205).

Uruguay

Under the *Constitution* of 17 November 1966, amended on 8 December 1996, statutes and the decrees of the local governments which have the force of law, may be declared unconstitutional by reason of form or content, in accordance with the *Constitution* (Article 256). The Supreme Court of Justice has original and exclusive jurisdiction in the hearing and deciding of such matters, and must render its decision in accordance with the requirement for final decisions (Article 257). The declaration of the unconstitutionality of a statute and the inapplicability of the provisions affected thereby, may be requested by any person who considers that their direct, personal, and legitimate interests have been affected:

- by means of a lawsuit, which must be filed before the Supreme Court of Justice;
- by an objection of unconstitutionality, which may be made in any judicial proceedings.

A judge or court hearing any judicial proceeding, may also request a review of the constitutionality of a statute and its applicability, before rendering a decision (Article 258). In such a case, the proceedings are suspended and the case is referred to the Supreme Court of Justice.

Decisions of the Supreme Court refer exclusively to a concrete case and have effect solely on the proceedings for which they are rendered (Article 259).

Venezuela

Constitutionalisation first began in 1811. However, the *Constitution* of 1961, following the constitutional tradition of the *Constitution* of 1858 (the supremacy of the *Constitution*) established the Supreme Court of Justice as a body empowered to exercise the constitutional review of statutes and other state regulations. At the same time, Article 20 of the *Civil Code* allows all courts in concrete cases to declare all normative acts as void when they are considered unconstitutional. In such a way the diffuse system was introduced. As a diffuse system it has an *incidenter* character and the judges have *ex officio* power. Decisions have a declaratory, *ex tunc* and *pro praeterito* effect (and/or retroactive effect). Despite its non-application in a concrete case, a particular regulation is still valid, because the *Constitution* reserved the determination of the nullity of a statute only for the Supreme Court of Justice. Due to the fact that the principle of *stare decisis* is not applied, a concrete decision is not binding on an individual judge or other judges and courts, which may change their opinion at any time.

To avoid eventual conflicts between judgments concerning constitutional matters, a concentrated system of constitutional review was introduced in parallel by the *Constitution* of 1858. This *Constitution* even introduced a popular complaint on the basis of which the then Supreme Court could declare provincial legislative acts null and void. This power of the Supreme Court was preserved also after the constitutional reform of 1864, despite the extraction of the popular complaint and that the member states of the then federative state received the status of petitioner in such cases. The mentioned power was preserved by the *Constitution* of 1893 until the *Constitution* of 1961 (amended on 16 March 1983), which is still in force. On the basis of this *Constitution*, the activities of the Court are regulated in detail by the *Supreme Court of Justice Basic Act* of 1976. However, the jurisdiction of the Supreme Court was extended to all state regulations. By the same *Act*, the legal basis of the popular complaint was created. The *Constitution* does not require that a particular petitioner have an individual legal interest; the *Supreme Court of Justice Basic Act* has limited such a wide formulation with the condition that the disputed statute must violate the rights and interests of the petitioner. The popular complaint is not bound by a particular term and does not fall under the statute of limitations. Proceedings before the Supreme Court following such a complaint have an objective character. Complaints may be refused by decisions, which have *erga omnes* and *res judicata* effect. Decisions declaring statutes as null and void also have *erga omnes* effect and an absolute character *res judicata*. In such cases review is repressive. Furthermore, the Venezuelan system has featured a preventive review since 1854 exercised by the Supreme Court on the request of the President of the Republic before the promulgation of the relevant statute. The effect of decisions is different depending on the kind of proceedings. If the proceedings are of a diffuse character, the decisions have *inter partes* and *pro praeterito* and/or *ex tunc* effect. Decisions in the concentrated Venezuelan system have *erga omnes* effect. They are constitutive, *pro futuro*, as well as with *ex nunc* effect. The *Supreme Court of Justice Basic Act* of 1976 did not regulate such matters and determined that the Supreme Court alone has to determine the effect of its decisions.

In addition, the system of Venezuela also includes *amparo* proceedings (*derecho de amparo*), which was introduced by Article 49 of the *Constitution* of 1961 with the aim to protect basic rights and freedoms. However, even the former *Constitutions* of Venezuela included *habeas corpus* proceedings (limited only to the protection of personal freedom). *Amparo* proceedings are now regulated by the *Ley Organica de Amparo sobre derechos y garantias constitucionales* of 22 January 1988.

The Former British Colonies of Latin America (The West Indies)

These countries (Barbados, Guiana, Jamaica, and Trinidad and Tobago) did not adopt the English legal system, which does not include a special institution for constitutional review.

Therefore, in the mentioned countries constitutional review is exercised by the highest judicial body in the country: the High Court, the Court of Appeals, and the Privy Council. Constitutional review was introduced concerning the implementation of the principle of the separation of powers, which prevents the usurpation of the judicial function by the legislature.

In contradistinction with the English system, most of the British Commonwealth countries, in particular in the West Indies region, adopted the diffuse system of judicial review. The system of constitutional review in these countries mainly follows the general trends of the diffuse system. However, concerning constitutional matters, in these countries the Supreme Court has the jurisdiction of final appeal. Some countries explicitly empowered courts to exercise constitutional or judicial review, sometimes explicitly this power was assigned to the Supreme Court, *e.g.* Trinidad and Tobago. There the High Court of Justice is empowered also to interpret the *Constitution*.

H. Systems of Constitutional Review in Countries with a Federal State Structure

Constitutional review in the proper sense of the word, taken however from the theoretical point of view, can develop only when instead of the principle of the sovereignty of Parliament[154], there prevails the idea of the supremacy of the *Constitution*,[155] and when constitutional review is performed by a special body, independent of the legislative and executive power.[156] Such approaches were characteristic of development after World War II. On the other hand, constitutional review also involves the principle of the vertical separation of powers. It emerged in federal states, whereby constitutional review was supposed to exert supervision over the federal legislature in relation to member states. In Austria and Switzerland, countries with a tradition in the field of constitutional review, the respective body empowered to perform constitutional review was introduced only on the federal level. In Germany constitutional review was introduced on the federal level as well as on the level of provinces. A similar system was introduced in the former Yugoslavia (1963), as well as in Slovenia and other constituent republics of the former Yugoslavia (1963). After the introduction of constitutional review on the federal level, constitutional review has been adopted in Russia since 1990 also by the federal entities of the Russian Federation. The structure of constitutional review on the federal as well as on the level of member states is still preserved in the present Federal Republic of Yugoslavia and in Bosnia and Herzegovina. A certain special position is accorded to Argentina, where the democratic transformation process in a Federal State first developed in its units, marked by the gradually increasing introduction of elements of constitutional review of different intensity by the individual provinces (Tucuman).

Such a structure of constitutional review was not adopted in the former Czechoslovak Republic; there the Constitutional Court was established only on the federal level. In spite of the efforts in Kwazulu-Natal, constitutional review was created only on the level of the South African Federal State.

Some other federations did not adopt the constitutional review on the level of member states, e.g. Brazil, Canada, Comoros, India, Malaysia, Nigeria, Togo, and the U.S.A., where the respective function has been provided by the Supreme Court or by the Constitutional Court.

In Hong Kong, as a special Administrative Territory of China (after 1 July 1997), a specific system of constitutional review was introduced, where the function of constitutional review is performed predominantly by the Parliament (the National People's Congress) and/or a certain parliamentary body (the Constitutional Committee).

[154] Where the representative body itself decides on the constitutionality of its laws.

[155] Whereunder the Constitution is the basis and the source of all state power.

[156] Not by the Parliament itself, but either by the regular courts or by a special body, such as the Constitutional Court or some other body.

In Switzerland, the Federal Court cannot evaluate federal statutes, generally binding resolutions and ratified international agreements, and in cantons the constitutional review was not introduced. The only federal legislative decisions subject to constitutional review are orders issued by the Federal Executive (Federal Council). The Federal Court exercises its constitutional jurisdiction chiefly with respect to legislative acts and decisions issued by the Cantons. Other disputes brought before the Swiss Federal Court are as follows: conflicts of jurisdiction between Federal and cantonal authorities and disputes concerning voting rights.

On the other hand, some Constitutional Courts are empowered to decide on the conformity of the Constitutions of specific State Regions with the (main) State Constitution (*e.g.*, Georgia, as regards the Abkhasian territory and Uzbekistan, as regards the territory of Karakalpakstan. In addition, the local Karakalpakstan Constitutional Court (the Constitutional Committee of the Karakalpakstan Republic) also exists.

GERMANY

The first integral system of constitutional review on the federal level as well as on the level of member states was introduced in Germany. Beside the Federal Constitutional Court (*Bundesverfassungsgericht*), the member states (*Laender*) established their own Constitutional Courts. Their titles are sometimes "the Constitutional Court (*Verfassungsgerichtshof*)", and sometimes "the State Court (*Staatsgerichtshof*)". All member states except Schleswig-Holstein adopted the constitutional review. At first the Province of Berlin did not establish such a Court in spite of the respective basic provisions in the Berlin Constitution. In addition, the Federal Constitutional Court developed a certain limited system of legal protection as regards the Berlin Province. However, the Constitutional Court of Berlin was finally established by the *Constitutional Court Act of 8 November 1990*. The Schleswig-Holstein Province, on other hand, under the Federal Constitution transferred the function of constitutional review to the Federal Constitutional Court. In addition, the *Constitution of Schleswig-Holstein* did not institute a Constitutional Court on the local level[157]. Until 1993, among the five new German member states, only Sachsen, Sachsen-Anhalt and Brandenburg introduced the constitutional review[158]. However, the constitutional review was not introduced in all German member states with the same intensity. One of the most famous Courts is the Constitutional Court of Bavaria, situated in Munich, because of its tradition. As a matter of fact, the constitutional review in Bavaria has its roots in the Bavarian Constitutions of 1850 and of 1919.

Provincial Constitutional Courts were established in the following German Provinces:

- Baden-Wuerttemberg (based in Stuttgart);
- Bavaria (based in Munich);

[157] *See* Pestalozza, C., *Verfassungsprozessrecht*, Muenchen, C.H. Beck'sche Verlagsbuchhandlung, 1991, p. 372-377.

[158] *See* Schlaiach, K., *Das Bundesverfassungsgericht*, Muenchen, C.H. Beck'sche Verlagsbuchhandlung, 1994, p. 72.

- Berlin (based in Berlin);
- Bremen (based in Bremen);
- Hamburg (based in Hamburg);
- Hessen (based in Wiesbaden);
- Niedersachsen (based in Buckeburg);
- Nordrhein-Westfalen (based in Muenster);
- Rheinland-Pfalz (based in Koblenz);
- Saarland (based in Saarbrücken).

The powers of the Constitutional Courts did not follow any common model, so there are some differences between present Constitutional Courts. In addition, between the Federal Constitutional Court and Provincial Constitutional Courts powers are separated with regard to the principles which represent the general grounds for the separation of powers between the Federal State and the member states. Accordingly, the Federal Constitutional Court is empowered to decide in all cases of federal constitutionality (concerning conformity with the Federal Constitution), while the Constitutional Courts of the member states are empowered to decide in cases of Provincial constitutionality (concerning conformity with their Provincial Constitutions). However, both proceedings can be simultaneous and parallel if the same regulation is concerned. In such cases both Courts (the Federal and the Provincial) coordinate their proceedings. As a rule, the freedom to decide on such issues as "foreign" law is limited, provided that the competent Constitutional Court has already decided the case with *erga omnes* effect. Thus, Provincial Constitutional Courts are bound by the decisions of the Federal Constitutional Court concerning matters of Federal constitutional law, whereas, the Federal Constitutional Court is bound by the decisions of Provincial Constitutional Court cases concerning matters of Provincial constitutional law. The relationship between the Federal Constitutional Court and the Constitutional Courts of member state is expressly determined not only in the German system, but also in some other systems (*e.g.* the FRY).

THE RUSSIAN FEDERATION

Under the *Constitution of the Russian Federation* of 12 December 1993, the Constitutional Court of the Russian Federation consists of 19 judges (Article 125). The Court, on the request of the President of the Federation, the State *Duma*, one-fifth of the members of the Federation Council of Representatives of the State *Duma*, the Government of the Federation, the Supreme Court of the Federation, the Supreme Arbitration Court of the Federation, or bodies of the legislative and executive branches of members of the Federation, resolves cases concerning compliance with the *Constitution* of the Federation of:

- federal statutes, normative acts of the President of the Federation, the Federation Council, the State *Duma* and the Government of the Federation;
- republican constitutions, charters, as well as statutes and other normative acts of members of the Federation published on issues pertaining to the jurisdiction of

bodies of State power of the Federation and the joint jurisdiction of bodies of State power of the Federation and bodies of State power of members of the Federation;

- agreements between State bodies of the Federation and bodies of State power of members of the Federation, and agreements between bodies of State power of members of the Federation;
- international agreements of the Federation that have not entered into force.

In addition, the Constitutional Court resolves jurisdictional disputes:

- between the Federal State bodies;
- between State bodies of the Federation and State bodies of the members of the Federation;
- between supreme State bodies of members of the Federation.

The Constitutional Court of the Federation, in proceedings following complaints concerning the violation of the constitutional rights and freedoms of citizens and requests from courts, reviews the constitutionality of the statute applied or due to be applied in a concrete case in accordance with proceedings determined by federal statute.

The federal Constitutional Court, on the request of the President of the Federation, the Federation Council, the State *Duma*, the Government of the Russian Federation, or legislative bodies of members of the Federation, interprets the federal *Constitution*.

Acts and their provisions deemed unconstitutional do not have force thereof. International agreements of the Federation may not be enforced and applied if they violate the federal *Constitution*.

The Federal Constitutional Court on request of the Federation Council rules on compliance with established proceedings when charging the President of the Federation with state treason or other serious crimes.

Judges of the federal Constitutional Court are appointed by the Federation Council following nomination by the President of the Federation (Article 128).

The powers of the federal Constitutional Court are established by federal statute.

In the Russian Federation the Constitutional Courts of the following federal entities were established in addition to the federal Constitutional Court: Adigea (based in Mojkop); Baskhiria (based in Ufa); Buryatia (based in Ulan-Ude); Dagestan (based in Mahačkala); Irkutska Oblast (based in Irkutsk); the Kabardino/Balkar Republic (based in Nalčik); Karelia (based in Petrozavodsk); Koma (based in Siktivkar); Northern Ossetia (based in Vladikavkaz); Tatarstan (based in Kazan) and Tuba (based in Kizil); and Yakutia/Sakha (based in Yakutsk). Subsequently, Constitutional Courts were also introduced in the following federal units: Altai, Chuvachia, Inguchia, Kakasa, the Karachewo-Cherkez Republic, Khalmukia, Marii-el, Udmurtia. Particularities of constitutional review systems of federal entities are presented in detail in *Chapter XIV*.

Particularities of the Constitutional Review in Some Countries/Constitutional Review in the New Democracies.

Argentina

Particularities of the Argentinean constitutional review system are presented in detail in Chapter XIV. Particularities of the Constitutional Review in Some Countries/Central and South America/The Particular Systems of Constitutional Review/Argentina.

The Former SFRY and Present FR of Yugoslavia

Before 1963 the Yugoslav system for the protection of constitutionality and legality included the review of the constitutionality and legality of rules under the principle of self-review within the parliamentary system. The authors of the project that introduced constitutional review came to the conclusion that this review lacked efficiency because - in so far as it was practiced - it was mainly oriented to the conformity of the policy expressed in some rules and less to legality in its literal meaning. As far as the latter is concerned it was too tolerant, and therefore inefficient. This led to a search for a new solution to these problems. Practice, however, revealed that legislative and executive bodies were, mainly for objective reasons, unable to review the constitutionality and legality of the rules objectively and critically, because they were themselves their authors.

The experiences from elsewhere in the world proved the same - it was a period of many new constitutional review systems. On these grounds it was generally believed that the protection of the constitutionality and legality of rules would favour special autonomous bodies, independent of the legislative and executive powers. In this period more and more countries introduced special bodies of constitutional review, especially Constitutional Courts, whereof the main task was to evaluate the conformity of legal rules with the Constitution as well as to abrogate and annul unconstitutional or illegal rules. Such decisions issued by the Constitutional Court actually have the power of Law, because they affect everyone to whom such invalidated provisions refer; as such this encroaches upon the sphere of the legislature or other measure-imposing bodies. Leaving decisions on such disputes to a third, neutral, body which is supposed to issue decision mainly with reference to reasons based on constitutional law and after certain proceedings before the Constitutional Court, actually entails the de-politicisation of such disputes and minimizes arbitrariness, which is in the interest of the stabilisation of the legal system. Constitutional review was expected to contribute to the faster and more efficient elimination of unconstitutional and illegal phenomena and negative tendencies; at the same time it should also introduce more democratic methods and flexibility when solving such problems. If such functions were performed by government bodies, they would, according to the then belief, not only deal with the problems of legality, but would also interpose themselves as eager political agents.

Hence, this all led to the introduction of special constitutional bodies, whereof the constitutional review would limit the field of legislative, and partly also executive, power, and which would be, above all, apolitical supervisory bodies of special types, featuring various additional, distinctly judicial, powers, including the basic power to review the constitutionality of statutes. The intention of the then Yugoslav constitutional order was that the new Constitutional Courts were supposed to act as a part of the parliamentary system and not as classical judicial bodies such as might be inferred from the name itself. This, however, did not mean that the decision-making process of Constitutional Courts could be identified with the legislative function. The then theory on constitutional law, however, did not accept Kelsen's view whereunder decisions issued by the Constitutional Court relating to the constitutionality of statutes is actually a legislative function, but rather considered that in such cases decisions issued by Constitutional Courts should be understood as individual acts rather than general acts. On the introduction of constitutional review, the political aspect of constitutionality and legality was attributed great importance. At the same time Constitutional Courts should have the least possible restriction on the method of their operation, their preparations for decisions, discussions and decision-making process (except for the basic rules of procedure specified by law). In all cases, however, Constitutional Courts depended on applications lodged by petitioners or proponents.

The *1963 Yugoslav Federal Constitution* as well as the 1963 *Constitutions* of former constituent republics introduced the constitutional review on the federal as well as on the level of constituent republics. The *Constitution of the Republic of Slovenia of 1963* (Official Gazette SRS, No. 10/63) envisaged the first former constituent republic Constitutional Court[159].

The constitutional courts were a new institution for the protection of constitutionality and legality that had not existed in the former constitutional system: the Constitutional Court as an independent body with precisely specified powers in the field of constitutionality and legality protection, a special body in addition to the bodies of the parliamentary system in the narrow sense of the word and in addition to the already existing bodies within the system of ordinary justice. At first constitutional review was concerned with discussions on its compatibility with the principle of the unity of powers, as this was the leading principle of the legal system. The actual turning-point in favour of the introduction of the constitutional review into the legal system was brought about by the positive attitude of the leading political structure to the institution of the constitutional review in the proceedings preceding the adoption of the *Constitution of 1963*. In addition to the Federal Constitutional Court in charge of protecting federal constitutionality, constituent republic constitutional courts were

[159] The *Constitutional Court Act* (Official Gazette SRS, Nos. 39/63 and 1/64) specified the power of and the proceedings before the Constitutional Court; it determined that it should start functioning on 15 February 1964. The Assembly of the SRS elected the first President and eight judges of the Constitutional Court on 5 June 1963 (the resolution on their election was published in the Official Gazette SRS, No. 22/63). The President and the judges were sworn in before the President of the Assembly on 15 February 1964. The first Rules of Procedure of the Constitutional Court were adopted on 23 February 1965 (Official Gazette SRS, No. 11/65).

also established in charge of protecting constituent republic constitutionality; they did not represent a different instance in relation to the Federal Constitutional Court.[160]

The *Constitution* of 1974 reorganized the position and the powers of the Slovenian Constitutional Court (Official Gazette SRS No. 6/74); more detailed provisions on powers and proceedings were defined in the *Constitutional Court of the Socialist Republic of Slovenia Act* (Official Gazette SRS, No. 39/74 and 28/76); new *Rules of Procedure of the Constitutional Court* were also adopted (Official Gazette SRS, No. 10/74).

Under constituent republic Constitutions of 1974 the jurisdiction of their constitutional courts was based on the separation of jurisdictions between the Federation and the constituent republics and Autonomous Provinces; each of these constitutional courts acted with due institutional independence in compliance with the powers specified in the constitution of the appropriate level, whereby the constitutional courts were in no hierarchical relation to one another and the Federal Constitutional Court was not an instance above other constitutional courts, nor was the constituent republic Constitutional Court an instance above provincial constitutional courts. However, the then Federal Constitutional Court was empowered to decide on jurisdictional disputes between the constitutional courts of constituent republics and/or Autonomous Provinces. The proceedings before the constitutional courts followed the rules of procedure adopted by the constitutional courts themselves, pursuant to the idea that the proceedings before the Constitutional Court should omit formality and any bureaucratic approach to the benefit of efficiency and promptness. Therefore, elements of traditional and contradictory judicial proceedings were omitted from the rules of procedure.

Accordingly, the constitutional courts were established and their powers were specified in compliance with the *Constitution*. In individual constituent republics and autonomous provinces their position and the respective proceedings were also specified in detail in *Constitutional Court Acts* or even in internal regulations that, as a rule, regulated only their organization and internal operation. Individual constitutional courts had different numbers of members. The constitutional court judges were elected by the Parliaments, their term of office was eight years without the possibility of re-election to the same Court. The President of the Constitutional Court was elected from among the judges for a shorter term of office, most often for a period of 4 years, without the possibility of re-election to the same office. The judges enjoyed parliamentary immunity.

On the one hand, stress was laid on the autonomy and the independence of the Constitutional Court, on the other hand, the courts stressed the need for cooperation with government bodies and the protection of constitutionality and legality, because the Constitutional Court could not be an isolated and closed institution.

---

[160] In practice, such relations between Constitutional Courts were not easily established, which was also due to inadequate and inaccurate distinctions between the legislative powers of the Federation and the constituent republics, and, in particular, as then believed by the Slovenian Constitutional Court, due to the not very reasonable specification of the powers of the Federal Constitutional Court. The constitutional review in both Autonomous Provinces (Vojvodina, Kosovo), introduced in 1972, existed till 1991, when the jurisdiction of the Serbian Constitutional Court was extended over the whole territory of the constituent Republic of Serbia.

This initial period was characterized by a small number of applications lodged with the Constitutional Courts (also due to the relatively low normative power of the constituent republics), and individual petitions prevailed. In spite of the rare notion that the powers of constitutional courts should be extended, in particular to electoral cases, impeachment, the constitutional review of referendums, the preventive constitutional review of international treaties, or even to the constitutional review of the then citizens' associations, officially the opinion was adopted that the usefulness of the constitutional judiciary should be preserved in the legal system, without extension of its powers. The constitutional courts should limit themselves to constitutionality and legality, whereas all other questions relating to the individual belong to the sphere of other bodies outside the constitutional courts.

The present constitutional review in the FRY has been carried out by the Federal Constitutional Court and the Constitutional Courts of the Republic of Serbia/the FRY and Montenegro/the FRY. The *Constitution of the FRY* (Official Gazette FRY, No. 1/92) and the *Federal Constitutional Court Act* (Official Gazette FRY, No. 36/92) regulate the organization, proceedings, as well as the powers of the Federal Constitutional Court. The *Constitution of the Republic of Serbia* (Official Gazette, No. 1/90) and the *Proceedings Before the Constitutional Court of Serbia and the Legal Effect of its Decisions Act* (Official Gazette, No. 32/91), the *Constitution of the Republic of Montenegro* (Official Gazette, No. 48/92) and the *Constitutional Court of Montenegro Act* (Official Gazette, No. 44/75) regulate the organization, powers and the proceedings before the Constitutional Court of both constituent republics. The constitutional courts of the constituent republics are independent of the Federal Constitutional Court[161]. The Federal Constitutional Court does not have the position of the highest court, or even the position of a "Supreme Court". The Federal Constitutional Court is composed of seven members (Para. 1 of Article 2 of the *Federal Constitutional Court Act*) with a tenure of 2 years. The Powers of the Federal Constitutional Court under Article 124 of the *Federal Constitution* reflect the relation between the Federation and constituent republics. The Federal Constitutional Court decides on:

- the conformity of the Constitutions of constituent republics with the *Federal Constitution* (*in meritum*);
- the conformity of laws and executive regulations with the *Federal Constitution* and with ratified international agreements (the unconstitutional law/executive regulation can be abrogated);
- the conformity of the laws and executive regulations of constituent republics with Federal Law (the illegal law/executive regulation can be abrogated);
- the conformity of other federal regulations with Federal Law;
- the conformity of acts and activities of political parties with the *Federal Constitution* and Federal Law;
- constitutional complaints in relation to violations of constitutional rights by individual acts;

[161] See Srdić, *Pravna zaštita pred Ustavnim sudom*, Beograd, Službeni glasnik, 1993, p. 25.

- jurisdictional disputes between Federal bodies and constituent republics and between constituent republics themselves;
- appeals in relation to violations of rights concerning Federal elections.

BOSNIA AND HERZEGOVINA[162]

e.1. According to the Dayton Agreement, the Constitutional Court (Annex 4, Article VI) has appellate jurisdiction over constitutionality issues arising out of a judgment of any other court in Bosnia and Herzegovina (Article VI para. 3 (b); this may include human rights disputes (cf. Article II).

The Court is to have jurisdiction over issues referred to it by any court in the country on whether a law on whose validity its decision depends, is compatible with the *Constitution*, with the *European Convention for Human Rights and Fundamental Freedoms and its Protocols* or with rules of public international law pertinent to the court's decision (Article VI para 3 (c)).

It also has jurisdiction to decide any dispute between the entities that arises under the *Constitution* between the Entities (the Federation of Bosnia and Herzegovina and the Serbian Republic of Bosnia) and the central Government, and between the Entities themselves, or between institutions of Bosnia and Herzegovina including the question of the compatibility of an *Entities' Constitution* with the *Constitution of Bosnia and Herzegovina* (Article VI, para. 3 (a)).

The Court is composed of nine members: four from the Federation of Bosnia and Herzegovina, two from the Serbian Republic of Bosnia and three non-citizens of Bosnia and Herzegovina from countries selected by the President of the European Court of Human Rights.

e.2. The Constitution of the Serbian Republic of Bosnia: The Constitutional Court (Article 120 - Article 125) decides on:

- the conformity of laws, other regulations and general enactments with the *Constitution*;
- the conformity of regulations and general enactments with the law;
- conflicts of jurisdiction between agencies of legislative, executive and judicial authorities;
- conflicts of jurisdiction between agencies of the Republic, and regions, cities and municipalities;
- the conformity of programs, statutes and other general enactments of political organisations with the *Constitution* and the law.

In accordance with *Amendment XLII*, the Constitutional Court monitors constitutionality and legality by providing constitutional bodies with opinions and

[162] Working Document 1 CDL - 020/96 prepared by the Secretariat of the Venice Commission of the Council of Europe.

proposals for enacting laws to ensure the "protection of the freedoms and rights of citizens".

The Constitutional Court may initiate proceedings on constitutionality and legality itself. Moreover, anyone "can initiate such proceedings.

The Court is composed of 7 Judges with a tenure of 8 years, after which they cannot be re-elected. The President of the Constitutional Court is elected by the National Assembly for a three-year term, after which he cannot be re-elected. Its proceedings, the legal effect of its decisions and other questions of its organization and work are regulated by law.

e.3. The Constitution of the Federation of Bosnia and Herzegovina (proposed in the Washington Agreement of February 1994): The primary functions of the Constitutional Court (Chapter IV, Section C, Articles 9-13) are to resolve disputes between Cantons; between any Canton and the Federation Government; between any Municipality and its Canton or the Federation Government; and between or within any of the institutions of the Federation Government.

It also determines, on request, whether a law or a regulation is in accord with the *Constitution of the Federation*. The Supreme Court, the Human Rights Court or a Cantonal Court has the obligation to submit any concerns of whether an applicable law is not in accord with the *Constitution* to the Constitutional Court. Decisions are final and binding.

According to the *Federation Constitution* (Chapter II, A, Article 6) "all courts . . shall apply and conform to the rights and freedoms provided in the instruments listed in *Annex to the Federation Constitution* (this includes the *European Convention for Human Rights and Fundamental Freedoms*).

The Court is composed of nine Judges.

XVI. International Associations of Bodies Exercising Constitutional/Judicial Review:

Generally speaking, the role of constitutional review has been expanding; at the same time individual constitutional courts increasingly share more common elements regarding organization, proceedings, and rationales for their decisions and opinions. An important stimulus is provided also by the integrational tendencies in constitutional justice.

An example of such a semi-official conduit is the European Conference of Constitutional Courts established in 1972 in Dubrovnik in the former Yugoslav Federation, which includes almost 40 European and non-European countries[163] . This is possible due to the already existing similar functional principles, common to all constitutional systems. The Conference exists as a forum for the international exchange of opinions in the field of constitutional review. These are meetings of "pure" constitutional courts and other corresponding institutions of constitutional review. The work of constitutional courts is, in many respects, of far-reaching importance. They contribute to the strengthening and better articulation of constitutional case-law.

The chronicle of Conferences to date:

I. Dubrovnik, from 17 October to 20 October 1972

II. Baden-Baden, from 14 October to 16 October 1974

III. Rome, from 20 October to 22 October 1976

IV. Vienna, from 16 October to 18 October 1978

V. Lausanne, from 26 October to 28 October 1981

VI. Madrid, from 23 October to 25 October 1984

VII. Lisbon, from 27 April to 29 April 1987

VIII. Ankara, from 7 May to 10 May 1990

IX. Paris, from 10 may to 13 May 1993

X. Budapest, from 4 May to 9 May 1996

XI. Warsaw, from 16 May to 20 May 1999

Since 1972 constitutional courts have been cooperating within this informal Conference of constitutional courts. Such periodical working meetings are important from many points of view. The Conference entails a certain wider form than traditional bilateral and informative contacts between constitutional courts, and provides an extension and deepening of such contacts. Following a period of development,

[163] The Full members of the Conference are: Andorra, Austria, Belgium, Bulgaria, Croatia, the Czech Republic, Cyprus, France, Germany, Hungary, Italy, Liechtenstein, Lithuania, Malta, Poland, Portugal, Russia, Romania, Slovakia, Slovenia, Spain, Switzerland, Turkey. The associated members are: Albania, Armenia, Belarus, Bosnia and Herzegovina, the FYROM, Georgia and Moldavia. The current candidates for the Conference are: Ukraine and Uzbekistan.

constitutional case-law became stronger and deeper. The courts established working contacts and exchanged opinions, which finally resulted in a loose association.

The initiators of the first meeting of the Conference of constitutional courts in Dubrovnik were the Federal constitutional court of the former Yugoslav Federation and the Constitutional, Courts of Italy and the Federal Republic of Germany. Subsequently the Constitutional Court of Austria, the French Constitutional Council and the Swiss Federal Supreme Court also joined. It was decided that the courts would meet every three years, and that a particular preliminary preparatory meeting of presidents and secretaries would be held in the country of the particular court which was next due to host the Conference.

The participants of the first Conference underlined first of all the general importance of professional meetings for the development of international cooperation between the constitutional courts, as well as for better understanding and protection of constitutionality and legality irrespective of all the differences between various social, economic and political systems. The Conference is the sole international forum where basic questions on constitutional review can be discussed on a comprehensive comparative basis.

The first contact committee of the Conference was composed of the Constitutional Courts of Austria, Germany, Italy and Yugoslavia. The international cooperation resulted from an initiative by the Federal Constitutional Court of Yugoslavia. Following this initiative, the first Conference was held from 17 to 20 October 1972 in Dubrovnik. The Conference discussed the powers of the constitutional courts as well as the effects of their decisions. The first Conference was attended by the following Constitutional Courts and other institutions exercising constitutional review: Austria, France, Germany, Italy, Romania, Switzerland and Yugoslavia.

This group (or association) of constitutional courts is not an institutionalised body; it works if necessary on the request of one of its members. Its competencies are the preparatory activities for the conference, and the determination of conference topics. This lax association is mainly guided by the mentioned constitutional courts as well as by the Swiss Federal Court, which also has a long tradition. Subsequently, some other courts joined this leading group, e.g. the Constitutional Courts of Spain and Portugal, as well as the French Constitutional Council.

The Conference is an instrument which has promoted the usefulness of constitutional review, including the constitutional protection of human rights and freedoms. The Conference has supported the introduction of the constitutional review in particular countries where such an institution had not been known before. In addition, the Conference has contributed to the strengthening of the status of the constitutional court within the national legal system of every country hosting the Conference.

The location and topic of the next Conference are decided during the previous Conference. The official language of the Conference is the language of the country (of the constitutional court) hosting the Conference. Reports on the Conference have been predominantly published in the European Human Rights Magazine. The Conference has not adopted its own permanent rules of procedure; every Conference has adopted new rules of procedure, but the respective text has remained unchanged.

The activities of the Conference are closed to the public. However, the public is informed of the ceremonial opening and of the final official report of the Conference. No formal conclusions of the Conference concerning proposed and/or discussed topics or questions have been reached, but in any case a final official report has to be accepted and published. The body which initiates and reaches decisions in practice is a select group of presidents and secretaries general of various constitutional courts. The President of each Conference is the President of the Constitutional Court hosting the Conference. In principle, the decisions of the Conference are issued by consensus.

The organisational costs of the Conference are divided between the members. Each delegation covers its own travel and accommodation expenses. The Constitutional Court organising the conference covers the main part of the organisational costs.

The number of delegation members is limited to 4 judges and a secretary, however this number is often exceeded. Participation in the Conferences was mainly limited to European countries, along with some observers, or associated members from other parts of the world. Furthermore, the Conference has not been attend by the constitutional courts of the member states of federal countries.

The Conferences are meetings of "pure" constitutional courts and other sate institutions exercising constitutional review. The Conference participants are the constitutional courts which have already been organisers of Conferences, as well as constitutional courts which have been accepted as members of the Conference on the basis of written requests and submitted reports concerning the activities of their Courts. The Conference does not have a permanent Secretary, it works only as a select group and in plenary sessions (the assembly of the officially participating constitutional courts).

The Commission for Democracy through Law (the Venice Commission) of the Council of Europe, established in 1990, includes almost 50 European and non-European countries; The Commission homepage[164] also includes many links to Internet sites with information on constitutional courts or equivalent bodies of member states, associate members and Commission observers.[165]

The first attempts to establish the Venice Commission were presented at the European Conference of Constitutional Courts, which was held in 1987 in Lisbon. The greatest supporters of this idea were the then presidents of the Constitutional Courts of Italy and Germany. The Commission was formally established at the Conference of

164 http://www.coe.fr//

165 Members appointed by the member States of the partial agreement: Albania, Austria, Belgium, Bulgaria, Croatia, the Czech Republic, Cyprus, Denmark, Estonia, Finland, the Former Yugoslav Republic of Macedonia, France, Germany, Greece, Hungary, Iceland, Ireland, Italy, Latvia, Liechtenstein, Lithuania, Luxembourg, Malta, Moldavia, Netherlands, Norway, Poland, Portugal, Romania, San Marino, Slovakia, Slovenia, Spain, Sweden, Switzerland, Turkey and Ukraine. Associate members: Armenia, Azerbaijan, Belarus, Bosnia and Herzegovina, Georgia. Observers: Argentina, Canada, Japan, Kyrgyzstan, Uruguay, the U.S.A. and the Vatican. South Africa has a special cooperative status.

European Foreign Ministers of January 1990 in Venice. Therefore, the Commission was called the Venice Commission. In May of 1990 the Charter of the Commission was adopted on the basis of a special agreement, and closed with the Council of Europe. The member states of the Council of Europe are not members of the Venice Commission automatically. It is necessary to apply for membership on the basis of an appropriate document.

The first session of the Commission was in 1991 in Italy. The Venice Commission also has some sub-commissions, which have been dealing with theoretical and practical problems related to the constitutional systems in the member states. The Commission includes 37 full members, five associated members and eight observers. The members of the Commission are mainly European countries, however also some non-European countries are represented[166].

The main task of the Commission is to promote the principle of the Separation of Powers, the principle of the Rule of Law and a Social Welfare State, support the development of the judicial review of constitutionality as well as to promote the development of the information bases of bodies exercising constitutional review in member states. Beside the countries with constitutional review systems with a long tradition, there are member states where this institution is still in the process of being adopted and developed.

The aim of the activities of the Venice Commission is to implement the principles of the European legal heritage in national constitutional and legal systems. The seat of the Commission is in Strasbourg, the permanent meeting place is in Venice. The members of the Commission are mainly lawyers and experts in constitutional law. An important form of the Commission's activities are specialized seminars, the so-called *UniDem* seminars, where global problems are discussed which concern all constitutional systems, *e.g.* human rights protection, referendums, the federal structure of states, constitutional review, *etc.*

The results of the Commission's activities are as follows:

- the establishment of a common documentation centre;
- a collection of data concerning the activities of constitutional courts, in English, French and in national languages;
- the CODICES database (case-law, systemic legislation, literature);
- a CD-ROM containing case-law, Constitutions and Constitutional Court Acts, as well as the text of the European Convention for the Protection of Human Rights and Fundamental Freedoms;
- the Bulletin on Constitutional Case-Law;
- a systematic thesaurus in French and English, which is implemented as a standard in the preparation of different documents for a common data base;

[166] Argentina, Canada, Japan, Morocco, Paraguay, South Africa, South Korea and the USA.

- a Network for the cooperation of bodies exercising constitutional review, on the Internet;
- E-mail conferences between member states of the Venice Commission;
- a connection with the data base of the newly established Association of French speaking constitutional courts;
- the *UniDem* seminars and workshops in the member states, in which complex topics concerning constitutional review are discussed following the proposals of host countries;
- comparative analyses of particular institutions of constitutional review (the composition of constitutional courts, their powers, the elections of judges, the term of office, *etc.*).

The CIS Conference of New Democracies was founded in October 1997 in Yerevan, Armenia.[167] The first organised meeting of the newly established Conference was held in Minsk in June 1998.

The South American Group of Constitutional Courts was founded in 1992 in San Jose, Costa Rica, where the first conference of this group of countries was held, and includes 10 Countries. The first conference of this group of countries was also held there. In addition, a Group of Spanish Speaking Constitutional Courts was established (the Ibero-American Conference of Constitutional Review), composed of such countries as Costa Rica, Guatemala, Paraguay, Venezuela, Mexico, Nicaragua, Peru, Brazil, Spain, and Portugal. The first conference of this Group was held in Lisbon (constitutional review in general), the second in Madrid (the individual complaint before the constitutional court), but the third one in Guatemala City in 2000.

The Arab Group of Constitutional Courts and Constitutional Councils was founded on 25 and 26 February 1997 in Cairo, Egypt, where the first conference of this group of countries was held, and comprises 11 Countries[168]. The first conference adopted the Charter of the Group regulating its organization and activities.

In addition, the West African Association of the Supreme Courts using the French Language (A.O.A.-H.J.F.) was established on 10 November 1998 in Cotonou (Benin). The Association supports cooperation between institutions that promote the development of the role of the judiciary concerning the consolidation of democracy and the principle of the Rule of Law.

---

[167] The Conference as a consultative body includes the following countries: Armenia, Belarus, Kazakhstan, Kyrgyzstan, Russia and Tadjikistan.

[168] Tunisia, Algeria, Sudan, Palestine, Kuwait, Libanon, Libya, Egypt, Morocco, Mauritania and Yemen.

The Association of Constitutional Courts using the French Language - A.C.C.P.U.F., established in 1997 in Paris, includes 49 European and non-European countries.[169]

The first conference of this Association was held in Paris in 1997, the second in Beirut in September 1998.

Another more recent feature tending to integrate information systems are (1) the information system of European and some non-European constitutional/judicial review bodies, managed by the Venice Commission of the Council of Europe since 1991, and (2) the recently developed Internet connection of the constitutional courts. Furthermore, the mentioned associations, particularly the A.C.C.P.U.F., are also more or less supported by a computerised documentation service or a respective centre.

[169] Albania, Algeria, Armenia, Belgium, Benin, Bulgaria, Burkina Faso, Burundi, Cambodia, Cameroon, Canada, Cape Verde, the Central African Republic, Chad, Comoros, Congo, Djibuti, Egypt, Equatorial Guinea, France, the FYROM, Gabon, Guinea, Guniea Bissao, Haiti, the Ivory Coast, Laos, Lebanon, Luxembourg, Madagascar, Mali, Mauritania, Mauritius, Moldavia, Monaco, Morocco, Niger, Poland, Romania, Senegal, the Seychelles, Slovenia, Switzerland, Syria, Togo, Tunisia, Vanuatu, Vietnam, Zaire.

XVII. The Basic Goals, Some Tendencies and the Logic of the Development of Systems of Constitutional Review

The protection of constitutionality and legality is reflected in the constitutionally assured protection of constitutionality and legality (the judicial review of constitutionality). This was introduced on the basis of the realization that also State bodies can violate the constitution, and was more firmly established with written constitutions. The ideal ground of constitutional review involves the principle that the constitution is the highest legal act, which in the hierarchy is above all other general legal acts (and particular statutes). Constitutional review is the highest remedy among the legal remedies for the protection of constitutionality and legality. It would be excessive to assert that it is impossible to consider as constitutional such constitutional systems which do not have an appropriate legal guarantee of constitutionality. However, it is necessary to take into consideration the fact that the protection of constitutionality by different forms of judicial review is one of the most important guarantees for the enforcement of the socio-political system determined by the constitution.

Constitutional justice (in particular concerning the European model of constitutional review) is a part of the political system and its basic function is to protect the socio-political relations determined by the constitution, whose legal basis is dependent on different systems of constitutional review. For the implementation of constitutionality and legality, appropriate social and political guarantees are necessary[170]. Only once the appropriate social conditions are fulfilled, does the judicial review of constitutionality become reasonable and important, because only then can constitutionality be implemented also by legal remedies. Constitutional review is as such a legal form which attempts to assure the consideration of the constitution by repressive remedies. In comparison with other legal remedies, constitutional review protects and implements the constitution as the highest legal and political act. Therefore, constitutional justice is the highest protector of constitutionality. As such, the institution it is not a part of the ordinary judiciary. It is a special institution which can not be identified with the judiciary, legislature or with some other legal activity. Constitutional justice has a special function which is of a legal and political nature. Its aim is, in case of necessity, to (indirectly) assure the basic rights and freedoms of humans and citizens by repressive remedies. Constitutional justice is a part of the political system which endeavours to protect in a legal form basic socio-political relations. Therefore constitutional justice differs from the judiciary in that it has a completely different function - *i.e.* protection on the grounds, *i.e.* the Constitution, of a given social and political order. Constitutional justice and review can act only within a stable social and political system, where the social forces are ready to respect the decisions of bodies exercising the judicial review of constitutionality. Although constitutional review is fundamentally of a repressive character, it may have a preventive function within a

[170] *See* Rupnik, J., Ustavnost, demokracija in politični sistem, Založba Obzorja Maribor 1975, p. 15-150.

stable political system. Simply the existence of constitutional review should influence the consideration of the constitution.

Theory distinguishes wider and narrower senses of constitutional review. Constitutional review in a wider sense of the word means the deciding of constitutional disputes in a judicial form with the aim to protect the constitution. In a narrower sense of the word, constitutional review is an evaluation of the conformity of statutes with the constitution, *i.e.* the review of the constitutionality of statutes. Constitutional review can act only within the system of a compact (rigid) constitution. If the constitution may be changed only by ordinary statute, *i.e.* by ordinary legislative procedure, the judicial review of constitutionality would be without sense. The more the constitution is compact (rigid) the more it corresponds to the judicial review of constitutionality.

It is possible to speak about "real" constitutional review when the material meaning of constitutionality is taken into consideration. Constitutional review reflects the realization that also legislative bodies can violate the basic rights of humans and citizens. Therefore, constitutional review is closely bound with the consideration of such rights.

The constitution is a basic legal and political act. Therefore, constitutional disputes are legal concerning form, and political concerning contents. Because the constitution is a legal and political act, it is clear that the protection and implementation of the constitution is a basic question of every democratic political system. The basic function of constitutional justice is the protection of the constitution. In this function constitutional justice also reviews the activities of legislative and administrative bodies. This role of constitutional justice necessarily has a political nature. The specific nature of constitutional justice is reflected in the possibility of reviewing legislative and administrative bodies.

Constitutional review may not contradict itself. Therefore the bodies that carry out the judicial review of constitutionality must consider some unwritten rules. Among others, these include that the constitutional review exercising the review of the constitutionality of statutes must interpret the constitution in accordance with valid social and political principles. In addition, the constitutional court must equally evaluate the unconstitutionality of statutes form the point of view of the contents as well as from the point of view of formal constitutionality. The basic principles and the basic rights are the framework which determines the competence of the legislature. Consequently, the constitutional court is bound by basic human rights, although it protects these rights indirectly when evaluating the conformity of a statute with the constitution. Such conformity has to be material and formal. Constitutional review is, when necessary, the instrument of the rule of law. Furthermore, the rule of law involves the consideration of individuals as the subject of the political system, as well as constitutionality as a historically introduced political and legal category.

The basic function of the judicial protection of constitutionality is to decide if statutes and executive regulations are in conformity with the constitution. Therefore, the interpretation of the constitution is the basic activity of bodies exercising the judicial review of constitutionality. This interpretation entails a comparison of two regulations which are on different level of the legal hierarchy, *i.e.* a comparison of a lower regulation with a higher one. The basic aim of such interpretation is to give or to determine the appropriate meaning (the contents) of constitutionality as concerns a concrete case, however, having an *erga omnes* effect. This comparison involves the comparison of the contents and the form.

Constitutional review in the world has reflected and still reflects different social and political interests, depending on particular social and political relations within concrete political systems. Therefore it is impossible to speak about a certain positive or negative function of this institution. In any case, the function of constitutional review is the protection of social and political regulation. Constitutional review is a legal remedy, by its contents and consequences it can intervene into political circumstances. It may be taken to be one of the most important guarantees for the secure stability of a particular political system, because it potentially limits the self-interest of the highest bodies of authority, in particular the legislative, executive and administrative branches.

XVIII. Conclusion

Enclosed Materials

1. Bibliography on Comparative Constitutional/Judicial Review General:

Boeckenfoerde, Ernst Wolfgang, Verfassungsgerichtsbarkeit: Strukturfragen, Organization, Legitimation, NJW 1999, Heft 1, p. 9-17

Capeletti, M., *The Judicial Process in Perspective*, Chapt. 3, published in 58 Cal. L. Rev. 1017(1970), published also in Beatty D., Comparative Constitutional Law, Faculty of Law, University of Toronto, Spring 1994, p. I-1/I-11.

Mavčič, A., Slovenian Constitutional Review, Its Position in the World and Its Role in the Transition to a New Democratic System, Ljubljana. Založba Nova revija, 1995

Mavčič, A., The Slovenian Constitutional Review, An Exception Among Systems and Experiences in the New Democracies, Journal of Constitutional Law in Central and Eastern Europe, No. 4/2 (1997), p. 169

Mavčič, A., *The Citizen as an Applicant Before the Constitutional Court*, Report on the Seminar organised by the European Commission for Democracy through Law, in conjunction with the Constitutional Court of Georgia on Contemporary Problems of Constitutional Justice, Tbilissi, Georgia, 1-3 December 1996, Offprint.

Mavčič, A., *The Role of the Slovenian Constitutional Court in Legal Transition*, Report on the Conference on Constitutional Transition, CCT'97, Hong Kong, 29 May - 1 June, 1997, Offprint.

Mavčič, A., *The Nature and Effects of Decisions of the Slovenian Constitutional Court, the Temporary Order as an Element of the Constitutional Review Proceedings*, Report on the Colloquium ueber Grundfragen der Verfassungsgerichtsbarkeit in Mittel- und Osteuropa, das Max-Planck-Institut fuer auslaendisches oeffentliches Recht und Voelkerrecht, Heidelberg, 17-18 April, 1997, Offprint.

Mavčič, A., *The Protection of Fundamental Rights by the Constitutional Court and the Practice of the Constitutional Court of the Republic of Slovenia*, Report on the Seminar "The Protection of Fundamental Rights by the Constitutional Court", Venice Commission of the Council of Europe, Brioni, Croatia, 23-25 September 1995, Proceedings, p. 204.

Mavčič, A., *The Protection of Fundamental Rights by the Constitutional Court*, Report on the Constitutional Dimension of Judicial Reform and Judicial Organization Seminar, Kyrgyzstan, Bishkek, 17-18 June 1997, Offprint.

Mavčič, A., *The Issue of the Judicial Review of the Constitutionality of the Laws in a Newly Emerged Democracy: Slovenia*, The EU/Tacis Program Support to the Constitutional Court of Uzbekistan, Seminar in Tashkent, 11-15 September 1997, organised by the European Commission and the Greek Research Institute Center of European Constitutional Law, Themistocles and Dimitris Tsasos Foundation, Offprint.

Mavčič, A., *Human Rights Protection with the Help of the Individual Complaint*, The Venice Commission of the Council of Europe, Workshop on the Functioning of the Constitutional Court of the Republic of Latvia, Riga/Latvia, 3-4 July 1997, organized by the Constitutional Court of the Republic of Latvia, Offprint.

Mavčič, A., *The Constitutional Court, Different Models of Operation as Regards Systems of Federal States*, The Venice Commission of the Council of Europe, Workshop on the Relationship between Central Constitutional Courts and Constitutional Courts of Federal Entities, Petrozavodsk, the Republic of Karelia (Russian Federation), 22-24 September 1997, Offprint.

Mavčič, A., *The Development and Functions of Constitutional Courts, The Use of Case Law*, The Rule of Law, The Use of the European Convention on Human Rights, Standards Used to Review Government Actions, the Equal Protection Clause, Workshop organised by the European Union, Council of Europe, International Human Rights Group, Office of the High Representative, Sarajevo, Bosnia and Herzegovina, 24-25 November 1997, Offprint.

Mavčič, A., *The Budget of the Constitutional Court, Control and Management with Respect to the Independence and Autonomy of the Court*, Workshop organised by the Venice Commission of the Council of Europe, Kiev, Ukraine, 19-21 January 1998, Offprint and Proceedings.

Mavčič, A., *The Protection of Human Rights by Bodies Exercising Constitutional/Judicial Review*, Conference of Constitutional Courts, organised by the CIS, Minsk, Belarus, 3-4 June 1998, Offprint and Proceedings.

Mavčič, A., *The Particularities of the Legal Information System of the Constitutional Court of Slovenia*, International conference organised by the Association pour le développement de l'informatique juridique, Paris, France, 22-23 October 1998, Offprint and Proceedings.

Mavčič, A., The Slovenian Constitutional Review as an Example of a System in the Process of Transition , International conference organised by the Pontificia Universidad Catolica de Chile, Facultad de Derecho, Santiago, Chile, 5-7 November 1998, Offprint and Proceedings.

Mavčič, A., *The Presentation of Constitutional Review Matters on the Internet*, International conference organised by the Istituto per la Documentazione Giuridica del Consiglio Nazionale delle Ricerche, Florence, Italy, 2-5 December 1998, Offprint and Proceedings, CD-ROM.

Mavčič, A., *The Hierarchy of Legal Norms in the Constitutional Systems of the Associated Countries/The Slovenian System*, TAIEX, European Communities, Vienna, Austria, 14 December 1998, Proceedings.

Mavčič, A., *The Constitutional Law of Slovenia*, Kluwer International, Belgium/The Netherlands, 1998, 320 p., English.

Mavčič, A., *The Constitution of Slovenia*, Kluwer International, Belgium/The Netherlands, 1998, 70 p., English.

Rupnik, J., *Ustavnost, demokracija in politični sistem* (Constitutionality, Democracy and the Political System, (Slovene), Maribor, Založba Obzorja, 1975.

Wuertenberger, T., *Verfassungsrechtliche Streitigkeiten in der zweiten Haelfte des 18. Jahrhunderts*, Grundrechte, soziale Ordnung und Verfassungsgerichtbarkeit, Festschrift fuer Ernst Benda zum 70. Geburtstag, C.F. Mueller Juristischer Verlag Heidelberg, p. 442-456.

2. Bibliography on Africa:

Durieux, Andre: *Le controle de la constitutionnalite des lois dans divers Etats africains*, p. 213-238, published in Actualite du controle juridictional des lois, Travaux des Sixiemes, Jurnees d'etudes juridiques Jean Dabin, Bibliotheque de la Faculte de Droit de l'Universite Catholique de Louvain, Bruxelles, 1973

El-Morr, Awad, *The Supreme Constitutional Court of Egypt and the Protection of Human and Political Rights*, Islam and Public Law, Classical and Contemporary Studies, Graham&Trotman, p. 229-260.

Kumado, C. K., *The Judicial Review of Legislation in Ghana since Independence*, The Black Law Journal, Volume 5, Number 1, p. 208-230

Kader, Asmal, *Constitutional Courts - a Comparative Survey*, The Comparative and International Law Journal of Southern Africa, Volume 24, Number 1, March 1991, p. 315-340 *La Cour Constitutionnelle de la Republique Gabonaise*, Libreville: Multipress, 1996, p. 9.

Moderne, Franck, *L'evolution des juridictions constitutionnelles dans les etats d'Afrique francophone et la Republique Malgache*, Les institutions constitutionnelles des etats d'Afrique francophone et de la Republique Malgache, La Vie du Droit en Afrique, Paris 1979, p.185-209

Mubako, Simbi, *Fundamental Rights and Judicial Review: The Zambian Experience*, The Zimbabwe Law Review, Volume 1&2, 1983-1984, p. 97-132

Bahbouhi, Tahar, *Peut-on parler de controle de constitutionnalite des lois dans la theorie islamique?*, Revue juridique poilitique et economique du Maroc, Numero 18, Decembre 1985, p. 59-87

Conac, Gerard, *Les cours supremes en Afrioue*, II La jurisprudence, Paris 1989, p. 172

Reyntjens, F., *Constitutiones Africae*, Volume I, II, III, Bruxelles-Paris, 1988

Bendourou, Omar, *Le Conseil Constitutionnel Algérien, Revue du Droit Public et de la Science Politique en France et a l'Etranger*, Paris, 4-1991, novembre-decembre 1991, p.1617-1640

Owona, Joseph, *Droit constitutionnel et regimes politiques africains*, Paris 1985

Conac, Gerard, *La Constitution Malgache du 19 aout 1992*, Afrique contemporaine, Trimestriel no 166, avril-juin 1993, p. 56

Constitution de la Republique du Zaire, Bureau du President, Kinshasa, 1988

Moyrand, Alain, *La normalisation constitutionnelle au Tchad*, Centre d'études d'Afriue Noire, Travaux et Documents, no 26-1990, p. 47-49

Ngom, Benoit Saaliu, *L'arbitrage d'une democratie en Afrique: La Cour supreme du Senegal*, Presence Africaine, Paris-Dakar, 1989

The Constitution of the Federal Republic of Nigeria, Official Gazette, No 29, Lagos-3rd May 1989, chapter 76, p. 143

Constitution du Burkina Faso, Imprimerie de la Direction Générale des editions Sidwaya, Ouagadougou, septembre 1991

The Constitution of the Republic of Namibia, The Materials of the Max-Planck-Institut, Heidelberg (Afr/Nam IX A:1)

Constitution de la Republique Gabonaise (Loi no 3/91 du 26 mars 1991), Direction des Publications Officielles, Libreville, 1991

Verfassungsentwurf der Nationale Union fuer die totale Unabhaengigkeit von Angola UNITA, Unita/Klemmerberg Verlag, Bammental/Heidelberg, 1990, p. 34-35

Bartolomei, Jacopo, Bartolomei, Maria Rita, *L'organizzazione costituzionale in Costa D'Avorio*, profili e problemi, Milano, 1990, p. 213-219

Brewer-Carias, Allan R, *Judicial Review in Comparative Law*, Cambridge, 1989

Brehme, Gerhard, *Verfassung und Verfassungswirklichkeit in Laenderd Asiens und Afrikas*, Berlin, 1984, p. 28

Blaustein, Flanz, *Constitutions of the Countries of the World*, Oceana Publications, Inc., New York, Release 1983-1993

3. Bibliography Concerning Asia:

Beer, Lawrence Ward, Constitutionalism in Asia - Asian Views of the American Influence, Berkeley-Los Angeles-London, 1979

Beer, Lawrence Ward, Constitutional Systems in Late Twentieth Century Asia, Asia Law Series - School of Law, University of Washington, Number 12, 1991

Brehme, Gerhard, Verfassung und Verfassungswirklichkeit in Laenderd Asiens und Afrikas, Berlin, 1984, p. 28

Chiba, Masaj, Asian Indigenous Law (In Interaction with Received Law), London, 1986, p. 195

The Constitution of The Kingdom of Thailand, Foreign Law Division, Office of the Judicial Council, Bangkok, 1991

Dudeja, Vijay Lakshmi, Judicial Review in India, London, 1988

Espiritu, Caesar, Law And Human Rights in the Development of ASEAN, Singapore, 1986, p. 23 and p. 66

Heuser, Robert, Die Interpretation der Verfassung durch die Versammlung der Hohen Richter in Taiwan, published in Dieter Eikemeier/Herbert Franke: State and Law in East Asia (Festschrift Karl Buenger), Wiesbaden 1981, p. 255-271

Human Rights Watch: Human Rights in Iraq (Middle East Watch), New York, 1990, p. 22-38

Jenckel, Hans Wilhelm, Das Rechtssystem der Republik Singapur, Frankfurt/Main, 1986

Judicial Council, The Council of State of Thailand, Office of the Council of State, Thailand, Bangkok, 1991, Materials of the Max-Planck-Institut Heidelberg (OA/Thai:IX B1)

Judicial Council Act, Office of the Council of State, Thailand, Bangkok, 1991, Materials of Max-Planck-Institut Heidelberg (OA/Thai:IX B2)

Mei Dong, Chen, Viewing the Chinese Review Organ for Unconstitutionality in Comparison with the Review System for Unconstitutionality Worldwide, Law in East and West, Tokyo, 1988, p. 463-481

Merz, Juergen, Die Mongolei auf dem Weg zu pluralistischer Demokratie und Marktwirtschaft - Die neue Verfassung von 1992, Verfassung und Recht in Uebersee (Law and Politics in Africa, Asia and Latin America, 26. Jahrgang-1.Quartal 1993, Nomos-Verlag, Baden-Baden 1993, p. 82-100

Pakistan, Human Rights Violations and the Decline of the Rule of Law, London, 1982, p. 8-15

Prasad, Ganesh, The Right to Constitutional Remedies in the Indian Constitution, Allahabad, 1989, p. 60

Seizelet, Eric, La reforme de la justice constitutionnelle en Coree du Sud, Revue française de Droit constitutionnel, no 9/1992, p. 141-151

Suffian bin Hashim Tan Sri, Mohamed, An Introduction to the Constitution of Malaysia, Kuala Lumpour, 1972

The Constitution of Nepal, Law Books Management Committee, Katmandu, December 1981

Von Bruenneck, Alexander, Verfassungsgerichtsbarkeit in den westlichen Demokratien, Baden-Baden (Nomos), 1992

Wang, Shibu, La legislation elaborée par l'administration en Chine, (Revue internationale de droit compare), Journées de la Société de legislaion comparée, Anée 1991, no. special vol. 13, p. 127-133

Wesley-Smith, Peter, Constitutional & Administrative Law in Hong Kong (Text and Materials), Volume One and Two, Hong Kong, 1987, p. 206-213

Zamudio, Hector Fix, Los tribunales constitucionales y los derechos humanos, Mexico, 1985

Yueh-Sheng Eeng, The Grand Justices En Masse, Its Evolution And Function, The Republic o China Constitutional Court (Grand Justices Council) Reporter, Interpretations, Volume One, Taipei, December 2000, p. 21-24

4. Bibliography Concerning Central and South America:

Bazan, Mario Pelaez, *Hacia la justica constitucional (Tribunal de Garantias Constitucionales*, Lima, 1984

Belaunde, Domingo Garcia, *La accion de inconstitucionalidad en el derecho comparado*, El Derecho, Jurisprudencia general, Tomo 146, Buenos Aires 1992, p. 859-866

Brewer-Carias, Allan R., *Judicial Review in Comparative Law*, Cambridge, 1989

V. Bruenneck, Alexander, *Verfassungsgerichtsbarkeit in den westlichen Demokratien*, Baden-Baden (Nomos), 1992

Carnegie, A.R., *The Judicial Review of Legislation in the West Indian Constitutions*, Public Law - The Constitutional and Administrative Law of the Commonwealth, Spring 1971, p. 276-287

Di Lorio, Ana, *El control de constitucionalidad (Sistemas)*, Revista Juridica Argentina La Ley, Buenos Aires, t. 1992-B, p. 1030-1041

Favoreu, Louis, Jolowicz John Anthony, *Le Controle Juridictionnel des Lois*, Paris/Aix-en-Provence 1986

Gonzalez,P. S., Sanchez, Trevijano, Hernandez, Eduardo Martinez, *Los derechos fundamentales y libertades publicas en la constitucion Colombiana de 1991*, Revista de Derecho Politico, Madrid, No. 35/1992, p. 369-401

Martinez, Juan Manuel Goig, *La protection de los derechos humanos en la nueva constitucion Colombiana*, Revista de Derecho Politico, Madrid, No.35/1992, p. 405-415

Mendes, Gilmar Ferreira, *Die Abstrakte Normenkontrolle vor dem Bundesverfassungsgericht und vor dem brasilianischen Supremo tribunal Federal*, Scfriften zum Oeffentlichen Recht, Band 607, Berlin, 1991

Valle-Riestra, Javier, *El Tribunal de Garantias Constitucionales, El Caso de los Votos Nulos y Blancos*, Lima, 1986

Verfassungsgerichtsbarkeit in der Gegenwart: Laenderberichte und Rechtsvergleichung (Internatonales Kolloquium), Max-Planck-Institut fuer auslaendisches oeffentliches Recht und Voelkerrecht, Koeln-Berlin 1962

Zamudio, Hector Fix, *Los tribunales constitucionales y los derechos humanos*, Mexico, 1985

APPENDIX I
EVOLUTION DE LA JUSTICE CONSTITUTIONNELLE

L'institution d'organes juridictionnels suprêmes pour veiller à la constitutionnalité et à la légalité n'est pas une découverte des Etats modernes.

Le droit de la Grèce antique distinguait le *nomos* (que l'on pourrait dans un certain sens comparer aux lois constitutionnelles actuelles) du *psephisma* qui pourrait à notre époque être appelé règlement.[171] Les Grecs avaient introduit le principe fondamental selon lequel le règlement (*psephisma*), indépendamment de son contenu, ne devait pas être en contradiction avec le *nomos*, ni dans sa forme ni dans son contenu. L'adoption d'un *psephisma* inconstitutionnel avait deux conséquences. En premier lieu, le membre de l'organe législatif qui avait proposé un règlement inconstitutionnel était responsable pénalement, ce qui pouvait donner motif au droit général de recours. En second lieu, les *psephismata* qui étaient contraires aux *nomoi* étaient considérés comme nuls. Dans leurs décisions, les juges athéniens, bien que liés en principe aux deux fondements, c'est-à-dire aux lois et aux règlements, n'étaient tenus aux règlements que si ceux-ci étaient conformes aux lois constitutionnelles.

Dans l'ancien Empire germanique, des éléments de justice constitutionnelle sont relevés dès 1180. Les organes juridictionnels de l'époque statuaient surtout à propos de litiges portant sur la compétence entre les détenteurs du pouvoir, mais aussi partiellement sur les violations des droits. Le contrôle de la constitutionnalité des lois est apparu sous diverses formes tout au long de l'histoire du droit allemand, avant d'être introduit par la Constitution de Weimar dans le sens compris aujourd'hui. Par ailleurs, des formes antécédentes de justice constitutionnelle existaient en France jusqu'au milieu du XIIIe siècle. Au Portugal, le Code Philippe a introduit la justice constitutionnelle au début du XVIIe siècle.

La Cour fédérale autrichienne est en 1867 devenue compétente pour résoudre les litiges concernant la compétence et la protection des droits politiques de l'individu face à l'administration. Parallèlement, la Cour d'Etat statuait alors sur les accusations mettant en cause l'Etat et ses lois. La Cour constitutionnelle avec compétence exclusive de statuer sur la constitutionnalité des lois a été fondée par la Constitution de 1920, avant tout grâce aux théoriciens du droit autrichiens, Adolf Merkel et Hans Kelsen. La Constitution fédérale suisse de 1848 prévoyait certes l'introduction de la justice constitutionnelle, mais c'est la Constitution révisée en 1874 qui attribua à la Cour suprême des compétences de justice constitutionnelle plus étendues.

En Norvège, à partir de 1890, la jurisprudence a introduit le contrôle de la constitutionnalité des lois. Avant la Première Guerre mondiale, la Roumanie a mis en place la justice constitutionnelle suivant le modèle américain et avant la Seconde

[171] Capeletti, M., The Judicial Process in Perspective, Chapt. 3, pub. dans 58 Cal. L. Rev. 1017 (1970), pub. aussi dans Beatty D., Comparative Constitutional Law Faculty of Law, University of Toronto, Spring 1994, p. 1-6.

Guerre mondiale, d'autres pays ont introduit des organes juridictionnels destinés à veiller au respect de la constitutionnalité: Tchécoslovaquie (1920), Liechtenstein (Staatsgerichtshof, 5/11-1925), Grèce (1927), Egypte (1941), et Espagne (1931).

Le droit aragonais, du XIIIe au XVIe siècle, connaissait le contrôle et la garantie des droits constitutionnels sous forme de procédures qui sont de fait les précurseurs des recours constitutionnels modernes: recurso de agravios, firma de derecho in manifestacion de personas. Ces formes initiales de droits garantissant la justice constitutionnelle ont retenti largement, repris dans les systèmes ramifiés de contrôle constitutionnel en Espagne (1978), au Portugal (1976) et en Amérique latine (par exemple au Mexique dès les constitutions de 1857 et 1917, et au Brésil dans les constitutions de 1890 et 1946).

La justice constitutionnelle est en principe inconnue dans le système juridique britannique moderne,[172] pourtant, l'histoire du droit anglais en connaît des éléments individuels.[173] L'Amérique du Nord a repris les idées anglaises de la primauté de la Constitution et du contrôle de la constitutionnalité des lois.[174] En 1803, l'affaire Marbury v. Madison a été déterminante pour le développement de la justice constitutionnelle. En effet, elle a donné l'occasion à la Cour suprême américaine de statuer sur l'inconstitutionnalité de la loi. Peu à peu, cette compétence s'est finalement imposée, bien qu'une affaire comparable n'ait été portée devant cette cour que plus tard, en 1857.

L'introduction du contrôle de la constitutionnalité des lois a progressé en plusieurs vagues. La première déferle tout de suite après la Seconde Guerre mondiale.[175] La seconde apparaît dans les années 1970,[176] en réaction aux régimes dictatoriaux en place auparavant dans certains pays. L'introduction en 1963 de la justice constitutionnelle en ex-Yougoslavie suivant à la fois le modèle autrichien et allemand était une particularité; en effet, les systèmes socialistes d'alors n'étaient pas, par principe, compatibles avec l'idée de justice constitutionnelle. La troisième vague d'introduction de la justice constitutionnelle arrive dans les années 1990 dans les pays de l'Est européen.[177]

[172] Bien que la Chambre des Lords se charge de certaines fonctions de contrôle de la constitutionnalité des lois, ce qui en réalité représente un contrôle parlementaire.

[173] Par exemple, le principe de la primauté de la constitution, qui date de 1610 ; l'usage de l'accusation publique - impeachment dont la source remonte au Moyen Age tardif.

[174] Dès la fin du XVIIIe siècle, les tribunaux américains ont adopté diverses décisions sur la non validité de certaines lois anglaises dans les Etats d'Amérique du Nord. Selon la Constitution de 1787, la Cour suprême (fédérale) n'avait cependant pas de compétences explicites en matière de justice constitutionnelle.

[175] Par exemple : Brésil (de nouveau en 1946), Japon (1947), Birmanie / Myanma (1947), Italie (1948), Thaïlande (1949), Allemagne (1949), Inde (1949), France (1958), Luxembourg (1950), Syrie (1950), Uruguay (1952), Chypre (1960), Turquie (1961), Algérie (1963) et Grèce (1968).

[176] Espagne et Portugal

[177] Pologne (1982), Hongrie (1984) et ex-Union soviétique (1988), et plus récemment dans la Communauté des Etats indépendants (Arménie, Géorgie, Biélorussie, Moldavie, Azerbaïdjan, Tadjikistan, Ouzbékistan, Kirghizstan, Kazakhstan, etc). Dans le cadre de la Fédération Russe, les Cours constitutionnelles sont introduites même au niveau des républiques fédérées (Iakoutie, Bachkirie, Komis, Tatarie, Carélie, Adyghes, Bouriatie, Daghestan, Oblast de Irkoutsk, République de Karbadino-Balkare, Ossétie du Nord, Touva, Altaï, Ingouchie, Kalmoukie, République de Karatchevo-Tcherkess, Mariis, Oudmourtie, Khakass, Tchouvachie).

A. Modeles actuels de justice constitutionnelle

Le modèle "américain" - judicial review model tire son origine de l'affaire Marbury/Cour suprême des USA en 1803. Aux Etats-Unis, les questions relevant du droit constitutionnel sont jugées par tous les tribunaux à compétence générale (justice constitutionnelle décentralisée ou diffuse) selon une procédure tout à fait ordinaire (*incidenter*). En règle générale, les décisions ont un effet seulement *inter partes*. La décision de la Cour sur la non-conformité de la loi avec la constitution est en règle générale rétroactive, c'est-à-dire *ex tunc* (elle a des conséquences *pro praeterito*).[178]

Le nouveau modèle commonwealth[179] ne peut être rangé ni dans le modèle américain ni dans le modèle européen. Sa spécificité est que la justice constitutionnelle relève exclusivement de la compétence de la Cour suprême qui est constituée de juges réguliers, sans nomination politique. Il s'agit en règle générale d'un contrôle préventif et la fonction de la Cour suprême est de nature consultative, bien qu'un jugement de sanction soit également possible. Les décisions ont un effet *erga omnes*.

Le modèle "autrichien" (continental, européen - constitutional review) découle du modèle de Kelsen, établi en 1920. Sa base est le principe de la primauté de la Constitution et le principe de la primauté du Parlement. La constitutionnalité des lois est appréciée par des Cours constitutionnelles particulières constituées de juges spécialement qualifiés ou par des Cours suprêmes de large compétence avec des départements spécialisés en la matière. Il s'agit donc d'une justice constitutionnelle centralisée à procédure spéciale (*principaliter*). Les décisions s'imposent en règle générale comme *erga omnes*. Les organes juridictionnels de cette justice constitutionnelle peuvent avoir diverses dénominations.[180]

---

178 Ce système a été adopté par les pays suivants :
- En Europe : Danemark, Suède, Norvège, Irlande, Estonie ;
- En Afrique : Botswana, Gambie, Ghana, Guinée, Kenya, Malawi, Namibie, Nigeria, Seychelles, Sierra Leone, Tanzanie ;
- Au Proche Orient : Israël, Iran ;
- En Asie : Bangladesh, Fidji, Hong Kong (avant le 1/7-1997), Inde, Japon, Kiribati, Malaisie, Etat fédéré de Micronésie, Nauru, Népal, Nouvelle Zélande, Palau, Papouasie-Nouvelle-Guinée, Singapour, Tibet (selon la Constitution des Tibétains en exil, le 14/6-1991), Tonga, Tuvalu, Vanuatu, Samoa occidentales ;
- En Amérique du Nord : USA, Canada ;
- En Amérique Centrale et du Sud : Argentine, Bahamas, la Barbade, Bolivie, Saint Domingue, République Dominicaine, Grenade, Guyana, Haïti, Jamaïque, Mexique, Saint-Christophe et Niévès, Trinité-et-Tobago.

179 Ile Maurice

180 a) Cours constitutionnelles
- En Europe: Albanie, Andorre, Autriche, Biélorussie, Bulgarie, Bosnie (Cour constitutionnelle internationale, Cour constitutionnelle de la Fédération Bosnie et Herzégovine, Cour constitutionnelle de la République serbe Bosnie et Herzégovine), République tchèque, Monténégro, Croatie, Italie, lettonie, Lituanie, Luxembourg, Hongrie, Macédoine, Malte, Moldavie, Allemagne (avec les lander de Bade-Wurtemberg, Bavière, Brême, Hambourg, Hesse, Basse-Saxe, Rhénanie du Nord-Westphalie, Rhénanie-Palatinat, Sarre, Saxe, Saxe-Anhalt, Brandebourg), Pologne, Roumanie, Russie (avec les Cours constitutionnelles des unités fédérales : Adyghes, Bachkirie, Bouriatie, Daghestan, Oblast de Irkoutsk, Iakoutie/Sakha, Carélie, République de Karbadino-Balkare, Komis, Ossétie du Nord, Tatarie, Touva, Altaï, Ingouchie, Kalmoukie, République de Karatchevo-Tcherkess, , Mariis, Oudmourtie, Khakass, Tchouvachie), Slovaquie, Slovénie, Espagne, Serbie, Turquie, Ukraine, République fédérale de Yougoslavie ;
- En Afrique: Angola, Bénin, Burundi, République de Centrafrique, Egypte, Guinée-Equatoriale, Gabon, Afrique du Sud, Madagascar, Mali, Rwanda, Togo ;
- Au Proche Orient: Chypre, Irak avant le régime actuel, Palestine, Syrie ;
- En Asie: Corée du Sud, Kirghizstan, Mongolie, Sri Lanka, Thaïlande, Géorgie (avec la Cour constitutionnelle de la région autonome de Adjarie), Tadjikistan, Ouzbékistan (avec le Comité constitutionnel de la République de Karakalpackie), Azerbaïdjan, Arménie, Tchétchénie ;
- En Amérique Centrale et du Sud: Chili, Surinam, Province de Tucuman (Argentine).

b) Les Cours suprêmes et leurs départements spécialisés
- En Europe : Belgique, Islande, Liechtenstein ;
- Au Proche Orient : Yémen ;
- En Afrique : Burkina Fasso, Tchad, Niger, Soudan, Zaïre, Ouganda (1995), Erythrée, Zambie ;

Le modèle mixte (continental américain) comprend des éléments du système diffus et du système centralisé. Malgré la compétence de la Cour constitutionnelle ou de la Cour suprême en matière de justice constitutionnelle (ou de son département spécialisé), tous les tribunaux de certains pays ont le droit de ne pas appliquer les lois qu'ils considèrent comme inconstitutionnelles.[181]

Le modèle "français" (continental) est basé sur le modèle du *Conseil constitutionnel français* (1958), où les affaires de droit constitutionnel sont jugées par des organes particuliers de justice constitutionnelle (avant tout le Conseil constitutionnel) ou des départements spéciaux de Cours suprêmes à compétence générale (contrôle constitutionnel centralisé) à partir d'une procédure particulière *(principaliter)*, tenant compte du fait que l'appréciation de la constitutionnalité est le plus souvent de nature préventive (consultative).[182]

D'autres organes de contrôle constitutionnel existent quand cette fonction est réalisée conformément au principe d'autocontrôle par un organe de travail spécialisé du législateur (par exemple le Conseil d'Etat, le plus souvent le parlement, etc.).[183]

Les systèmes n'ayant pas de justice constitutionnelle sont:

En Europe: la Grande Bretagne (bien que les compétences de la Chambre des Lords présentent certains éléments de contrôle constitutionnel préventif); les Pays-Bas (avec des exceptions et considérant notamment que l'intégration dans les institutions européennes a influencé la rupture survenue dans le principe fondamental du système juridique néerlandais qui ne permettait pas la justice constitutionnelle);

En Afrique: Lesotho, Liberia, Libye.

- En Asie : Philippines ;
- En Amérique Centrale et du Sud : Costa-Rica, Nicaragua, Panama, Paraguay, Uruguay.

c) Conseil d'Etat
- Au Proche Orient : Liban ;
- En Afrique : Cameroun, Mauritanie, Sénégal ;
- En Asie : Kazakhstan, Cambodge.

[181] Les organes de juridiction constitutionnelle sont :
a) Les Cours constitutionnelles
- En Europe : Portugal ;
- En Amérique Centrale et du Sud : Equateur, Guatémala, Colombie, Pérou.

b) Les Cours Suprêmes ou leurs départements specializes
- En Europe : Grèce, Suisse (tenant compte du fait que le système suisse est un système de justice constitutionnelle limitée, la Cour fédérale ne pouvant statuer sur les lois fédérales, les résolutions obligatoires en général et les traités ratifiés) ;
- En Asie : Indonésie, Taiwan ;
- En Afrique : Iles du Cap-vert ;
- En Amérique Centrale et du Sud : Brésil, Salvador, Honduras, Vénézuéla.

[182] En Europe : France ;
En Afrique : Algérie, Comores, Djibouti, Maroc, Mozambique, Côte-d'Ivoire.

[183] En Europe : Finlande ;
Au Moyen Orient : Bahrein, Koweït, Oman ;
En Afrique : Congo, Ethiopie, Guinée Bissau, Sao Tomé et Principe, Tunisie, Zimbabwe ;
En Asie : Afghanistan, Birmanie/Myanma, Brunei, Laos, Chine, Hong Kong (après 1/7.1997), Corée du Nord, Pakistan, Vietnam, Turkménistan ; Australie;
En Amérique Centrale : Cuba

Les institutions internationales exerçant des fonctions particulières de justice constitutionnelle:

- La Cour européenne des droits de l'homme - Strasbourg (recours européen);
- La Cour de justice des communautés européennes - Luxembourg (action pour annuler un acte, action pour manquement à l'encontre du Conseil des ministres ou de la Commission de la Communauté, résolution de questions préalables par contrôle concret à la demande des Cours des Etats membres);
- La Cour de l'AELE - Genève (résolution des différends entre les pays membres de l'AELE et contrôle concret à la demande des Cours des pays membres de cette organisation);
- *Comision y la Corte Interamericanas de los Derechos Humanos;*
- *Tribunal de Justicia del Acuerdo de Cartagena;*
- Projet d'instituer La Corte Centroamericana de Justicia como Tribunal Constitucional de Centroamerica.

Les associations internationales d'institutions qui exercent le contrôle de la constitutionnalité

On constate une expansion notable de la justice constitutionnelle dans le monde et, parallèlement, toujours plus d'éléments communs entre les Cours constitutionnelles elles-mêmes au niveau de l'organisation, de la procédure, des motifs des décisions et des avis. Ces faits s'expliquent par le respect de principes identiques immanents à tout système constitutionnel. Les tendances à l'intégration des justices constitutionnelles sont de même très encourageantes. Au niveau international, des échanges d'idées en la matière se font par des relations de nature mi-formelle. Sous de nombreux aspects, les rencontres de travail périodiques des Cours constitutionnelles ont une signification de grande portée: grâce à elles, la jurisprudence constitutionnelle s'affirme et s'approfondit.

La Commission européenne pour la démocratie par le droit du Conseil de l'Europe (Commission de Venise) a été instituée en 1990. Elle englobe pays européens et pays non-européens en tant que membres à part entière, membres associés et pays observateurs.[184]

Les premiers efforts pour fonder une telle commission ont été présentés en 1987 à la Conférence des Cours constitutionnelles européennes à Lisbonne. Le plus fort soutien apporté à cette idée est venu des présidents respectifs des Cours constitutionnelles italienne et allemande de cette période. La Commission a été fondée formellement en

[184] **Membres à part entière** (les pays du Conseil de l'Europe membres de la Commission choisissent les nouveaux sur la base d'un accord spécial) : Albanie, Autriche, Belgique, Bulgarie, Croatie, République tchèque, Chypre, Danemark, Estonie, Finlande, Macédoine, France, Allemagne, Grèce, Hongrie, Islande, Irlande, Italie, Lettonie, Liechtenstein, Lituanie, Luxembourg, Malte, Moldavie, Pays-Bas, Norvège, Pologne, Portugal, Roumanie, San Marin, Slovaquie, Slovénie, Espagne, Suède, Suisse, Turquie et Ukraine.
Membres associés : Arménie, Azerbaïdjan, Biélorussie, Bosnie et Herzégovine, Géorgie.
Pays observateurs : Argentine, Canada, Japon, Kirghizstan, Uruguay, USA, et Vatican. L'Afrique du Sud et la Corée du Sud ont un statut de coopération particulier.

1990 à la Conférence des ministres des affaires étrangères européens, à Venise. Pour cela, la commission s'appelle aussi Commission de Venise. En mai 1990, les statuts de la Commission ont été adoptés, sur la base d'un accord particulier, en liaison avec le Conseil de l'Europe. Les pays membres du Conseil de l'Europe ne sont pas automatiquement membres de la Commission de Venise. Pour y adhérer, le pays candidat doit en faire la demande sur la base d'un document approprié.

La tâche principale de la Commission est de promouvoir le principe de la division des pouvoirs et les principes de l'Etat de droit à caractère social, de soutenir les progrès de la justice constitutionnelle et d'encourager le développement des bases d'information des organes juridictionnels pour le contrôle de la constitutionnalité dans les pays membres. En effet, hormis les pays où les systèmes de justice constitutionnelle ont une tradition, dans d'autres pays membres, cette institution n'en est qu'à son stade de formation et de croissance.

La Conférence des Cours constitutionnelles de la Communauté des Etats indépendants (nouvelles démocraties) a vu le jour en octobre 1997 à Erevan, Arménie.[185] La première rencontre organisée, c'est-à-dire le premier séminaire professionnel international de cette Conférence, s'est tenu à Minsk en juin 1998.

Le groupe des organes juridictionnels pour le contrôle constitutionnel dans les pays d'Amérique latine a été fondé en 1992 à San José, Costa Rica où s'est également tenue la première conférence des organes de justice constitutionnelle qui réunit dix pays. Plus tard, en réponse à l'initiative de la Cour constitutionnelle espagnole, la Conférence ibéro-américaine des Cours constitutionnelles a été instituée. Elle réunit les Cours constitutionnelles dont la langue de travail est l'espagnol et le portugais.

L'Association des Cours constitutionnelles ayant en partage l'usage du français (A.C.C.P.U.F.), fondée en 1977 à Paris, elle regroupe 49 pays européens et non européens.[186] La première conférence de cette association s'est tenue à Paris en 1997, la deuxième à Beyrouth en septembre 1998.

La Conférence des Cours constitutionnelles européennes

B. Bibliographie - conférence des cours constitutionnelles européennes

Deset godina rada ustavnog suda Jugoslavije, Beograd, oktobra 1973, ed. USJ, p.113

Die Hierarchie von Verfassungsnormen und ihre Funktion beim Schutz der Grundrechte, VIII. Konferenz des Europaeischen Verfassungsgerichte, EuGRZ 1990, p. 453

[185] La Conférence est un organe consultatif qui réunit les Cours constitutionnelles des pays suivants : Arménie, Biélorussie, Kazakhstan, Kirghizstan, Fédération Russe et Tadjikistan.

[186] Albanie, Algérie, Arménie, Belgique, Bénin, Bulgarie, Burkina Faso, Burundi, Cambodge, Cameroun, Canada, Iles du Cap-Vert, République Centrafricaine, Tchad, Comores, Congo, Djibouti, Egypte, Guinée Equatoriale, France, Macédoine, Gabon, Guinée, Guinée Bissau, Haïti, Côte-d'Ivoire, Laos, Liban, Luxembourg, Madagascar, Mali, Mauritanie, Ile Maurice, Moldavie, Monaco, Maroc, Niger, Pologne, Roumanie, Sénégal, Seychelles, Slovénie, Suisse, Syrie, Togo, Tunisie, Vanuatu, Vietnam, Zaïre.

Etudes: VIIeme Conférence des Cours constitutionnelles européennes, Annuaire International de Justice Constitutionnelle, III/1987, GERJC, d'Aix-Marseille, 1989, p. 15

Faller Hans Joachim, *Zur Entwicklung der nationalen Verfassungsgerichte in Europa*, EuGRZ 1986, p. 42

Machacek Rudolf, *Verfahren vor dem VfGH*, 2. Auflage, Manz Wien, 1992, p. 41

Mavčič Arne, *Mednarodna konferenca ustavnih sodišč*, Pravna praksa, no. 8/93, p.19

Peta konference europskih ustavnih sudova, Pravni život, 3/82, p. 387

Zierlein Karl-Georg, *Entwicklung und Moeglichkeiten einer Union: Die Konferenz der Europaeischen Verfassungsgerichte*, Festschrift fuer Wolfgang Zeidler, Band 1, Walter de Gruyter Berlin-New York, 1987, p.315

C. Chronologie des conférences des cours constitutionnelles européennes tenues jusqu'a ce jour

- Dubrovnik, du 17/10 au 20/10-1972
- Baden-Baden, du 14/10 au 16/10-1974
- Rome, du 20/10 au 22/10-1976
- Vienne, du 16/10 au 18/10-1978
- Lausanne, du 26/10 au 28/10-1981
- Madrid, du 23/10 au 25/10-1984
- Lisbonne, du 27/4 au 29/4/-1987
- Ankara, du 7/5 au 10/5-1990
- Paris, du 10/5 au 13/5-1993
- Budapest, du 4/5 au 9/5-1996
- Varsovie, du 16/5 au 20/5-1999

Depuis 1972, les Cours constitutionnelles sont liées de façon informelle par la Conférence des Cours constitutionnelles européennes. Dans la pratique et sous maints aspects, les rencontres de travail périodiques des Cours constitutionnelles (congrès) ont une signification de grande portée. Il s'agit d'une forme de coopération élargie qui vient compléter les contacts bilatéraux et informatifs traditionnels existant déjà entre les Cours constitutionnelles, une liaison qui permet à la fois d'étendre et d'approfondir les relations. Car tout au long de son développement, la jurisprudence constitutionnelle s'est affermée et apprfoondie. Les Cours ont établi entre elles des relations de travail, elles ont échangé des idées, ce qui les a finalement amenées à instituer entre elles une association souple.

L'origine de la Ière convocation de la Conférence des Cours constitutionnelles européennes à Dubrovnik vient d'une impulsion donnée par les Cours constitutionnelles ex-yougoslave, italienne et allemande (RFA). Se sont immédiatement associés à ce noyau la Cour constitutionnelle autrichienne, le Conseil constitutionnel français et la Cour suprême suisse. Dès le début, il a été décidé que les Cours constitutionnelles se réuniraient tous les trois ans, une réunion préparatoire des présidents et des secrétaires étant convoquée préalablement à la Cour constitutionnelle du pays organisateur de la rencontre.

La décision, quant au lieu et à la thématique de la prochaine conférence (congrès), est adoptée lors du congrès en cours.

Les débats de la Conférence ne sont pas publics, les médias ne rendent compte que de l'ouverture solennelle du congrès et du rapport final. La Conférence n'adopte aucune résolution formelle quant aux thèmes proposés et traités, mais un communiqué final est adopté et publié. En pratique, parmi les organisateurs des congrès, c'est le groupe restreint des présidents et des secrétaires généraux des Cours constitutionnelles qui est l'organe dont la fonction est de présenter des initiatives et d'adopter des résolutions. Le président de la Cour constitutionnelle organisatrice et hôte préside le congrès. En règle générale, la Conférence décide par consensus.

Les frais d'organisation de la Conférence se répartissent entre les membres du groupe restreint, ce faisant, chaque délégation prend en charge ses frais de voyage et de séjour au lieu du congrès. La Cour constitutionnelle organisatrice de la rencontre supporte la plus grande part des frais d'organisation.

Le nombre des membres de chaque délégation est généralement limité à 4 juges et au secrétaire général; toutefois, dans la pratique, ce nombre est souvent dépassé. Jusqu'à présent, la participation aux congrès s'est limitée en général aux Cours européennes, tenant compte du fait qu'aucune Cour constitutionnelle au niveau d'unités fédérales n'y a participé (par exemple les Cours constitutionnelles des Lander allemands).

Il s'agit de rencontres des Cours constitutionnelles au vrai sens du terme et d'autres institutions d'Etat analogues ayant compétence en justice constitutionnelle. Le cercle restreint de la Conférence est composé des Cours constitutionnelles qui étaient à l'origine les organisatrices de la Conférence et des Cours constitutionnelles qui ont été ensuite acceptées après avoir présenté une demande d'admission écrite accompagnée d'un document sur leurs activités en la matière. Jusqu'en 1997, la Conférence n'avait pas de secrétariat permanent; elle fonctionnait seulement comme "groupe restreint" et en assemblées plénières (assemblée de tous les participants du moment).[187]

Lors de la réunion préparatoire d'octobre 1997 à Varsovie, le secrétariat permanent de la Conférence a été élu. Il est composé des représentants des Cours constitutionnelles autrichienne, allemande et suisse, du Conseil constitutionnel français, et de la Cour du pays où se tient le congrès. À cette occasion, la Conférence a reçu le soutien logistique de la Commission européenne pour la démocratie par le droit (Commission de Venise) auprès du Conseil de l'Europe. À la réunion de Varsovie - du 16/5 au 20/5-1999 - le Règlement de la Conférence a également été adopté.

---

[187] Actuellement, la Conférence réunit les membres à part entière suivants : Andorre, Autriche, Belgique, Bulgarie, Croatie, République tchèque, Chypre, France, Allemagne, Hongrie, Italie, Liechtenstein, Lituanie, Malte, Pologne, Portugal, Fédération Russe, Roumanie, Slovaquie, Slovénie, Espagne, Suisse, Turquie.
Les membres associés sont : Albanie, Arménie, Biélorussie, Bosnie et Herzégovine, Macédoine, Géorgie, Moldavie.
Les candidats à la Conférence sont : l'Ukraine et l'Ouzbékistan.

APPENDIX II
A TABLUAR PRESENTATION OF CONSTITUTIONAL/ JUDICIAL REVIEW AROUND THE WORLD

Here follows a tabular presentation of different models of constitutional courts as special bodies that as protectors of constitutionality enjoy a certain legal superiority in relation to the other branches of power. From an organisational point of view, it is possible to distinguish different current models of constitutional/judicial review. Furthermore, constitutional courts are here also presented from the point of view of their powers excercised in accordance with constitutional and statutory regulations in force. In addition, a map presents the mentioned constitutional and judicial review models arranged by main regions: Europe, Eastern Europe, Africa, Asia, the Middle East as well as North, Central and South America. These models are presented by different colours.

Constitutional-Judicial Review	CONSTITUTIONAL COURT		HIGH COURT or SPECIAL SENATE of the HIGH COURT			CONSTITUTIONAL COUNCIL				
Country	European Model	Mixed European-American Model	European Model	American Model	Mixed European-American Model	French Model	European Model	Other Institutional Forms of the Constitutional-Judicial Review	Without Constitutional-Judicial Review	New Common-wealth Model
EUROPE										
Albania	■									
Andorra	■									
Austria	■									
Belgium			■							
Belarus	■									
Bosnia	■									
- Serbian Bosnia	■									
Bulgaria	■									
Croatia	■									
Czech Republic	■									
Denmark				■						
Estonia				■						
Finland								■		
France						■				
FRY	■									
- Kosovo			■							
- Montenegro	■									
- Serbia	■									
Germany	■									
- Baden-Württemberg	■									
- Bavaria	■									
- Brandenburg	■									
- Berlin	■									
- Bremen	■									
- Hamburg	■									
- Hessen	■									
- Niedesachsen	■									
- Nordrhein-Westfalen	■									
- Rheinland Pfalz	■									
- Saarland	■									
- Sachsen	■									
- Sachsen-Anhalt	■									
Greece					■					
Hungary	■									
Iceland			■							
Ireland				■						
Italy	■									
Latvia	■									
Liechtenstein			■							
Lithuania	■									
Luxemburg	■									
Macedonia	■									
Malta	■									
Moldavia	■									
Monaco			■							
Netherlands									■	
Norway				■						
Poland	■									
Portugal		■								
Romania	■									
Russia	■									
- Adigea	■									
- Altai	■									
- Bashkiria	■									
- Buryatia	■									
- Chechnya	■									
- Chuvashia	■									
- Dagestan	■									

Constitutional-Judicial Review / Country	CONSTITUTIONAL COURT: European Model	CONSTITUTIONAL COURT: Mixed European-American Model	HIGH COURT or SPECIAL SENATE of the HIGH COURT: European Model	HIGH COURT or SPECIAL SENATE of the HIGH COURT: American Model	HIGH COURT or SPECIAL SENATE of the HIGH COURT: Mixed European-American Model	CONSTITUTIONAL COUNCIL: French Model	CONSTITUTIONAL COUNCIL: European Model	Other Institutional Forms of the Constitutional-Judical Review	Without Constitutional-Judicial Review	New Common-wealth Model
- Ingushia	■									
- Irkutskaya Oblast	■									
- Karbardino-Balkar	■									
- Khakassia	■									
- Karachaewo-Cherkez	■									
- Karelia	■									
- Kalmikia	■									
- Komy	■									
- Marii-El	■									
- Northrn Ossetia	■									
- Tatarstan	■									
- Tuva	■									
- Udmurtia	■									
- Yakutia	■									
Slovakia	■									
Slovenia	■									
Spain	■									
Sweden				■						
Switzerland					■					
Turkey	■									
Ukraine	■									
United Kingdom									■	
AFRICA										
Algeria						■				
Angola	■									
Benin	■									
Botswana				■						
Burkina Faso			■							
Burundi	■									
Cameroon			■							
Cape Verde					■					
Central African Rep.	■									
Chad			■							
Comoros						■				
Congo								■		
Djibouti						■				
Egypt	■									
Eritrea			■							
Ethiopia								■		
Equatorial Guinea	■									
Gabon	■									
Gambia				■						
Ghana				■						
Guinea				■						
Guinea Bissau								■		
Ivory Coast						■				
Kenya				■						
Lesotho									■	
Liberia									■	
Libya									■	
Madagascar	■									
Malawi				■						
Mali	■									
Mauritius										■
Mauritania							■			
Morocco						■				
Mozambique						■				
Namibia				■						

Constitutional-Judicial Review / Country	CONSTITUTIONAL COURT: European Model	CONSTITUTIONAL COURT: Mixed European-American Model	HIGH COURT or SPECIAL SENATE of the HIGH COURT: European Model	HIGH COURT or SPECIAL SENATE of the HIGH COURT: American Model	HIGH COURT or SPECIAL SENATE of the HIGH COURT: Mixed European-American Model	CONSTITUTIONAL COUNCIL: French Model	CONSTITUTIONAL COUNCIL: European Model	Other Institutional Forms of the Constitutional-Judical Review	Without Constitutional-Judicial Review	New Common-wealth Model
AFRICA - continue										
Niger			■							
Nigeria				■						
Rwanda	■									
Sao Tome &Principe								■		
Senegal							■			
Seychelles				■						
Sierra Leone				■						
South Africa	■									
Sudan			■							
Swaziland				■						
Tanzania				■						
Togo	■									
Tunisia								■		
Uganda			■							
Zaire			■							
Zambia			■							
Zimbabwe								■		
THE MIDDLE EAST										
Bahrain								■		
Cyprus	■									
Iran				■						
Israel				■						
Kuwait								■		
Lebanon							■			
Oman								■		
Palestine	■									
Syria	■									
Yemen			■							
ASIA, AUSTRALIA										
Afghanistan								■		
Armenia	■									
Australia								■		
Azerbaijan	■									
Bangladesh				■						
Brunei								■		
Burma								■		
Cambodia							■			
China								■		
Fiji				■						
Hong Kong								■		
Georgia	■									
- Adjaria	■									
India				■						
Indonesia					■					
Japan				■						
Kazakhstan							■			
Kiribati				■						
Kyrgyzstan	■									
Laos								■		
Malaysia				■						
Micronesia				■						
Mongolia	■									
Nauru				■						
Nepal				■						
New Zealand				■						
North Korea								■		
Pakistan								■		
Palau				■						

Constitutional-Judicial Review	CONSTITUTIONAL COURT		HIGH COURT or SPECIAL SENATE of the HIGH COURT			CONSTITUTIONAL COUNCIL		Other Institutional Forms of the Constitutional-Judical Review	Without Constitutional-Judicial Review	New Common-wealth Model
Country	European Model	Mixed European-American Model	European Model	American Model	Mixed European-American Model	French Model	European Model			
Papua New Guinea				■						
Philippines			░							
Singapore				■						
South Korea	■									
Sri Lanka	■									
Taiwan					░					
Tajikistan	■									
Thailand	■									
Tibet				■						
Tonga				■						
Tuvalu				■						
Turkmenistan								░		
Uzbekistan	■									
- Karakalpakstan	■									
Vanuatu				■						
Vietnam								░		
Western Samoa				■						
NORTH AMERICA										
Canada				■						
USA				■						
CENTRAL AND SOUTH AMERICA										
Argentina				■						
- Buenos Aires				■						
- Chaco				■						
- Entre Rios				■						
- Formosa				■						
- La Rioja				■						
- Nequen				■						
- Rio Negro				■						
- Santiago del Estero				■						
- Tucuman	■									
Bahamas				■						
Barbados				■						
Belize				■						
Bolivia				■						
Brazil					░					
Chile	■									
Colombia		■								
Costa Rica			░							
Cuba								░		
Dominica				■						
Dominican Republic				■						
Ecuador		■								
El Salvador					░					
Grenada				■						
Guyana				■						
Guatemala		■								
Haiti				■						
Honduras					░					
Jamaica				■						
Mexico				■						
Nicaragua			░							
Panama			░							
Paraguay			░							
Peru		■								
St. Kitts/Nevis				■						
Surinam	■									
Trinidad and Tobago				■						
Uruguay			░							
Venezuela					░					

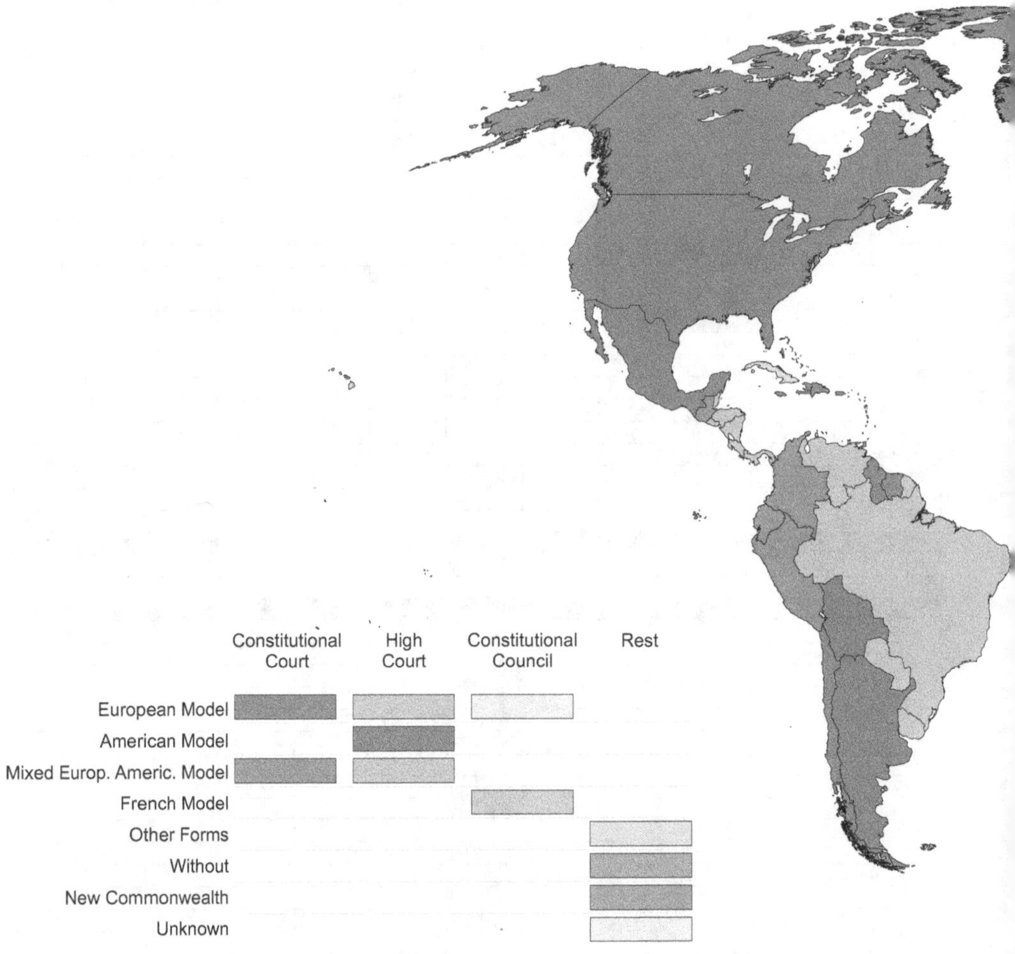

The **"Austrian" (Continental - Constitutional Review) Model** (based on Kelsen's Model of 1920, involving the interconnection of the principle of the supremacy of the *Constitution* and the principle of the supremacy of the Parliament), whereunder constitutional matters are dealt with by specialized Constitutional Courts with specially qualified judges or by ordinary Supreme Courts or high courts or their special chambers (concentrated constitutional review) in special proceedings *(principaliter)*. As a rule it is an abstract review, although a concrete review is also possible. In addition to the *a posteriori* review, *a priori* review is also foreseen. The decisions have an *erga omnes* effect with reference to the absolute authority of the institution by which they are taken.

The **"American" - Judicial Review Model** (based on the *Marbury Case (1803)*, dealt with by the Supreme Court of the United States, and on John Marshall's doctrine), whereunder constitutional matters are dealt with by all ordinary courts (a decentralized or diffuse or dispersed review) under ordinary court proceedings *(incidenter)*. It is a specific and *a posteriori* review, whereby the Supreme (high) Court in the system provides for the uniformity of jurisdiction. In the diffuse system, the decisions as a rule take effect only *inter partes* (except for the principle *stare decisis*, whereunder the courts in the future abide by the ruling). In principle the decision concerning the unconstitutionality of a statute is declaratory and retrospective, *i.e. ex tunc* (with *pro praeterito* consequences).

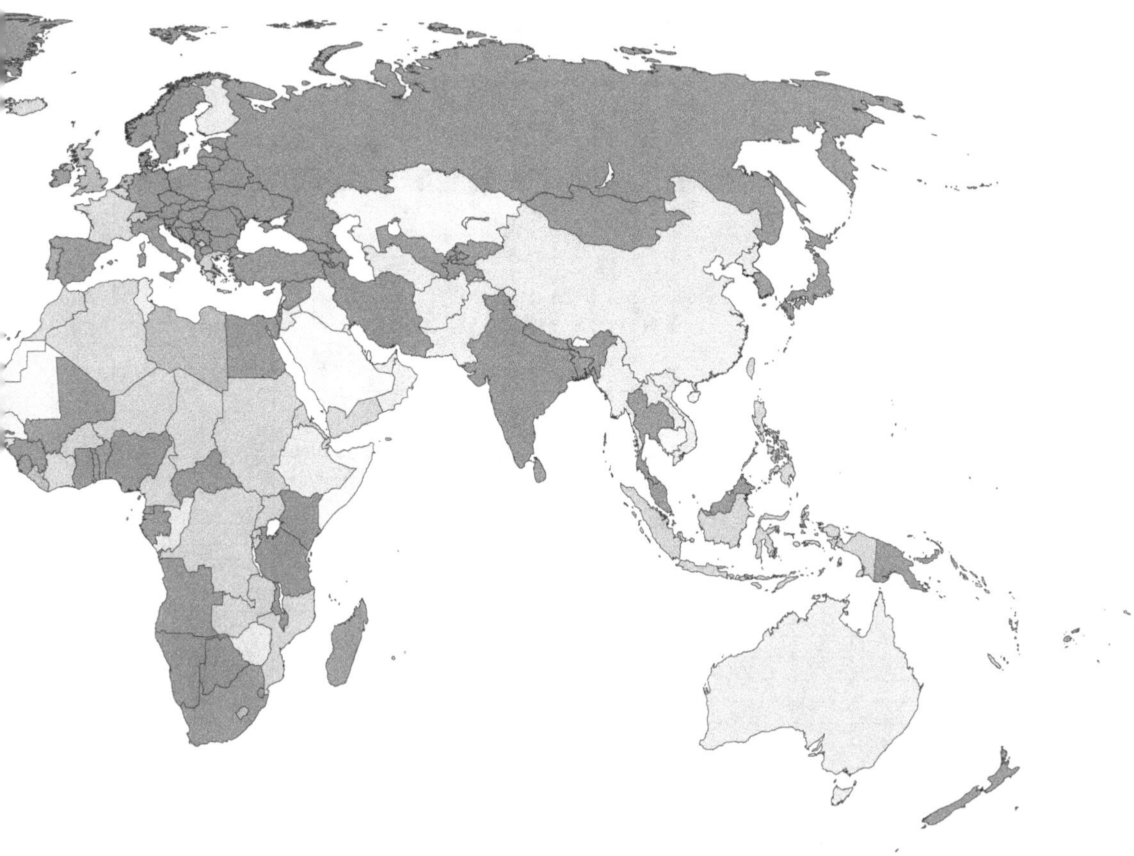

The **"Mixed" (American Continental) Model** with the elements of both a diffuse and concentrated system; despite the constitutional review power of the central Constitutional or Supreme Court (or its special chambers), all ordinary courts in the particular country are entitled to not apply laws deemed as not in conformity with the *Constitution*.

The **"French" (Continental) Model** (based on the model of the French Constitutional Council - *Conseil Constitutionnel* - of 1958), where constitutional matters are subject to review by special bodies of constitutional review (most often the Constitutional Council) or by special chambers of ordinary Supreme Courts (concentrated constitutional review) in special proceedings *(principaliter)*, provided that constitutional review is mainly of a preventative (consultative) character (although these systems also have a repressive form of constitutional review, in particular with reference to electoral matters).

Other Bodies with the Power of Constitutional/Judicial Review (the National Council, Parliament or specialized parliamentary bodies, etc.).

The **New (British) Commonwealth Model *(Mauritius)*** cannot be classified either under the American or the European model. It is characterized by a concentrated constitutional review under the jurisdiction of the Supreme Court consisting of ordinary judges without political nomination; as a rule, it involves preventative *(a priori)* review and the consulting function of the Supreme Court, although repressive *(a posteriori)* review is also possible; decisions take an *erga omnes* effect.

Constitutional-Judicial Review / Country	PREVENTIVE REVIEW: Constitution	PREVENTIVE REVIEW: International Agreements	PREVENTIVE REVIEW: Statutes	PREVENTIVE REVIEW: Regulations	PREVENTIVE REVIEW: Acts of the President of the State	PREVENTIVE REVIEW: Acts of Territorial Units	PREVENTIVE REVIEW: Other General Acts	A POSTERIORI REVIEW – Abstract Review: Constitution-	A POSTERIORI REVIEW – Abstract Review: International Agreements	A POSTERIORI REVIEW – Abstract Review: Statutes	A POSTERIORI REVIEW – Abstract Review: Parliamentary resolutions	A POSTERIORI REVIEW – Abstract Review: Regulations	A POSTERIORI REVIEW – Abstract Review: Acts of the President of the State	A POSTERIORI REVIEW – Abstract Review: Local Government Statutes	A POSTERIORI REVIEW – Abstract Review: General Acts - Exercise of Public Powers	A POSTERIORI REVIEW – Abstract Review: Other General Acts	A POSTERIORI REVIEW – Abstract Review: National Norms versus Treaties	A POSTERIORI REVIEW – Abstract Review: Regional Agreements	A POSTERIORI REVIEW: Concrete Review
EUROPE																			
Albania		■								■		■					■		
Andorra		■																	
Austria			■						■	■		■				■			■
Belgium										■									
Belarus		■	■	■			■												
Bosnia										■									
- Serbian Bosnia										■		■							
Bulgaria		■								■			■				■		■
Croatia										■						■			■
Czech Republic										■		■					■		■
Denmark																			
Estonia		■								■									■
Finland			■																
France		■	■				■												
FRY										■		■		■			■		
- Montenegro										■		■							
- Serbia										■		■		■		■			
Germany		■	■							■									■
- Baden-Württemberg								■		■									
- Bavaria										■									■
- Brandenburg																			
- Berlin										■									
- Bremen																			■
- Hamburg										■									■
- Hessen										■									
- Niedesachsen										■									■
- Nordrhein-Westfalen										■									
- Rheinland Pfalz								■		■									
- Saarland								■		■									
- Sachsen																			
- Sachsen-Anhalt																			
Greece									■	■									
Hungary		■	■							■		■				■	■		■
Iceland																			
Ireland			■																
Italy			■							■									■
Latvia									■	■	■	■	■	■			■		
Liechtenstein									■	■		■							
Lithuania		■							■	■		■	■						■
Luxemburg																			
Macedonia										■						■			
Malta																			■
Moldavia	■	■							■	■		■	■						
Monaco																			
Netherlands																			
Norway																			
Poland		■	■							■		■				■	■		■
Portugal			■	■															
Romania			■				■												■
Russia		■	■						■	■		■	■	■					■
- Adigea									■	■		■	■						■
- Altai																			
- Bashkiria									■	■			■	■					■
- Buryatia		■								■		■	■	■				■	■
- Chechnya																			
- Chuvashia																			
- Dagestan		■						■		■		■		■				■	■

Constitutional-Judicial Review	PREVENTIVE REVIEW							A POSTERIORI REVIEW											
								Abstract Review											
Country	Constitution	International Agreements	Statutes	Regulations	Acts of the President of the State	Acts of Territorial Units	Other General Acts	Constitution-	International Agreements	Statutes	Parliamentary resolutions	Regulations	Acts of the President of the State	Local Government Statutes	General Acts - Exercise of Public Powers	Other General Acts	National Norms versus Treaties	Regional Agreements	Concrete Review
- Ingushia																			
- Irkutskaya Oblast										X		X		X				X	
- Karbardino-Balkar									X	X		X				X		X	
- Khakassia																			
- Karachaewo-Cherkez																			
- Karelia		X								X		X		X				X	X
- Kalmikia																			
- Komy										X		X		X				X	X
- Marii-El																			
- Northrn Ossetia			X	X						X		X	X	X		X			
- Tatarstan									X	X		X	X						
- Tuva									X	X									
- Udmurtia																			
- Yakutia									X	X		X	X	X					X
Slovakia										X		X		X		X	X		
Slovenia		X								X		X		X	X	X	X		X
Spain		X	X							X				X					X
Sweden																			
Switzerland	X																		
Turkey			X							X						X			
Ukraine		X								X		X	X	X					
United Kingdom																			
AFRICA																			
Algeria		X	X		X					X			X						
Angola										X		X							
Benin										X									
Botswana																			
Burkina Faso		X	X																
Burundi		X	X	X			X												
Cameroon		X	X				X		X	X									
Cape Verde		X								X		X							X
Central African Rep.	X	X	X	X			X												
Chad			X				X		X	X									
Comoros		X	X	X			X		X	X		X							
Congo		X	X	X					X	X		X							X
Djibouti			X				X												X
Egypt										X		X							
Eritrea										X		X							
Ethiopia																			
Equatorial Guinea										X									
Gabon		X	X	X															X
Gambia																			
Ghana																			
Guinea		X	X		X														
Guinea Bissau																			
Ivory Coast		X	X																
Kenya																			
Lesotho																			
Liberia																			
Libya																			
Madagascar		X	X	X	X		X		X	X		X	X			X			X
Malawi										X									
Mali		X	X													X			
Mauritius			X							X									
Mauritania									X	X		X							
Morocco			X																
Mozambique										X		X							
Namibia			X	X						X									

Constitutional-Judicial Review	PREVENTIVE REVIEW							A POSTERIORI REVIEW											
								Abstract Review											
Country	Constitution	International Agreements	Statutes	Regulations	Acts of the President of the State	Acts of Territorial Units	Other General Acts	Constitution-	International Agreements	Statutes	Parliamentary resolutions	Regulations	Acts of the President of the State	Local Government Statutes	General Acts - Exercise of Public Powers	Other General Acts	National Norms versus Treaties	Regional Agreements	Concrete Review
AFRICA - continue																			
Niger			■				■												■
Nigeria																			
Rwanda										■									
Sao Tome &Principe																			
Senegal									■	■									
Seychelles										■									■
Sierra Leone																			
South Africa			■			■				■									■
Sudan										■		■							
Swaziland																			
Tanzania																			
Togo			■				■												■
Tunisia		■	■																
Uganda										■						■			
Zaire										■									
Zambia			■							■									■
Zimbabwe																			
THE MIDDLE EAST																			
Bahrain																			
Cyprus			■				■	■		■				■					■
Iran																			■
Israel																			
Kuwait										■		■							
Lebanon										■									
Oman																			
Palestine										■									
Syria			■							■									
Yemen										■		■	■						
ASIA, AUSTRALIA																			
Afghanistan										■		■							
Armenia		■								■		■	■						
Australia																			
Azerbaijan		■							■	■		■	■	■					■
Bangladesh																			
Brunei																			
Burma																			
Cambodia			■							■									■
China																			
Fiji																			
Hong Kong																			
Georgia		■								■		■	■	■					■
- Adjaria																			
India																			
Indonesia			■																
Japan																			
Kazakhstan		■	■																■
Kiribati																			
Kyrgyzstan								■		■									■
Laos																			
Malaysia										■									■
Micronesia																			
Mongolia										■		■	■						
Nauru																			
Nepal																			
New Zealand																			
North Korea																			
Pakistan																			
Palau																			

Constitutional-Judicial Review	PREVENTIVE REVIEW							A POSTERIORI REVIEW											
								Abstract Review											
Country	Constitution	International Agreements	Statutes	Regulations	Acts of the President of the State	Acts of Territorial Units	Other General Acts	Constitution-	International Agreements	Statutes	Parliamentary resolutions	Regulations	Acts of the President of the State	Local Government Statutes	General Acts - Exercise of Public Powers	Other General Acts	National Norms versus Treaties	Regional Agreements	Concrete Review
Papua New Guinea																			
Philippines									■	■		■	■			■			
Singapore																			
South Korea										■									■
Sri Lanka			■																
Taiwan										■									■
Tajikistan		■								■		■	■	■		■			
Thailand			■				■												■
Tibet																			
Tonga																			
Tuvalu																			
Turkmenistan																			
Uzbekistan								■	■	■		■	■	■					
- Karakalpakstan																			
Vanuatu																			
Vietnam																			
Western Samoa																			
NORTH AMERICA																			
Canada																			
USA																			
CENTRAL AND SOUTH AMERICA																			
Argentina																			
- Buenos Aires																			
- Chaco																			
- Entre Rios																			
- Formosa																			
- La Rioja																			
- Nequen																			
- Rio Negro																			
- Santiago del Estero																			
- Tucuman			■	■						■		■	■						
Bahamas																			
Barbados																			
Bolivia										■						■			
Brazil								■		■									
Chile		■	■							■									
Colombia										■									
Costa Rica			■					■	■	■									■
Cuba								■		■									■
Dominica																			
Dominican Republic																			
Ecuador			■							■		■	■			■			
El Salvador										■		■	■						
Grenada																			
Guyana																			
Guatemala		■	■							■		■							■
Haiti																			
Honduras										■									■
Jamaica																			
Mexico										■									
Nicaragua										■									
Panama										■		■	■						■
Paraguay										■									■
Peru			■							■									
St. Kitts/Nevis																			
Surinam																			
Trinidad and Tobago																			
Uruguay										■									■
Venezuela			■							■									

Constitutional-Judicial Review	Interpretation of the Rule				Legislative Initiative			Jurisdictional Disputes					
Country	Constitution	Statutes	Implementation of the Rule	Omissions of Statutory Regulating	Citizen	Constitutional Court	Legislative Procedures	Between the Hightest State Bodies	Between State and Local/Regional Unites	Between Local/-Regional Unites	Between Courts and State Bodies	Other Jurisdictional Disputes	Between the Constitutional Courts of Federal Entities
EUROPE													
Albania	■							■	■				
Andorra													
Austria					■				■	■	■	■	
Belgium													
Belarus													
Bosnia									■	■			
- Serbian Bosnia								■	■				
Bulgaria	■							■	■				
Croatia												■	
Czech Republic									■				
Denmark													
Estonia													
Finland													
France		■											
FRY								■	■	■			■
- Montenegro									■	■	■		
- Serbia											■		
Germany	■							■	■	■			
- Baden-Württemberg								■					
- Bavaria								■					
- Brandenburg													
- Berlin								■					
- Bremen								■					
- Hamburg								■					
- Hessen								■					
- Niedesachsen								■					
- Nordrhein-Westfalen								■					
- Rheinland Pfalz			■										
- Saarland								■					
- Sachsen													
- Sachsen-Anhalt													
Greece											■		
Hungary	■			■	■				■			■	
Iceland													
Ireland													
Italy				■				■	■	■			
Latvia													
Liechtenstein													
Lithuania													
Luxemburg													
Macedonia								■	■				
Malta													
Moldavia	■												
Monaco													
Netherlands													
Norway													
Poland		■						■					
Portugal				■									
Romania					■								
Russia	■		■					■	■	■			
- Adigea	■					■		■	■				
- Altai													
- Bashkiria	■		■			■		■	■	■			
- Buryatia	■					■		■	■	■			
- Chechnya													
- Chuvashia													
- Dagestan	■	■				■		■	■				

Constitutional-Judicial Review	Interpretation of the Rule		Implementation of the Rule	Omissions of Statutory Regulating	Legislative Initiative			Jurisdictional Disputes					
Country	Constitution	Statutes			Citizen	Constitutional Court	Legislative Procedures	Between the Hightest State Bodies	Between State and Local/Regional Unites	Between Local/-Regional Unites	Between Courts and State Bodies	Other Jurisdictional Disputes	Between the Constitutional Courts of Federal Entities
- Ingushia													
- Irkutskaya Oblast	■		■					■	■	■			
- Karbardino-Balkar			■			■		■					
- Khakassia													
- Karachaewo-Cherkez													
- Karelia						■		■	■	■			
- Kalmikia													
- Komy	■					■		■	■	■			
- Marii-El													
- Northrn Ossetia						■							
- Tatarstan						■		■	■	■			
- Tuva			■			■							
- Udmurtia													
- Yakutia	■					■			■			■	
Slovakia	■							■					
Slovenia								■	■	■	■		
Spain					■			■	■	■			
Sweden													
Switzerland									■	■			
Turkey													
Ukraine								■	■	■		■	
United Kingdom													
AFRICA													
Algeria													
Angola													
Benin													
Botswana													
Burkina Faso													
Burundi	■					■							
Cameroon								■	■	■			
Cape Verde													
Central African Rep.							■	■	■				
Chad								■					
Comoros													
Congo													
Djibouti													
Egypt		■									■		
Eritrea	■												
Ethiopia													
Equatorial Guinea		■											
Gabon	■							■					
Gambia													
Ghana													
Guinea													
Guinea Bissau													
Ivory Coast													
Kenya													
Lesotho													
Liberia													
Libya													
Madagascar	■	■						■	■				
Malawi													
Mali								■					
Mauritius													
Mauritania													
Morocco													
Mozambique								■					
Namibia	■												

Constitutional-Judicial Review / Country	Interpretation of the Rule: Constitution	Interpretation of the Rule: Statutes	Implementation of the Rule	Omissions of Statutory Regulating	Legislative Initiative: Citizen	Legislative Initiative: Constitutional Court	Legislative Initiative: Legislative Procedures	Jurisdictional Disputes: Between the Hightest State Bodies	Jurisdictional Disputes: Between State and Local/Regional Unites	Jurisdictional Disputes: Between Local/-Regional Unites	Jurisdictional Disputes: Between Courts and State Bodies	Jurisdictional Disputes: Other Jurisdictional Disputes	Jurisdictional Disputes: Between the Constitutional Courts of Federal Entities
AFRICA - continue													
Niger	■							■					
Nigeria									■	■			
Rwanda													
Sao Tome &Principe													
Senegal								■					
Seychelles				■									
Sierra Leone													
South Africa								■	■	■			
Sudan	■	■											
Swazi													
Tanzania													
Togo													
Tunisia													
Uganda	■			■									
Zaire	■												
Zambia													
Zimbabwe													
THE MIDDLE EAST													
Bahrain													
Cyprus												■	
Iran													
Israel													
Kuwait													
Lebanon													
Oman													
Palestine		■											
Syria													
Yemen												■	
ASIA, AUSTRALIA													
Afghanistan	■												
Armenia													
Australia													
Azerbaijan	■	■						■					
Bangladesh													
Brunei													
Burma													
Cambodia	■	■											
China													
Fiji													
Hong Kong													
Georgia								■					
- Adjaria													
India									■				
Indonesia		■											
Japan													
Kazakhstan	■							■					
Kiribati													
Kyrgyzstan	■												
Laos													
Malaysia									■				
Micronesia													
Mongolia								■					
Nauru													
Nepal													
New Zealand													
North Korea													
Pakistan									■				
Palau													

Constitutional-Judicial Review	Interpretation of the Rule				Legislative Initiative			Jurisdictional Disputes					
Country	Constitution	Statutes	Implementation of the Rule	Omissions of Statutory Regulating	Citizen	Constitutional Court	Legislative Procedures	Between the Hightest State Bodies	Between State and Local/Regional Unites	Between Local/-Regional Unites	Between Courts and State Bodies	Other Jurisdictional Disputes	Between the Constitutional Courts of Federal Entities
Papua New Guinea	■												
Philippines			■										
Singapore													
South Korea								■	■	■			
Sri Lanka	■												
Taiwan	■	■						■					
Tajikistan								■					
Thailand								■					
Tibet													
Tonga													
Tuvalu													
Turkmenistan													
Uzbekistan	■	■											
- Karakalpakstan													
Vanuatu													
Vietnam													
Western Samoa													
NORTH AMERICA													
Canada													
USA													
CENTRAL AND SOUTH AMERICA													
Argentina													
- Buenos Aires													
- Chaco													
- Entre Rios													
- Formosa													
- La Rioja													
- Nequen													
- Rio Negro													
- Santiago del Estero													
- Tucuman										■	■	■	
Bahamas													
Barbados													
Bolivia										■			
Brazil				■						■			
Chile													
Colombia													
Costa Rica													
Cuba													
Dominica													
Dominican Republic													
Ecuador			■					■					
El Salvador								■					
Grenada													
Guyana													
Guatemala								■					
Haiti													
Honduras													
Jamaica													
Mexico									■	■			
Nicaragua								■	■	■		■	
Panama													
Paraguay													
Peru								■		■			
St. Kitts/Nevis													
Surinam													
Trinidad and Tobago													
Uruguay													
Venezuela													

Constitutional-Judicial Review					Constitutional Complaint				Capacity for offices			Impeachment			
Country	Political Parties	Referendum	Elections	Confirming of Elections of Deputies	Human Rights Protection	Communal Const. Complaint	Legal Initiative	Nationalisation	President of the State	Other State Representatives	Presidential Oath	President of the State	Other State Representatives	Special Kinds of Powers	Other Tasks Imposed to the Court by the Constitution/Statute
EUROPE															
Albania	■		■		■							■			
Andorra					■										
Austria		■	■	■	■							■	■	■	
Belgium															
Belarus															
Bosnia															
- Serbian Bosnia	■														
Bulgaria	■		■	■					■	■		■	■	■	
Croatia	■	■	■		■				■			■			■
Czech Republic	■		■		■	■						■		■	
Denmark															
Estonia															
Finland															
France		■	■	■					■	■				■	
FRY	■		■		■										
- Montenegro	■	■	■		■							■			■
- Serbia	■		■												
Germany	■		■	■	■	■						■		■	■
- Baden-Württemberg			■	■		■							■		■
- Bavaria			■	■	■								■		■
- Brandenburg															
- Berlin		■	■	■	■									■	■
- Bremen					■								■		
- Hamburg			■	■										■	■
- Hessen		■			■										■
- Niedesachsen			■	■									■		■
- Nordrhein-Westfalen		■	■	■		■							■		■
- Rheinland Pfalz			■					■					■		■
- Saarland		■	■	■	■		■	■					■		
- Sachsen															
- Sachsen-Anhalt															
Greece		■	■	■											
Hungary		■			■							■			
Iceland															
Ireland															
Italy												■	■		
Latvia															
Liechtenstein					■										
Lithuania			■						■				■		
Luxemburg															
Macedonia	■				■							■			■
Malta			■		■										
Moldavia	■	■	■		■				■					■	
Monaco															
Netherlands															
Norway															
Poland	■				■				■						
Portugal	■	■	■						■						■
Romania	■	■	■						■						
Russia	■				■				■	■		■		■	
- Adigea					■				■			■			■
- Altai															
- Bashkiria	■				■				■			■			■
- Buryatia					■							■			
- Chechnya															
- Chuvashia															
- Dagestan					■							■	■		■

Constitutional-Judicial Review / Country	Political Parties	Referendum	Elections	Confirming of Elections of Deputies	Constitutional Complaint: Human Rights Protection	Constitutional Complaint: Communal Const. Complaint	Legal Initiative	Nationalisation	Capacity for offices: President of the State	Capacity for offices: Other State Representatives	Presidential Oath	Impeachment: President of the State	Impeachment: Other State Representatives	Special Kinds of Powers	Other Tasks Imposed to the Court by the Constitution/Statute
- Ingushia															
- Irkutskaya Oblast												■			
- Karbardino-Balkar					■										
- Khakassia															
- Karachaewo-Cherkez															
- Karelia					■							■	■		
- Kalmikia															
- Komy					■							■	■		■
- Marii-El															
- Northrn Ossetia															
- Tatarstan												■			
- Tuva															■
- Udmurtia															
- Yakutia	■								■	■		■			
Slovakia	■	■	■	■	■							■			
Slovenia	■			■	■							■	■		■
Spain					■		■							■	■
Sweden															
Switzerland					■										
Turkey												■	■		■
Ukraine				■	■							■	■		■
United Kingdom															
AFRICA															
Algeria		■	■						■			■		■	
Angola															
Benin					■										
Botswana															
Burkina Faso	■	■	■												
Burundi			■		■				■		■			■	
Cameroon		■	■												
Cape Verde					■										
Central African Rep.			■						■						■
Chad		■	■											■	
Comoros		■	■										■		
Congo		■	■		■										
Djibouti		■	■		■										
Egypt														■	
Eritrea												■			
Ethiopia															
Equatorial Guinea		■	■		■										
Gabon		■	■												
Gambia															
Ghana															
Guinea			■												
Guinea Bissau															
Ivory Coast		■	■									■		■	
Kenya															
Lesotho															
Liberia															
Libya															
Madagascar		■	■									■			
Malawi															
Mali		■	■		■										
Mauritius			■		■										
Mauritania		■	■						■					■	
Morocco			■												
Mozambique		■	■						■						
Namibia			■									■			

Constitutional-Judicial Review Country	Political Parties	Referendum	Elections	Confirming of Elections of Deputies	Constitutional Complaint				Capacity for offices			Impeachment		Special Kinds of Powers	Other Tasks Imposed to the Court by the Constitution/Statute
					Human Rights Protection	Communal Const. Complaint	Legal Initiative	Nationalisation	President of the State	Other State Representatives	Presidential Oath	President of the State	Other State Representatives		
AFRICA - continue															
Niger		■	■												
Nigeria			■												
Rwanda												■			
Sao Tome &Principe															
Senegal					■										
Seychelles															
Sierra Leone															
South Africa					■										■
Sudan					■										
Swazi															
Tanzania															
Togo														■	
Tunisia															
Uganda															
Zaire		■	■												
Zambia															
Zimbabwe															
THE MIDDLE EAST															
Bahrain															
Cyprus			■		■				■	■				■	
Iran															
Israel					■										
Kuwait															
Lebanon			■												
Oman															
Palestine															
Syria			■		■										
Yemen			■												
ASIA, AUSTRALIA															
Afghanistan														■	
Armenia	■	■	■						■			■		■	
Australia															
Azerbaijan	■				■				■			■			■
Bangladesh															
Brunei															
Burma															
Cambodia			■											■	
China															
Fiji															
Hong Kong															
Georgia	■	■	■	■	■							■	■		■
- Adjaria															
India															
Indonesia															
Japan															
Kazakhstan		■	■	■					■			■			
Kiribati															
Kyrgyzstan			■		■				■						
Laos															
Malaysia															
Micronesia															
Mongolia			■	■	■							■	■		
Nauru															
Nepal															
New Zealand															
North Korea															
Pakistan															
Palau															

Constitutional-Judicial Review					Constitutional Complaint				Capacity for offices			Impeachment			
Country	Political Parties	Referendum	Elections	Confirming of Elections of Deputies	Human Rights Protection	Communal Const. Complaint	Legal Initiative	Nationalisation	President of the State	Other State Representatives	Presidential Oath	President of the State	Other State Representatives	Special Kinds of Powers	Other Tasks Imposed to the Court by the Constitution/Statute
Papua New Guinea					■										
Philippines															
Singapore															
South Korea	■				■								■		
Sri Lanka			■		■									■	
Taiwan					■								■		
Tajikistan															■
Thailand															
Tibet															
Tonga															
Tuvalu															
Turkmenistan															
Uzbekistan					■									■	■
- Karakalpakstan															
Vanuatu															
Vietnam															
Western Samoa															
NORTH AMERICA															
Canada															
USA															
CENTRAL AND SOUTH AMERICA															
Argentina															
- Buenos Aires															
- Chaco															
- Entre Rios															
- Formosa															
- La Rioja															
- Nequen															
- Rio Negro															
- Santiago del Estero															
- Tucuman			■		■								■		
Bahamas															
Barbados															
Bolivia												■	■		
Brazil					■										
Chile	■	■		■								■			■
Colombia					■							■			
Costa Rica															
Cuba														■	
Dominica															
Dominican Republic															
Ecuador					■										■
El Salvador					■										
Grenada															
Guyana															
Guatemala					■										■
Haiti															
Honduras					■										
Jamaica															
Mexico															
Nicaragua					■										■
Panama					■										
Paraguay															
Peru															
St. Kitts/Nevis															
Surinam															
Trinidad and Tobago															
Uruguay															
Venezuela															

Constitutional-Judicial Review	Other Forms of Human Rights Protection												Constitutional Complaint			
Country	Ordinary Court Proceedings	Ha-beas Corpus	Mandado de Seguranca	Recurso de Proteccion	Ha-beas Data	Mandamus Prohibition Certiorari Quo warranto	Respondeat Superior	Amparo	Subsidiary Amparo	Mandado de Injuncao	Popular complaint	Indirect Constitutional Human Rights Protect.	Human Rights	Communes	Legal Initiative	Nationalisation
EUROPE																
Albania													■			
Andorra													■			
Austria													■			
Belgium												■				
Belarus												■				
Bosnia												■				
- Serbian Bosnia																
Bulgaria												■				
Croatia											■		■			
Czech Republic											■		■	■		
Denmark	■															
Estonia												■				
Finland	■															
France												■				
FRY											■		■			
- Montenegro											■		■			
- Serbia																
Germany													■	■		
- Baden-Württemberg														■		
- Bavaria											■		■			
- Brandenburg																
- Berlin													■			
- Bremen																
- Hamburg																
- Hessen													■			
- Niedesachsen																
- Nordrhein-Westfalen														■		
- Rheinland Pfalz																■
- Saarland													■			■
- Sachsen																
- Sachsen-Anhalt																
Greece	■															
Hungary											■		■			
Iceland	■															
Ireland	■															
Italy												■				
Latvia												■				
Liechtenstein											■		■			
Lithuania												■				
Luxemburg																
Macedonia											■		■			
Malta											■		■			
Moldavia																
Monaco																
Netherlands	■															
Norway	■															
Poland													■			
Portugal													■			
Romania																
Russia													■			
- Adigea													■			
- Altai																
- Bashkiria													■			
- Buryatia													■			
- Chechnya																
- Chuvashia																
- Dagestan													■			

Shaded cells are marked ■.

Constitutional-Judicial Review	Other Forms of Human Rights Protection												Constitutional Complaint			
Country	Ordinary Court Proceedings	Ha-beas Corpus	Mandado de Seguranca	Recurso de Proteccion	Ha-beas Data	Mandamus Prohibition Certiorari Quo warranto	Respondeat Superior	Amparo	Subsidiary Amparo	Mandado de Injuncao	Popular complaint	Indirect Constitutional Human Rights Protect.	Human Rights	Communes	Legal Initiative	Nationalisation
- Ingushia																
- Irkutskaya Oblast																
- Karbardino-Balkar													■			
- Khakassia																
- Karachaewo-Cherkez																
- Karelia													■			
- Kalmikia																
- Komy													■			
- Marii-El																
- Northrn Ossetia																
- Tatarstan																
- Tuva																
- Udmurtia																
- Yakutia												■				
Slovakia													■			
Slovenia											■		■			
Spain									■				■			■
Sweden	■															
Switzerland													■			
Turkey																
Ukraine													■			
United Kingdom	■															
AFRICA																
Algeria																
Angola																
Benin													■			
Botswana		■				■										
Burkina Faso																
Burundi											■					
Cameroon																
Cape Verde													■			
Central African Rep.											■					
Chad											■					
Comoros																
Congo											■					
Djibouti											■					
Egypt																
Eritrea																
Ethiopia																
Equatorial Guinea																
Gabon																
Gambia																
Ghana		■				■										
Guinea																
Guinea Bissau																
Ivory Coast																
Kenya		■				■										
Lesotho		■				■										
Liberia																
Libya																
Madagascar																
Malawi		■				■										
Mali																
Mauritius		■				■							■			
Mauritania																
Morocco																
Mozambique																
Namibia																

Constitutional-Judicial Review	Other Forms of Human Rights Protection												Constitutional Complaint			
Country	Ordinary Court Proceedings	Ha-beas Corpus	Mandado de Seguranca	Recurso de Proteccion	Ha-beas Data	Mandamus Prohibition Certiorari Quo warranto	Respondeat Superior	Amparo	Subsidiary Amparo	Mandado de Injuncao	Popular complaint	Indirect Constitutional Human Rights Protect.	Human Rights	Communes	Legal Initiative	Nationalisation
AFRICA - continue																
Niger											■					
Nigeria		■				■										
Rwanda																
Sao Tome &Principe																
Senegal													■			
Seychelles											■					
Sierra Leone		■				■					■					
South Africa											■					
Sudan													■			
Swazi		■				■										
Tanzania		■				■										
Togo																
Tunisia																
Uganda		■				■					■					
Zaire																
Zambia		■				■										
Zimbabwe		■				■										
THE MIDDLE EAST																
Bahrain																
Cyprus													■			
Iran											■					
Israel																
Kuwait																
Lebanon																
Oman																
Palestine																
Syria													■			
Yemen																
ASIA, AUSTRALIA																
Afghanistan																
Armenia																
Australia	■															
Azerbaijan																
Bangladesh		■				■										
Brunei																
Burma																
Cambodia											■	■				
China																
Fiji																
Hong Kong		■														
Georgia													■			
- Adjaria																
India		■				■										
Indonesia		■														
Japan	■										■					
Kazakhstan												■				
Kiribati																
Kyrgyzstan													■			
Laos																
Malaysia		■														
Micronesia																
Mongolia													■			
Nauru																
Nepal		■				■										
New Zealand																
North Korea																
Pakistan		■														
Palau																

Constitutional-Judicial Review	Other Forms of Human Rights Protection												Constitutional Complaint			
Country	Ordinary Court Proceedings	Ha-beas Corpus	Mandado de Seguranca	Recurso de Proteccion	Ha-beas Data	Mandamus Prohibition Certiorari Quo warranto	Respondeat Superior	Amparo	Subsidiary Amparo	Mandado de Injuncao	Popular complaint	Indirect Constitutional Human Rights Protect.	Human Rights	Communes	Legal Initiative	Nationalisation
Papua New Guinea													■			
Philippines		■				■										
Singapore		■														
South Korea													■			
Sri Lanka		■				■										
Taiwan		■					■						■			
Tajikistan																
Thailand																
Tibet																
Tonga																
Tuvalu																
Turkmenistan																
Uzbekistan													■			
- Karakalpakstan																
Vanuatu																
Vietnam																
Western Samoa																
NORTH AMERICA																
Canada		■														
USA	■	■				■	■									
CENTRAL AND SOUTH AMERICA																
Argentina								■			■					
- Buenos Aires											■					
- Chaco		■									■					
- Entre Rios											■					
- Formosa		■														
- La Rioja											■					
- Nequen		■									■					
- Rio Negro											■					
- Santiago del Estero											■					
- Tucuman																
Bahamas																
Barbados	■															
Bolivia		■						■								
Brazil		■	■		■					■	■					
Chile		■		■												
Colombia		■						■	■		■					
Costa Rica		■						■			■					
Cuba		■						■								
Dominica																
Dominican Republic		■						■								
Ecuador		■						■								
El Salvador		■						■			■					
Grenada																
Guyana	■															
Guatemala		■						■								
Haiti								■								
Honduras		■						■								
Jamaica	■															
Mexico		■														
Nicaragua		■						■								
Panama		■						■			■					
Paraguay		■						■			■					
Peru		■						■			■					
St. Kitts/Nevis																
Surinam																
Trinidad and Tobago	■															
Uruguay		■						■								
Venezuela		■						■			■					

INDEX

A

B

C

K

L

M

N

O

P

R

S

T

U

V

W

Y

Z

www.ingramcontent.com/pod-product-compliance
Lightning Source LLC
LaVergne TN
LVHW080043210926
848481LV00011B/3271
* 9 7 8 1 6 0 0 4 2 1 9 3 8 *